Hooked

ART AND ATTACHMENT

Rita Felski

THE UNIVERSITY OF CHICAGO PRESS • CHICAGO AND LONDON

The University of Chicago Press, Chicago 60637
The University of Chicago Press, Ltd., London
© 2020 by The University of Chicago .
Published 2020
Printed in the United States of America

29 28 27 26 25 24 23 22 21 20   1 2 3 4 5

ISBN-13: 978-0-226-72946-6 (cloth)
ISBN-13: 978-0-226-72963-3 (paper)
ISBN-13: 978-0-226-72977-0 (e-book)
DOI: https://doi.org/10.7208/chicago/9780226729770.001.0001

Library of Congress Cataloging-in-Publication Data

Names: Felski, Rita, 1956– author.
Title: Hooked : art and attachment / Rita Felski.
Description: Chicago ; London : The University of Chicago Press, 2020. | Includes
     bibliographical references and index.
Identifiers: LCCN 2020010303 | ISBN 9780226729466 (cloth) | ISBN 9780226729633
     (paperback) | ISBN 9780226729770 (ebook)
Subjects: LCSH: Aesthetics. | Experience. | Interest (Psychology) | Hermeneutics.
Classification: LCC BH301.E8 F45 2020 | DDC 111/.85—dc23
LC record available at https://lccn.loc.gov/2020010303

♾This paper meets the requirements of ANSI/NISO Z39.48-1992 (Permanence of Paper).

Hooked

Contents

Preface

"What's the hook?" The question calls up a certain picture: a big-shot producer, perhaps, leaning back in his chair and quizzing a hapless scriptwriter who is hawking her wares around Hollywood. Hooks are associated with blockbusters and bestsellers: cliff-hangers, charismatic characters, what Alfred Hitchcock called MacGuffins. The audience is reeled in, played for all its worth, left flapping and gasping on the line. "Hooked" does not jump to mind as an adjective of choice for admirers of Marcel Proust or Marcel Duchamp—where the preferred language is that of aesthetic distance or critical resistance. Scholars often pride themselves on being indifferent or impervious to hooks: ignoring the bait, with a disdainful flick of their tails they swim away.

Yet all of us are hooked, even if our lures are fashioned from differing stuff. To a certain kind of reader, the pull of *Ulysses* is stronger than that of *Game of Thrones*; devotees of Joseph Conrad or J. M. Coetzee are no less fervent than fans of Tom Cruise. Wresting the language of hooks away from charges of sticky sentiment and manipulative marketing, I clarify its broader relevance for aesthetic experience. Perhaps we find ourselves not just captured but *captivated*: that is to say, we come to value the experience of being bound, in ways that cut aslant the modern prizing of unrestricted agency and freedom. The following pages build an aesthetic that is premised on relation rather than separation, on attachment rather than autonomy. What do works of art do? What do they set in motion? And to what are they linked or tied?

A groundswell of voices in the humanities is calling for a course correction—an overhaul of the aims and methods of humanistic study. In contrast to the culture wars of previous decades, this reassessment is spearheaded by critics—feminist and queer scholars feature prominently—with zero nostalgia for the past but hopes for a less cynical and disenchanted future. An assortment of catchphrases echoes through these debates: surface reading, new formalisms, the affective turn, the return to beauty. What *Hooked* adds to this conversation—and what distinguishes it—is its stress on attachment: how people connect to art and how art connects them to other things.

Literary studies, for example, zigzags between historicism and formalism (the stocks of formalism are currently on the rise), but neither approach can shed much light on some fundamental questions. Why do people seek out works of art? What are their differing motives, interests, concerns? What are these encounters with artworks *like*? And how are they sustained, suppressed, or reconfigured in the spaces of the library or the classroom? (What is the relationship, in other words, between the arts and the humanities?) And here there is a rift between the general capacity for aesthetic response—most people can point to a movie or a novel or a piece of music that affects them strongly—and the very partial accounts of the aesthetic in academic writing, where it is equated with either Kantian disinterestedness or edgy transgression. Without denying differences between ordinary and academic interpretation (see especially chapter 4), I draw out similarities that are often overlooked. Meanwhile, as Bruno Latour points out, whether attachments are felt to be irrational or well founded depends entirely on their distance from one's own tastes and preferences. My high estimation of Bartók or Badiou is so patently justified as to need no explanation; meanwhile, your love of Taylor Swift or—god forbid— Habermas can only be the result of manipulation by outside forces.

The language of attachment may make some readers nervous— fearing that what follows is a brief for mawkish outbursts and self-indulgent meanderings. Yet attachments involve thought as well as feeling, values and judgments as well as gut response. And they are, of course, often ambivalent, fraught, or vexed. I avoid overpsychologizing or oversociologizing the word by forcing it into the exclusive ambit of particular disciplines. As it is used in this book, "attachment" can include, but by no means requires, warm and fuzzy feelings (irony, as we'll see, can be a powerful tie); it allows for, but does not stipulate, relations to a social group or collective (one can feel as closely connected to a film, a painting, or a song as to another person). Moreover, attachments should not be confused with roots; they are made and unmade over time, intensify or fade away, are oriented to the future as well as the past, can assume new forms and point in surprising directions. Dissenting from the view that bonds are nothing more than restraints, I strive to clarify what they create and make possible. Such a line of argument slices across boundaries between reason and feeling, self and other, text and context. An emphasis on tie-making rather than tie-breaking can inspire ways of thinking about art and criticism that are not tripped up by their own contradictions.

In an influential tradition of modern criticism, for example, poems and paintings are prized for being sovereign, self-contained, and severed from their surroundings. The task of the critic is to honor this autonomy by zeroing in on the specifics of form and medium: an arresting visual composition or a striking juxtaposition of words. The uniqueness of a work will come into view only if all distractions and external details are pushed aside; its separateness and singularity must be fully honored. An alternative approach that has been dominant in recent decades sees the language of politics as the only permissible way of accounting for these same works. Rather than being gloriously self-sufficient, they are now charged with sustaining inequality or opposing it—the scholar's task being to sort them into categories of the complicit or the resistant. While these two approaches might seem to be worlds apart, they are often combined in one of the most beguiling of modern mythologies. That art often retains a certain distance from everyday language and thought is imbued with an amplitude of political meaning; this separation is hailed as an act of refusal and thus of critical dissent. The very functionlessness of art, to channel Adorno, serves a critical function: in saying no to the world, it embodies a fragile moment of freedom from the tyranny of instrumental reason and the slick seductions of the marketplace.

This mythology—like many mythologies—is not so much false as it is partial. It crystallizes a stirring and influential ideal: an ethos of critical aloofness that has indisputably molded the self-image of modern artists and intellectuals. And yet their own fierce attachment to this vision undercuts the claim that art is solely a matter of distancing and estranging. That artists assail convention, excoriate the public, or inveigh against oppressive norms does not mean they are untied. Attachments vary in form, scale, intensity, and object; they can be forged to a handful of fellow malcontents rather than to a mass public; to artistic forms rather than to marketplace values; to patterns of words rather than to persons; to what is ideal rather than to what is real. In the very same breath that they insist artworks resist any form of appropriation, meanwhile, scholars deploy these same works to deliver a talk, score points against academic rivals, or build a tenure file. (Attachment is a matter not just of feeling, as we'll see, but of intellectual, ethical, or institutional ties.) In short, we need better ways of thinking about relations: as not just encroaching but enabling, as sustaining both aesthetic experiences and the work of criticism. The question of what attachment *means* needs to be rethought from the ground up.

I've long been drawn to cultural studies, feminism, and pragmatism—approaches that are attuned, in their differing ways, to relational styles of thinking. Most recently, actor-network theory has allowed me to appreciate more fully that ties do not destroy the distinctiveness of art but make it possible. ANT, as it is often called, allows us to circumvent a series of surprisingly stubborn dichotomies: art versus society, text versus context, sophisticated versus naive response. (The word "circumvent" is intentionally chosen; the point is not to interrogate or deconstruct such oppositions but to walk around them in order to arrive somewhere else.) And above all, the scission of the subjective versus the objective: I versus they. Any case for art cannot brush aside the salience of first-person response; it is via such response that artworks come to matter, to make claims upon us. (This is one reason I prefer to speak of attachment rather than mediation or translation.) And yet, the personal does not exclude the transpersonal; nor is the experiential at war with the argumentative or the analytical. (Attachment, as we'll see, is about much more than "love.")

What I take from ANT is a certain way of going about things rather than a theory or a self-contained system of ideas. *Hooked* makes no attempt to survey the history or premises of actor-network theory or to summarize the prodigious number of books and essays authored by its most influential thinker, Bruno Latour. Nor is it an attempt to create a "Latourian criticism"—whatever that might mean. Rather, it looks closely at how people connect to novels and paintings and films and music. ANT came on the scene several decades ago as a way of crafting more accurate descriptions of how science *works*. Rather than endorsing soul-stirring stories of heroic discovery or debunking science as nothing more than a smokescreen for capitalist interests, its practitioners followed scientists around in their laboratories and documented the precise details of what they did and said.

By analogy, then, an ANT perspective does not endorse a view of aesthetic experience as transcendent and timeless; but neither does it seek to demystify it by translating it into the categories of another domain—economics, politics, psychoanalysis—that is held to be more fundamental or more real. Instead, it slows down judgment in order to describe more carefully what aesthetic experiences are like and how they are made. Rather than seeking distance from such experiences, it strives to edge closer. Antoine Hennion has done groundbreaking work along these lines, transposing ANT into the fields of art, music, and practices of taste; his influence can be seen everywhere in the following pages. Hennion, however, holds the job description of sociologist; my own emphases, in speaking from and to the humanities, cannot help but fall differently. New questions come to the fore: how attachment relates to traditional accounts of aesthetic experience; to theories of interpretation; to the status of exemplary works in the humanities; to divisions between expert commentary and the responses of lay audiences. If ANT is to be carried over into the humanities, it will be altered, revised, reoriented, betrayed. What follows is, perhaps, less ANT than ANT-ish.

Attachment is often treated as something to be interrogated, while its antithesis gets off scot-free. *Hooked* begins (chapter 1) by flipping things around: looking quizzically at the deference to detachment as the quintessential philosophical ideal and definitive diagnosis of late modernity. Turning to Yasmina Reza's play *"Art,"* I note the existence of status distinctions that would interest Pierre Bourdieu while pointing out that aesthetic relations involve more than power relations. The attachment theory of psychologists John Bowlby and Donald Winnicott might offer a more positive resource, yet here again the specter of reductionism threatens: we cannot do justice to aesthetic attachments as long as we explain them in terms of something else. Art hooks up to many other things; but it is not based on them or encased by them. Meanwhile, caring for art involves more than pleasure or feeling; it also brings into play second-order assessments of why art matters.

The first "attachment device" I consider is *attunement*—those affinities, inclinations, stirrings that often fall below the threshold of consciousness (chapter 2). Why, for example, are we drawn to a painting or piece of music in ways we struggle to explain while being left cold by others whose merits we duly acknowledge? In recent decades, talk of the ineffable has often been taboo—seen as evidence of Romanticism, elitism, mysticism, or other thought crimes. Yet most people can point to novels or movies or music— whether Mozart or Mötley Crüe—that affect them strongly in ways they find hard to articulate. Doing justice to such experiences will mean moving beyond standard forms of phenomenological or sociological explanation and attending to the surprising as well as the scripted, the sensuous as well as the sense-full, yet without pitching aesthetic experience outside the social world. Ranging across diverse examples of attunement, with a focus on Zadie Smith's conversion to the music of Joni Mitchell, I reflect on the agency of artworks, the duration and rhythms of becoming attuned, and the question of art's presence.

The following chapter turns to *identification*—a widespread response to fiction that is often invoked by critics but rarely fully seen. And here arguments are commonly derailed by treating identification as synonymous with empathy, on the one hand, and with identity, on the other. Yet identifying has no neat fit with identity categories; meanwhile, it can trigger ethical, political, or intellectual affinities that have little to do with co-feeling. Here I disentangle several strands of identification: alignment, allegiance, recognition, and empathy. What people most commonly identify with are characters—who are alluring, arresting, alive, not in spite of their aesthetic qualities but because of them. Yet fictional and real persons also overlap: the confusion of character and author in certain genres of fiction; the merging of character and star when watching a film. Characters are hybrids patched together out of fiction and life. Reflecting on the allure of Camus's antihero Meursault, I coin the idea of ironic identification: a style of attachment-via-shared-disassociation that also permeates the contemporary humanities. Rather than being limited to naive readers or over-invested viewers, identifying turns out to be a defining aspect of what scholars do.

The fourth chapter considers academic *interpretation* as another circuit of connection: critics forge ties to the works they explicate, the methods they use, and the disciplinary identities they inhabit. Yet an explicit concern with attachment can also alter *how* we interpret. And here I consider the salience of scale and stance. I elaborate on how an ANT-ish approach is compatible with differences in scale—tracing works within networks as well as networks within works—while justifying my own focus on midlevel ties between works and audiences as fundamental to clarifying what art does and why it matters. Drawing on the recent work of David Scott and Toril Moi, I ask what exactly it might mean to be receptive or generous and how knowledge is related to acknowledgment. How, finally, might such questions be relevant to the classroom? Being exposed to unfamiliar works or being exposed differently to familiar ones, learning new techniques of analysis and habits of attention—such practices of analytical engagement can alter the vector of our attachments.

In *The Limits of Critique*, I raised the question of what kinds of responses art elicits: what perceptual changes it triggers, what affective bonds it calls into being. What would it mean, I wondered, to do justice to these responses rather than treating them as naive, rudimentary, or defective? To be less shamefaced about being shaken or stirred, absorbed or enchanted? To forge a language of attachment as intellectually robust and refined as our rhetoric of detachment?[1] The hill on which I'm prepared to die is my conviction that the social meanings of artworks are not encrypted in their depths—perceptible only to those trained in professional techniques of interpretation. Rather—or so *Hooked* contends—any such meanings can be activated or actualized only by their differing audiences: calling for a rethinking of the fundaments of aesthetic experience.

On Being Attached

How does a novel entice or enlist us; how does a song surprise or seduce us? Why do we bridle when a friend belittles a book we love or fall into a funk when a favored TV show comes to an end? Attachment, I've suggested, has more than one meaning: to be attached is to be affected or moved and also to be linked or tied. It denotes passion and compassion—but also an array of ethical, political, intellectual, or other bonds. *Hooked* makes a case for "attachment" as a vital keyword for the humanities. Why do works of art matter? Because they create, or cocreate, enduring ties.

To focus on attachment is to trace out relations without presuming foundations. To look closely at acts of connecting as well as what one is connected to; the transpersonal as well as the personal; things in the world as well as things in works of art. It is less a topic or a theme than a style of thinking, a way of becoming sensitized to issues that are often sidelined in scholarship. My argument edges forward crabwise by attending to examples: Zadie Smith's conversion to Joni Mitchell; Patricia Hampl being hammered by a Matisse; Mohsin Hamid's invitation to empathy in *Exit West*; feminist allegiances with *Thelma and Louise*; ironic identification with Camus's *The Stranger*; ties between paintings and friends in Yasmina Reza's *"Art"*; Geoff Dyer being turned off and then turned on by Tarkovsky's *Stalker*; Wayne Koestenbaum's affinity with a stentorian phrase from Brahms; the geography of emotion in Eva Hoffman's *Lost in Translation*; my twinge of recognition on reading Thomas Bernhard; David Scott's generosity toward Stuart Hall.

Why go about things this way? The goal, in Annemarie Mol's words, is "not to fight until a single pattern holds, but to add on ever more layers and enrich the repertoire."[1] Stabs at analysis are needed to clarify our attunement to a certain song and not another, or why "empathy" may feel like the wrong word for a felt affinity with a fictional character. And yet the piling up of examples can mess up tidy schemas: causing generalizations to crumble, thwarting our best efforts to pin down and pigeonhole. Aesthetic theories often rein in this unruliness by staking their claims on a selective vision, writing as if aesthetic experience were always disinterested or rapturous or ethically consequential or politically motivated. In doing so, they overlook important differences in how people respond to works of art.

Attachment doesn't get much respect in academia. It is often outsourced to others—naive readers, gullible consumers, small-town patriots, too-needy lovers—and treated as a cause for concern, a regrettable, if common, human software malfunction. The history of critique, remark Luc Boltanski and Eve Chiapello, pits detachment against attachment, mobility against stability. In contrast to the bourgeoisie glued to their possessions—or women bound to their families and children—modern artists and intellectuals strive to slip free of ties, taking their cues from the figure of the Baudelairean dandy.[2] The critical frameworks of the last half century largely echo and endorse this modernist vision; any specialness accruing to art lies in its power to desist or resist, to break bonds rather than make bonds. The language du jour is one of dislocating, disorienting, demystifying. But perhaps the true naïfs are those critics who imagine themselves free of attachments.

The fear of stickiness is the fear of being stuck in place, of having one's freedom constrained and one's mobility impeded. And yet things move, and we move with them; we travel, and our attachments come along for the ride. We are talking about Velcro rather than superglue: connecting parts that move against each other, that can often be unhooked and rehooked. Stickiness is not something to be regretted or repudiated, as the condition of those unable to slide through the world with sufficient dexterity and ease. It is, rather, a nonnegotiable aspect of being in the world. Our critical languages extol the merits of unbinding and unraveling, and yet our critical practices tell a different story.

Attachments, of course, are not always positive. We can be drawn to things that hurt or humiliate, that feed our narcissism or pander to our delusions, that shore up half-baked ideas or wrongheaded beliefs. The playing field, moreover, is conspicuously uneven. Female readers have—of sheer necessity—glommed on to male writers more than the other way around, while most of the world's cultures bear the imprint of a Western canon of art and beauty. Is there not a risk, then, of idealizing or romanticizing attachment? All attachment is optimistic, writes Lauren Berlant, and yet such optimism becomes cruel when we are drawn to things that diminish or damage us. And Sara Ahmed reflects on how stickiness can get us stuck; binding can become a form of blocking; people can become deeply attached, for example, to schemas of racist thought.[3]

Yet, as Ahmed goes on to say, there is a tendency among critics to treat ties *only* this way: as if the condition of being-attached were an inherent weakness or defect, as if ties served only as restraints and limits. The upshot is a one-sidedness that not only simplifies the attachments of others but leaves us floundering to account for our own. It is not a matter of idealizing ties but of facing up to the ubiquity and inescapability of ties. Even the most searing or skeptical of judgments depends on a prior, if unacknowledged, commitment. Scholars are adept at theorizing, historicizing, and politicizing the investments of others—while often remaining coy or evasive about their own. What do we feel obligated to? What keeps us up at night? Taking attachment seriously—which does not mean denying ambivalence, friction, or discomfort—means grappling with the issue of what carries weight. It has both affective and ethical force.

We might begin by noting that aesthetic experiences are actively sought out. People break open a novel or watch a movie or stop to look at a painting in the hope of gaining something: solace or self-understanding, a frisson of pleasure or an insight into the world or the self. (Without discounting such motives as impressing one's friends or gaining cultural capital, I propose that such explanations take us only so far.) Yet these expectations are often overridden and overwritten by the metalanguages of criticism. Joli Jensen puts it well: "to reduce what other people do to dysfunction or class position or psychic needs or socioeconomic status is to reduce others to uninteresting pawns in a game of outside sources and to glorify ourselves as somehow off the playing field, observing and describing what is really going on."[4] Whether their approach is critical or affirmative, critics feel obliged to read novels, films, and paintings closely, with due attention to detail—yet lay responses to such texts are often held at arm's length, explained away before being fully seen. Not only are such responses more multifaceted than critics acknowledge, but they are also less remote from their own practices than they might think. (That identification and attunement are not listed as course learning goals or pondered in the pages of *PMLA* does not mean they do not affect academic life.)

It is not that research on lay audiences is lacking—many such accounts have piled up over the years—and yet they've made barely a dent in prevailing views about what it means to be a sophisticated reader or discerning appreciator of art. Again and again—in the aside of an essay, the sotto voce remark at a lecture—assumptions are aired about the inevitable gulf between scholarly and lay response. One reason for the nonimpact of audience studies on the mainstream of the humanities surely lies in its splicing of these audiences into very specific demographics: studies of Harlequin romance readers or of Bruce Springsteen fans. The very framing of such responses as "other"—as the property of a group that is not one's own—lets critics off the hook. It allows them to keep such responses at arm's length; to dismiss them as being of merely sociological interest; to evade, in short, their normative implications for, and provocation to, a certain academic self-image. What Deidre Lynch writes of the study of English holds true for the humanities generally: oppositions between a specialized guild of interpreters concerned with knowledge and meaning and a broader public driven only by feeling and pleasure create a distorted picture of both.[5]

How to tackle this dichotomy of the clueless versus the critical, those who are stuck to their love objects versus those who have pried themselves free? Over the last few decades, cultural studies has assailed this opposition on behalf of popular audiences, rebutting portrayals of such audiences as passive, overly emotional, and entirely uncritical. But less has been written about the *other* side of the divide: how responses of more educated readers or viewers— including academics—are shaped by investments, how they are entangled and affectively thick. Feminist and queer scholars have done most work along these lines, yet their ideas are too rarely taken up in other fields. In his book on musical taste, Carl Wilson urges critics to cling less tightly to their defensive postures of detachment and coolness and to own up to their enjoyment, "with all its messiness and private soul tremors."[6] As his phrasing suggests, interests are not absent, even if they are unaccounted for. The most jaded of critics are invested, if only in their own upmanship—and often in a great deal more. We are always *oriented* in some way: turned toward or against certain possibilities of feeling, thought, and action.

Attachment, meanwhile, is not just a matter of emotion. The point is not to shunt from the objective to the subjective but from a language of bifurcation (art versus society, text versus context) to one of relation. Attachments are not only psychological but involve many forms of joining, connecting, meeting. This means zeroing in on differing kinds of ties. People can become attached in a quite literal sense: the dog-eared paperback that rides around town in a jacket pocket; the lyrics streaming through the headphones that are glued to a student's ears; the Matisse postcard that is propped up on a desk and carried from one sublet to the next. Attachments can be institutional (the novel that crops up every year on my syllabus), cognitive (the essay that gave me a new intellectual vocabulary), ethical or political (the core beliefs and commitments that shape how I react to a controversial film). These connections sustain not only experiences of art but perceptions of its value. To the Shakespeare scholar, there is a world of difference between *Henry IV Part 1* and *Part 2*; the Stephen King fan will be highly indignant if you confuse *Cujo* and *Christine*. It is via the forging of ties—the acquisition of know-how, the honing of attention, exposure to examples, input from friends or teachers or reviewers—that novels or pictures or films come to matter: that they become more present, more vivid, more real.

That attachments are *made* in this way is often acknowledged, but only in order to score a point. Over the last few decades, the rhetoric of "social construction" has been weaponized to weaken the status of artworks, to downgrade them to a shadow of their former selves. Actor-network theory's style of thinking, however, is additive, not subtractive. That various factors are involved—that our attachments are shaped by the world into which we are thrown—does not lessen the import of these attachments or their objects. The fabrication of things does not have to be played out *against* them—to diminish or undercut them—but can also be played out *with* them, remarks Antoine Hennion.[7] That ties to artworks must be made does not weaken their value; that we help create the work does not mean it cannot surprise us. How to account for the complexity of this co-making?

We need to do justice to what the artwork does. The poem intervenes; the painting arrests a nonchalant viewer; the movie makes something happen. Someone is drawn to a haunting refrain, a quirky narrator, a burst of pigment: features that beg to be described, detailed, captured. For the fan, the enthusiast, the aficionado, such qualities matter. This mattering is built into the meaning of attachment: that we are drawn to one thing and emphatically not to another; that its specialness is nonnegotiable; that we are riled when we see it being treated as a stand-in for something else. "A work of art *engages* us," writes Latour, "and if it is quite true that it has to be interpreted, at no point do we have the feeling that we are free to do 'whatever we want' with it. . . . Someone who says 'I love Bach' . . . receives from Bach, we might almost say 'downloads' from Bach, the wherewithal to appreciate him."[8] Works of art invite and enlist us; they draw us down certain perceptual or interpretive paths. They have their own distinctiveness and dignity, can affect us in ways we did not imagine or anticipate, are not just pawns in a game of social distinction or blank screens onto which we project our idées fixes.

And yet these works of art also need our devotion. Their existence depends on being taken up by readers or viewers or listeners, as figures through whom they must pass. Without these intermediaries, they are destined to fade away into nothingness, are reduced, in Latour's evocative words, to "failure, loss, or oblivion: abandoned stage sets, rolled up canvases, now useless accessories, incrusted palettes, moth-eaten tutus."[9] What an artwork affords is exceptionally hard to disentangle from our response; its qualities disclose themselves only as we attend to them. We make the artwork even as it makes us. Rebecca Solnit writes: "the object we call a book is not the real book, but its potential, like a musical score or seed. It exists fully only in the act of being read; and its . . . home is inside the head of the reader, where the symphony resounds, the seed germinates."[10] Artworks must be *activated* to exist.

Meanwhile, these works arrive at our doorstep already wreathed in interventions and appropriations of many kinds, thanks to the diligence of publishers, agents, teachers, friends, curators, reviewers, and, in some cases, long histories of commentary. These mediations are not extraneous to a work, to be yanked off like pesky vines encroaching on a pristine house wall. They form an essential part of it, shaping what we perceive and why it comes to matter in the first place. (Because this book was on the syllabus, I grew to love it; because I heard that song on the radio one rainy Tuesday, it became the anthem of my early twenties.) As Hennion puts it, there is never a naked face-to-face of subject and object; even if we brood over a page of prose in monastic solitude, the air is thick with the ghosts of the many coactors who made the encounter possible.[11] Attachments are a matter not only of individual receptiveness but also of catalysts, sparks, triggers—all those influences that steer us toward an affinity for certain works, in predictable but also in surprising ways.

An essay by Wayne Koestenbaum captures beautifully what is at stake: the triangulation among a work, its recipient, and a penumbra of influences. Koestenbaum reflects on being drawn, as a teenager, to the opening movement of a Brahms piano concerto. Puzzling over the sources of this enigmatic affinity, he is drawn into a labyrinthian line of questioning that testifies to the impossibility of nailing down a single or simple causal explanation:

> Was Brahms the object? Was it the particular interval (minor seventh? ninth?) that the opening phrase traversed? . . . Was my object the piano's affinity with the orchestra, an ensemble chained to the dominating, hubristic piano? Did I feel affinity with finger-wizard Rudolf Serkin, with maestro George Szell, or their imagined affinity? Was my object—affinity's bull's-eye—my piano teacher, a diminutive young woman who'd played that daunting concerto earlier, as a soloist with a college orchestra? Did I feel an affinity with this teacher, whose narcissism, and whose audacious virtuosity, I imagined as a nougat I wanted to eat? Did I feel an affinity with D minor itself, the signature of woe and of containment within that comforting category, woe? . . . Was I mesmerized by Brahms's affinity with Beethoven, or Brahms's ties to Schumann? . . . Did I feel an affinity with modernity or with tonality's rupture, even if tonality was not yet being destroyed, even if I'd be a fool to say that this opening phrase predicted Schoenberg?[12]

In this passage—which winds on for many more sentences—Koestenbaum spins out a tangled web of associations. He felt compelled by the stentorian ugliness of Brahms's theme: its avoidance of happiness and its testy rejection of optimism and productivity resonated with his own feelings of malaise. The music felt masculine, even paternal (a difficult father?); it seemed aggressive, ambitious, Promethean; it conveyed a refusal to cooperate, a desire to throttle the environment; its surliness spoke to his own youthful sentiments. He felt called by the music, summoned into an excited blur of fear, love, and disgust, drawn to an aura of dominant magnetism. It was an affinity, he observes, that his younger self might have described as satanic, anarchic, family destroying but that brought no intellectual program or coherent ideology in its wake.

How to account for this attachment? The essay's trail leads to the pianist, the conductor, Koestenbaum's piano teacher, Brahms's rivalry with Schumann, the history and tonality of modern music—but also, in another passage, back to the affective turbulence of a queer youth, with its "childhood bedroom, its carpet, its curtain-filtered sunshine, its pessimism, its cramps, its *Mod Squad*, its dead flies."[13] Koestenbaum's essay alerts us to what actor-network theory calls "distributed agency"—that attachments to artworks are the result not of a single all-powerful cause steering things behind the scenes but of different things coming together in ways that are often hard to pin down. Ties that are parceled out for analysis among differing disciplines—musicology, psychology, cultural sociology—turn out to be hopelessly entangled. The starting point of Koestenbaum's inquiry is his fascination with a specific musical theme, yet this affinity opens out on to an entire world.

Semidetached

Why has the idea of detachment commanded such unconditional loyalty and staunch support? The driving goal of modern thought, it often seems, is to wrest oneself free from a primordial immersion in the given. Whether one turns to Hegel or Foucault, it is only by distancing oneself from what exists that one can gain any kind of critical purchase on it. Alienation is, in this sense, an indispensable element of philosophy and politics; even when viewed in a negative light, it is taken to be irrevocable, a fundament of our historical condition. What defines modernity is a sundering of persons from any form of taken-for-granted community or unity. To be modern is to be ripped free of the bonds of tradition and superstition, to be borne along by shock waves of social upheaval and secular disenchantment. The only alternatives are the false consolations of naivete or nostalgia.

Yet this view of modernity as a drama of scission and separation, unbinding and loosening—what Charles Taylor calls the subtraction story—is in need of reappraisal. While some ties are broken, new ones are forged. Romantic love, for example, has assumed a previously inconceivable importance over the last two centuries, even while being thickly leavened with irony and ambivalence. As Eva Illouz has shown, it embodies a distinctively modern bond between persons that is implicated in struggles for social recognition.[14] To be sure, accelerating waves of mobility across countries and continents have led to a crumbling of communities based around village or tribe. And yet, as old groupings have disappeared, new ones have proliferated in urban and now virtual spaces: sexual minorities and political pressure groups; Star Wars fans and Wagner aficionados. We are not less connected but differently connected; contemporary tribes have their own totems, rituals, and professions of faith. Hiro Saito points out that cosmopolitanism is less a matter of transcending attachments—a condition of lonely exile—than of multiplying attachments to nonlocal and nonnational others.[15] And once we factor in the vast spectrum of nonhuman actors in late modernity— the smartphones, shower gels, serotonin inhibitors, and shoes that populate countless lives—we might well conclude that our condition is one of ever-greater entanglement, of proliferating ties and multiplying dependencies.

At a philosophical level, meanwhile, detachment has been hailed as a precondition for any form of knowledge. This preference makes a certain intuitive sense: by standing back from phenomena, we strive to achieve greater insight. Thinking presumes a degree of distancing: the ability to discriminate between stronger and weaker claims, to sort and sift among modes of reasoning. We scrutinize our own biases, strive to correct our blind spots. And yet a complete impartiality is neither possible nor desirable. Perhaps the best we can strive for—and here I'm pulled back to the landscape of my British childhood, those sedate pairs of houses, cozily coupled and snuggled together, so redolent of lower-middle-class respectability!—is to be *semidetached*. The semidetached house is a residential unit that is linked to its neighbor; sharing a structural wall, it cannot stand alone. By analogy, we can distance ourselves from a few things at a time but never from everything at once.[16] As certain questions move into the forefront of consciousness, others fade into the background. Moments of insight can emerge only against a horizon of unchallenged—indeed, unnoticed—assumptions. For one strand of modern thought (relevant figures would include Heidegger, Merleau-Ponty, Polanyi, Taylor) such embedding is not a closing off of possibility but the precondition of any form of meaningful engagement.

A striving for unbridled lucidity, writes Polanyi, can wreak havoc on understandings of complex phenomena, which invite us to "dwell in" things rather than to scrutinize them from afar.[17] Distance is not always better than closeness: the bird's-eye view will miss crucial details and telling anomalies; it may result in knowing less rather than more. The coherence of critical theories is their forte but also their frailty; while intellectually appealing and morally compelling, they can be a poor fit for the messiness of reality—or of art. Meanwhile, it is not a matter of discarding thought in order to embrace a rapturous state of vibrating, throbbing, and wordless gaping. To query the *doxa* of detachment is not to elevate feeling over thought but to reflect on their intertwining. As Hans-Georg Gadamer reminds us, prejudices—that is to say, prejudgments— are not obstacles to thought but the precondition for any kind of thought; as Donna Haraway points out, it is only from a situated perspective that any kind of objectivity can be achieved. Even the most abstract and high-flown speculation, even the most iconoclastic or ironic of postures, pivots on a connection to *something*.

How does aesthetic experience relate to such questions? In its narrow sense, the phrase has come to denote a pleasure in beauty for its own sake rather than for any moral, practical, or other entailments it might bring. In the *Third Critique*, Kant gives an account of such pleasure as it relates to judgments of taste: it is subjective, since it cannot be justified by appealing to concepts; and yet it is also normative, since we cannot help wanting others to share our judgment. Aesthetic pleasure differs from finding something agreeable, moreover, in involving a stance of disinterest. Formalist critics seized on this account to construct a full-blown theory of art. What defines an artwork, they argue, are its qualities of significant form; these qualities demand a specific kind of response, in which everyday concerns and commitments are suspended. According to Clive Bell, "to appreciate a work of art we need bring with us nothing from life, no knowledge of its ideas or affairs, no familiarity with its emotions, . . . nothing but a sense of form and colour and a knowledge of three-dimensional space."[18] Aesthetic experience comes to serve as an exemplary—perhaps *the* exemplary— form of detached experience, and what defines art is its potential to offer such an experience.

This line of thought has been assailed from all sides over the last half century. Politically minded critics disputed the view that art could be cut off from its contexts, citing countless examples of aesthetic judgments steered—sometimes in the most transparent fashion—by ideological interests. Philosophers of art in the analytical tradition were no less damning: not only was the idea of "aesthetic experience" hopelessly impressionistic, but it could not deliver any kind of tenable distinction between art and non-art. The significance of *Brillo Boxes*, Arthur Danto pointed out, had nothing to do with its discernible aesthetic properties calling forth a subjective response. It was a matter, rather, of grasping Warhol's work as a conceptual provocation to the prior history and understanding of art. In the case against aesthetics—widely charged with being romantic, reactionary, apolitical, or incoherent—the idea of "aesthetic experience" served as Exhibit A.[19]

Yet these polemics have gradually subsided, alongside a growing recognition that aesthetics encompasses far more than Kant, Bell, or Greenberg. And while its associations with racial and gender inequalities are now amply documented, critics have testified to the vital role of aesthetic expression as a source of solace for the disenfranchised. Such expression serves as a stylized barrier, Paul C. Taylor writes, that can be held up against the incursions of a hostile world. His study of black aesthetics, conceived as an assembly of diverse forms and practices, elaborates on how beauty, structure, and meaning have been embraced as a form of consolation as well as an act of defiance in the face of oppression.[20]

Meanwhile, Susan Sontag's sally against interpretation half a century ago is getting a newly attentive hearing, alongside her rallying call for an erotics of art. There is a sharpening sense of the limits of decoding and deciphering, a feeling that hermeneutics can turn into hermeneutering, as Richard Shusterman puts it: a scholarly suffocating of art's incandescent energies. Might the language of aesthetic experience be worth rescuing? It conveys, after all, a widespread intuition that encounters with art can be valuable, absorbing, meaningful, and distinctive—even if artworks are not the only source of aesthetic experience and not all artworks deliver such experience.[21] Can we do justice to this intuition without falling back into a view of art and aesthetics as cut off from the rest of life?

Noel Carroll offers one solution: aesthetic experience in its narrow sense exists, he proposes, but as one response among others, with no superior or honorific status. (He calls this solution a "de-flationary" account.) We can, after all, pay attention to the design of a painting or a sculpture, weighing up whether or not it hangs together, responding to its formal, sensuous, or expressive quali-ties. But we also have moral, intellectual, or political responses to artworks that are no less valid and that may be actively solicited by the works in question. Derek Attridge writes from within a differ-ent tradition, yet his position has certain parallels to Carroll's in acknowledging literary and nonliterary response, while also sepa-rating them from each other. "Though works of literature," he ob-serves, "may offer lessons on living, and this may be an important aspect of their social value, it is not *as literature that they do so*." Elsewhere, Attridge differentiates between the literariness of a text and other qualities it may possess, such as rhetorical effectiveness, emotive appeal, or an imaginative modeling of utopian projects.[22]

This might look like a promising line of thought—one that strives to be pluralist and ecumenical. Yet is it really feasible to distinguish so assuredly between aesthetic and other forms of re-sponse? Between the literariness of a work and the jostling crowd of influences pressing in from all sides? My crush on Kazuo Ishiguro's *The Unconsoled* (see chapter 2) is partly prompted by the inspired pairing of its matter-of-fact language with a weirdly off-kilter fic-tional world. But—pace Koestenbaum—can I definitively disentan-gle this affinity from the shadow of Kafka that falls over Ishiguro's writing and my reading; from a personal history that inclines me toward Central European themes and sensibilities; from an in-grained preference—inflected by personality and temperament—for writing that is subdued rather than showy (Kafka rather than Joyce; Coetzee rather than Rushdie)? Severed from everything that makes me who I am, could I have any kind of aesthetic response at all?

It is not just that I cannot unstick myself from my own attributes while having an aesthetic response. It is also that the "separate but equal" position conceives of reactions to artworks—like the fridge-freezer combos available for purchase at Lowe's and Best Buy—as existing *side by side*: I have an aesthetic *or* a moral-political re-sponse *or* an emotional response. And yet these are often blended in ways that make it impossible to pry them apart. It is not just that political or affective response is mediated by aesthetic properties, but that aesthetic properties can augment or intensify the force of such response. (As we'll see in the next chapter, it was *Thelma and Louise*'s refashioning of genre conventions and sublime visuals that rendered it a powerful source of feminist identification.) Works of art have the potential to stir up ethical and political emotions—empathy, anger, outrage, solidarity—*by dint of their aesthetic qualities.*

As Winfried Fluck remarks, "taking an aesthetic attitude toward an object does not mean, or at least does not necessarily mean, that we disengage the object or ourselves from reality.... [T]he aesthetic function may become dominant, but it does not become exclusive."[23] Aesthetic responses are often mixed: it is not a matter of either/or but both/and. In attending to the formal or aesthetic qualities of a work, we may briefly bracket practical urgencies, but this does not mean that all reference to reality is lost. Art's promise of insight or pleasure exists in relation to a larger world and often feeds back into that same world. Everyday reality is not eclipsed by art; it is *reconfigured* by it.

That aesthetic experiences are mixed, admittedly, does not mean that they are always mixed in exactly the same proportions. There may be times when worldly concerns seem to fade entirely away; there is a sense of being arrested by the sheer thereness, or presence, of an artwork (the timbre of Joni Mitchell's voice; the delicately etched ruffs of a Vermeer). A grain of truth adheres to the Kantian idea that aesthetic perception can distance us from real-world concerns—but there's no reason why this distancing should serve as the ideal or prototype against which all engagements with artworks are measured. Meanwhile, "disinterestedness" does not quite capture the quality of this attention, which possesses its own force and intensity. As Jean-Marie Schaeffer remarks, "the aesthete seeking a sublime painting is no less interested than a fetishist seeking a foot—or a shoe—that suits him."[24] Attending to the formal elements of art may bring into play varying affects or dispositions, from the reflective to the rapturous, from the ecstatic to the ironic. But there is no single aesthetic attitude, no defining mode of pure or disengaged contemplation, that unites them.

The phrase "aesthetic experience" comes, meanwhile, with a

great deal of baggage; it often conjures up a drama that is being played out in the shuttered cells of individual minds. Kant, admittedly, reckons with the intersubjective aspects of such experience (we want our judgments to be shared by others), while Dewey spins the idea of experience to stress its communal and democratic qualities. But the default scenario, in most accounts of what it means to have an aesthetic experience, is a dyadic encounter on an empty stage: a solitary self faces a self-contained work. And yet, as we've already seen, a host of other players are involved. Our feelings about a novel or film are colored by multiple factors: a trenchant or effusive review, its presence on a college syllabus, scraps of random knowledge about an author or director. "Literary evaluation," remarks James Wood, cannot be separated from "the general messiness of being alive. . . . Your love of Chekhov might be influenced by the knowledge that he named one of his dachshunds Quinine."[25] Differing things come together; the singular qualities of Chekhov's writings, to be sure, but also, perhaps, a battered biography unearthed in a secondhand bookstore, a course on Russian literature taken in college, a friend's account of an off-Broadway performance of *Uncle Vanya.*

It is here that the language of "attachment" offers a crucial reorientation: one that blends response with relations, the personal with the transpersonal. What phenomenology gets right is that aesthetic experience can happen only in the first person: no one can listen or read or look for you; no one else can have *your* response. To treat such experiences as symptoms of larger structures is to erase those very qualities that define them: their perceptual and sensual textures, their variability, the way they are experienced as "mine." And yet readers and viewers do not exist in a vacuum; many things must have happened before I can gawp in admiration at a Manet at the Met. Many of the questions raised by cultural sociologists are thus entirely a propos. *Aesthetic experience is mediated; aesthetic experience can feel intensely immediate.* Both propositions hold true, and neither negates or cancels out the other.[26]

Yet they are often opposed or, at the very least, dispatched to different disciplines: as if talk of absorption or aesthetic pleasure cannot coexist with accounts of ties. There is no zero-sum game where the more "social" the artwork is, the less "aesthetic" it must be! We acquire forms of know-how that help us to engage a text; yet this text also solicits us in certain ways. Meanwhile, perception is shaped by the input of others, such that the question of what comes from the artwork or from elsewhere is difficult to disentangle. You look at a painting, Latour remarks, and "a friend of yours points out a feature you had not noticed—you are thus *made to see* something. Who is seeing it? You of course. And yet wouldn't you freely acknowledge that you would not have seen it *without* your friend? So who has seen the delicate feature? Is it you or your friend? The question is absurd."[27] Our seeing often depends on the seeing of others.

Cue Yasmina Reza's *"Art"*: a play about three middle-aged Parisian men whose friendship is cast out of joint by the purchase of a painting. Finding out that friends dislike an artwork you love can cast a pall over your relationship: how could they be so insensitive or obtuse? Conversely, our aesthetic responses are often colored by the reactions of others, not necessarily—or not only—because we are sycophants anxious to conform, but because their input helps us to see what we could not perceive by ourselves. Philosophies of art, remarks Noel Carroll, stress its impact on the individual or society as a whole. Yet art "is not just a personal affair, nor is it only a force in society writ large. It is also a medium through which we forge our small-scale, face-to-face, everyday relations with others."[28] We often go to movies and concerts with friends, thrash out disagreements about a novel over a coffee or a beer; yet little has been written on the topic of art and friendship.

"Art" starts with Serge announcing that he has bought an expensive abstract painting by the artist Antrios: a large white canvas marked by almost invisible diagonal lines. His friend Marc is filled with a deep sense of unease; he laments Serge's willingness to be ripped off, his loss of discernment. His oldest friend has become a snob and an aesthete: someone who talks about deconstruction and drops the phrase "incredibly modern" into his conversation. In short, Marc feels betrayed and abandoned; Serge has become a stranger, with pretentious and incomprehensible tastes. "I love Serge," he mourns, "and I can't love the Serge who is capable of buying that painting." The acquisition of the Antrios frays the ties

of their friendship; the austere minimalism that enchants Serge feels like a personal affront to Marc.

Serge responds by going on the counterattack, accusing his friend of taking pride in being a philistine. He extols the beauty of the painting, enthusing over how its whiteness fades into a spectrum of very light grays. He has not simply acquired an Antrios, like some cynical speculator on the art market: he loves the Antrios! Yet Marc, bristling with resentment, cannot accept this love at face value but must cynically reduce it to venal motives. "You've denied," Serge says bitterly, "that I could feel a genuine attachment to it." Their needy and insecure friend, Yvan, attempts to placate both of them: agreeing with Marc that Serge has gone crazy; with Serge that Marc is being insufferable. We are invited to consider how attachments to friends and to artworks are intertwined.

From one perspective, Reza's play speaks to Pierre Bourdieu's arguments that taste is just a way of demarcating and sustaining cultural hierarchies. Not only does your background affect the kind of artworks you like (Bach rather than Barry Manilow, Rothko rather than Renoir), but you like them in different ways. To be highly educated is to be schooled in an "aesthetic disposition"—an appreciation of form in relation to the history of art—while those without such training fall back on commonsense criteria: moral or political subject matter, the realism of a painting or the hummability of a tune. From the latter perspective, modern art can only look like an elaborate con trick; for their part, meanwhile, those with advanced degrees can look down their noses at devotees of Thomas Kinkade or Celine Dion. Serge's attachment to his Antrios, in this light, signals not only his affluence but also his ease with a certain critical language. And here Marc is not wrong to perceive a dividing line: between those who "get" modern art and those who don't. Not just a division but a status hierarchy, one that leaves Marc, the engineer with a technical education, stranded on the wrong side, tongue-tied, maladroit, and resentful. (In his own apartment hangs a pseudo-Flemish landscape looking out on to Carcassonne.)

And yet the Antrios is not *only* a means of shoring up distinctions. It does other things too, though they will elude the gaze of a Bourdieusian sociologist intent on seeing art as nothing more than an exercise in symbolic domination. Like any work of art, it exists via its ties. Yet these ties involve far more than struggles over cultural capital: the four-part relation between the three friends and the painting is also an elaborate dance of intimacy and distance, fascination and frustration, self and other. Marc, Serge, and Yvan are forced to confront the question of who they are and how well they know, or don't know, each other. (An existential leitmotif of the play is posed by the offstage psychoanalyst Finkelzohn: are you what you think you are or what your friends think you are?) Encountering a new painting, viewers may intone critical pieties gleaned from the Sunday supplements to impress their friends, as Bourdieu might suggest. But they may also burst into tears for reasons they cannot explain (James Elkins on people crying in front of pictures), or set off on a yearlong pilgrimage to see other works by the same artist (Michael White's *Travels in Vermeer*), or slash a painting with a razor (Dario Gamboni on the history of artistic vandalism).[29]

They may even—though very rarely!—draw another picture on top of the picture. In a gesture of contrition and self-sacrifice, Serge offers a felt-tip pen to his aggrieved friend. Grabbing hold of the pen and sketching a skier with a little woolly hat on the Antrios, Marc defaces it—or, seen from another angle, he makes the painting his own. Abstract art is transformed into a representational image; whiteness now signifies the blinding sheets of a snow blizzard. The ink is washable, it turns out, and the Antrios has been returned to a pristine state by the play's conclusion. But it is Marc who intones the play's closing lines and is given the last word on the painting: "A solitary man glides downhill on his skis. / The snow is falling. / It falls until the man disappears back into the landscape. / My friend Serge, who's one of my oldest friends, has bought a painting. / It's a canvas about five foot by four. / It represents a man who moves across a space and disappears."[30]

"Art" ends with Marc affirming a tie to the painting and reaffirming his tie to Serge. He now glimpses something in the Antrios he did not see before; in altering the painting, he has also been altered by it. The final sentence of the play—"a man who moves across a space and disappears"—acknowledges absence as well as presence, points to what is indiscernible as well as what is visible. The painting has acquired a new salience for Marc; it now bristles

with meanings that exceed the schemas of the sociologist's questionnaire. And yet this semantic richness has little to do with "autonomous art" as it is usually understood. Marc's original dislike of the Antrios is wrapped up with his feelings for Serge and his resentment at being replaced by a painting; his change of heart and altered perception are inseparable from his desire to salvage their friendship. Nicolas Bourriaud coined the phrase "relational aesthetics" to describe new styles of staging and performing art in the 1990s; yet Reza's play proposes that abstract painting is no less relational, no less connected, no less entangled than any other kind. In *"Art"* she traces out relays of attachments between artworks and persons that neither Kant nor Bourdieu can help us to decipher, that cannot be explained in terms of either aesthetic disinterest or metaphors of capital. "Friendship," Reza has remarked, "is at least as strong and as difficult as love."[31]

Attachment Devices

My line of argument should not be confused with "attachment theory": the school of psychology associated with John Bowlby and Donald Winnicott that identifies infant-parent bonds as the driving force of human development. Some critics have turned to child psychology to explain aesthetic response, treating artworks as transitional objects that, like the toddler's blanket, help us to negotiate the relationship between self and other. Yet novels and paintings are hardly the equivalent of blankets or stuffed animals; relations to artworks differ in kind from attachments to mothers and other caregivers. The writer Tim Parks, for example, asks some sharp questions about the puzzle of aesthetic affinities: why a certain novel will gel with a reader while another work makes no sense; how putting down a book in frustration can be likened to choosing not to pursue a friendship. Yet his answer—that it is all down to early family dynamics, as explicated by the Ugazio school of psychology—cannot help but disappoint.[32]

In this way of thinking, aesthetic ties are translated into something else; in being explained, they are explained away. For Parks, this "something else" is family dynamics; for other critics, it may be repression and the unconscious or capitalism and the commodity form or discourses and institutions. The critic nails down a final cause, of which relations to artworks are held to be effects. The issue of causality can be tackled with varying degrees of finesse: Marxist critics have pounced on this question with the passion of medieval scholars debating the finer points of theological doctrine, discriminating between models of mechanical, expressive, and structural causality. Meanwhile, the Frankfurt Four (Lukács, Adorno, Brecht, and Benjamin) have crafted some of the most dazzling modern commentaries on art. While Marxist criticism is often seen as reducing art to ideology, these critics take pains to underscore art's *difference* from ideology—its relative autonomy, its critique of capitalist structures. And yet, despite their philosophical subtlety and sensitivity to form, art is ultimately explained via a language that is derived from these same structures (as a commentary on alienated consciousness or as a protest against reification).

There is a real sense here in which art still gets the short straw; the center of gravity—what ultimately matters—lies elsewhere. Even as it resists an economic logic, it is explicated in terms of the logic that it resists. How can the aesthetic force of novels, films, or paintings be given its due if it is defined as subordinate to something else? Here we can look to Latour's discussion of modes of being; art possesses its own form of reality that is not derived from, or dependent on, a more fundamental level of existence. And yet a mode of being is not synonymous with a *domain* of being. A mode, in contrast to a domain, has no clear edges, borders, or walls; differing modes—aesthetic, religious, economic, legal, political—overlap and interact at numerous points.

To question single-order causalities, in other words, is not to deny connectedness. Certain ideas honed in psychology, for example, can be helpful in discriminating between modes of aesthetic response. Meanwhile, that the publishing industry has been afflicted by a chain of corporate takeovers and is now controlled by a handful of multinationals certainly affects what people are able to read, as well as what authors may feel obligated to write. But psychology alone cannot explain why we are drawn to certain works rather than others; nor does literature's status as a commodity single-handedly determine its many uses. Art hooks up to many other things, as we'll see. However, it is not *based* on them, nor is it *encased* by them. While it is not separate, it is also not subordinate. It is here that common spatial metaphors lead us astray. Society, Latour remarks, does not have a top and a bottom (as if art were being held up by the pillars of a more fundamental reality). Nor does the macro contain the micro: a work of art encased within the larger box of culture, in turn enframed by the megacontainer of society or history, akin to a set of stacking Russian dolls.[33] The task is to account for distinctiveness without overlooking connectedness, to trace actual ties without presuming inevitable foundations.

Actor-network theory pivots on this very question. Born from the intellectual ferment of science and technology studies in the late 1970s, its influence has spread across many fields and disciplines, though its uptake in literary studies is only just beginning. This delayed reception is not surprising, given that its way of going about things is out of synch with how most critics are trained to think. ANT offers no obvious purchase on historical periods, national literatures, or political identities—the main categories around which the discipline is organized. It rejects the picture of a yawning gap between words and the world (the much-touted linguistic turn) and steers clear of concepts such as ideology, discourse, and representation. Meanwhile, Latour has been scathing about the institutionalization of practices of critique. "Entire Ph.D. programs are still running to make sure that good American kids are learning the hard way that facts are made up, that there is no such thing as natural, unmediated, unbiased access to truth, that we are always prisoners of language, that we always speak from a particular standpoint, and so on," he remarks, "while dangerous extremists are using the very same argument of social construction to destroy hard-won evidence that could save our lives."[34] At a time when climate change deniers are attacking the legitimacy of scientific knowledge and fake news has become a cliché, is a ratcheting up of skepticism really what we need?

While I'm more interested in doing ANT than explaining it, a brief gloss of the phrase is called for. "Actor" is used in a quite specific sense to denote the irreducible nature of phenomena; it refers to anything whose existence makes a difference. My coffee mug makes a difference in conveying a stimulant to my befogged brain; its handle makes a difference by inviting me to pick it up

in certain ways. A rock makes a difference by forcing water running downstream to flow around it rather than over it, while its
overhanging side makes a difference in providing shelter for tiny
water creatures. As such examples make clear, "actor" has nothing
to do with consciousness, will, or intention, let alone with autonomy or independence. Rather, it points to the distinctiveness of
phenomena as they interact in a mutually composed world. ANT
is sometimes called a "flat ontology" because it suspends our usual
sorting and ranking mechanisms—nature versus culture, persons
versus things—to grant the nonhuman world equal footing, to acknowledge its vital role in human affairs as well as its vast existence
beyond them. Such a suspension does not deny obvious differences
between quarks and sharks but steers clear of dualistic schemas
that prejudge these differences in damaging ways.

"Network" is another potential source of confusion. As used in
ANT, it does not imply a network-y shape of crisscrossing lines or
have anything to do with computer and media technologies (paeans
to a "network society"). Rather, it conveys an insight that is ap-
plicable to any historical milieu: things exist only via relations,
but these relations can take on radically variant forms. Networks
are groups of actors working together—whether persons, things,
plants, animals, machines, texts, or competences—and have no
necessary size, shape, or scale. A network can be made up of twenty-
two soccer players, a ball, a stretch of flat ground, a referee, the rules
of the game, and cheering spectators. Networks, however, can also
play havoc with geographical measures of distance and proximity:
I can be a few feet from someone in the next phone booth, remarks
Latour, and yet be much more closely connected to my mother, who
is located six thousand miles away. Some networks, of course, are
longer, sturdier, and more powerful than others; that actors are
treated symmetrically by ANT does not mean their effects are held
to be equal. The task, rather, is to account for what is often taken
for granted: how certain networks are able to gain support, enroll
allies, and extend their influence. And here, of course, researchers
are also implicated in the processes they are tracing; networks are
not just things we find but things we make.[35]

"Theory," finally, is also something of a misnomer. In the dialogue at the heart of *Reassembling the Social*, a student drops in

on a Latour avatar during office hours, seeking advice about how to apply ANT in a dissertation—only to meet with objections at every turn. Actor-network theory, it turns out, is less a theory of how to study things than of "how *not* to study them—or rather, how to let the actors have some room to express themselves."[36] It is not a matter of feeding a topic—whether paintings or presidential assassinations—into a whirring machinery of concepts or theories in order to spit out the desired result. We need to follow the actors, scrape our knees on the rough rocks of reality, expect to be disconcerted or perplexed. (ANT does not flinch at the word "reality"—yes, we see the world from a certain standpoint rather than a God's-eye view, but we can also make inquiries, correct our assumptions, create better descriptions.) This orientation might be called pragmatic; ANT is something that is performed—a way of proceeding and paying attention—rather than a series of propositions or a self-contained body of ideas.

ANT, then, is a confusing if not downright misleading name. (At one point, Latour declares his readiness to ditch all the problematic aspects of the term: "that is, actor, network, theory, without forgetting the hyphen!")[37] As a style of thinking, however, it coaxes us away from entrenched spatial models: base versus superstructure, macro versus micro—and, ultimately, Art versus Society. Humanists, for example, are very fond of pitting the singularity of the artwork against the overbearing sameness of social forces. As Caroline Levine remarks, they are highly sensitive to aesthetic form while being much less attuned to the "many different and often disconnected arrangements that govern social experience."[38] The invocation of society as if it were a self-evident reality begs the fundamental question: *which* associations—which specific formations or groupings of actors—are we talking about? And here a panoramic view misses a great deal of what is happening on the ground, the specific connections and conflicts between differing networks. "Minor forms can sometimes work against major ones," Levine remarks. "A woman poet can retreat to the boundaries of her bedroom to block the encroachment of some very tiresome networks in favor of a richer, more expansive world."[39]

To do actor-network theory, then, is to tackle the fundamental question of how actors—whether scallops or subway trains, springboks or box springs—exist via their relations. And yet, as this phrasing suggests, it soon runs into potential objections. Reflecting on the influence of ANT, Latour ruefully notes that freedom of movement has been gained via a loss of specificity. As the scholar of networks "studies segments from Law, Science, The Economy or Religion, she begins to feel that she is saying almost *the same thing* about all of them: namely that they are 'composed in heterogeneous fashion of unexpected elements revealed by the investigation.'"[40] The very portability of ANT can be a weakness as well as a strength; if everything can be described as a network of diverse actors, then everything begins to sound more or less the same. How can such an approach help us to capture the force of Derek Walcott's poetry or the extraordinary appeal of *Game of Thrones*? We might well concede that literary works connect up to many other things, while also insisting that they involve distinctive ways of writing, reading, experiencing, and evaluating. (That my edition of *The Turn of the Screw* was made out of paper from an Ohio factory forms part of its networked existence but is less relevant to my Tuesday seminar than James's words or the editorial commentary that encircles them.)

To speak well to the concerns of humanists, ANT needs to hook up to the concerns of aesthetics since the eighteenth century: *features* of the work and *experiences* of the work. This linking is an act of translating that leaves neither party unchanged: to translate, after all, is to transform, distort, betray. And we can return to the question of attachment, now placed in a fresh light. *Hooked* centers on attachments to artworks: considered for their own sake rather than as effects of a more fundamental reality. How are we hooked, enticed, reeled in? What affective, ethical, political, or temporal aspects come into play? And what kind of attachment devices are we talking about? In daily life, we regularly rely on hinges, clamps, buttons, zippers, Velcro, laces, knots, stitches, tape, stickers, and glue. What are their aesthetic equivalents?

The following chapters zero in on three forms of attachment: attunement, identification, and interpretation, as differing ways of paying attention, with varying entailments. Interpretation is often separated from—and opposed to—the two other forms of engagement, yet there is common ground as well as salient differences.

I inquire how the affordances of artworks hook up to affective dispositions, patterns of perception, ethical or political commitments, repertoires of response—such that our attention is distributed in certain ways and we become sensitized to certain qualities rather than to others. While drawing mainly on essays, memoirs, and works of fiction that capture the phenomenological thickness of aesthetic response, I also cite relevant examples of ethnographic research. As Kim Chabot Davis shows in a sequence of fine-grained studies, there can be dramatic variations in affective response and in ethical or political judgments even within very specific interpretive communities: academic feminist responses to *The Piano*; gay men who love *Kiss of the Spider Woman*; fans of the TV show *Northern Exposure*.[41] It is not a matter of tongues slotting smoothly into grooves over and over again. Responses cannot be corralled into tidy boxes; actors do not always hook up in expected ways; anomalies, surprises, exceptions are not uncommon.

One reason critics are sometimes leery of social explanations, after all, is that aesthetic experience can feel like a turn away from the social. There may be a purposeful act of refusal or renunciation, a spurning of communal bonds; an overwhelming sense of absorption where the rest of the world briefly fades into nothingness. Such perceptions need to be honored rather than brushed aside. That books could distance readers from their milieu was already a familiar theme in the eighteenth century; critics complained that novels weakened social ties by creating a sense of distaste for what was nearest. Reading can cast the world in a radically different light, inspire us to turn away from what we thought we cared about. Books unite, Leah Price remarks, but they also divide; people can hide behind books, burrow into books, defend themselves with books (a handy repellent for women eating alone in public!), and use them to escape dull spouses, demanding children, and the trials of daily life.[42] They promote acts of division as well as association.

Orhan Pamuk's *The New Life* opens with a dramatic account of being yanked out of everyday life. "I read a book one day and my whole life was changed. Even on the first page, I was so affected by the book's intensity I felt my body sever itself and pull away from the chair. . . . What if I raised my eyes from the book and looked around at my room, my wardrobe, my bed, or glanced out of the window, but did not find the world as I knew it?"[43] The protagonist feels compelled, impelled, propelled by the words he is reading; the shift in his sense of being is irrevocable; he cannot help feeling— though he realizes the absurdity of this view—as if the book were written only for him. A gulf yawns between his new and his former life; things that had once mattered now seem utterly without consequence. Looking at his mother, a mother whom he dearly loves, he is overcome with guilt at the gulf between them. "I was well aware," he remarks, "that my room was no longer the same old room, nor the streets the same streets, my friends the same friends, my mother the same mother."[44] Sitting down at the table, before a stew of meat and potatoes, braised leeks, a salad, he strives to engage in conversation, to help his mother clear away the dishes, to act as if his life has not been turned upside down. A fundamental scission has taken place—one that will propel Pamuk's protagonist on a long and arduous journey.

It is not uncommon, when reading, to have a sense of breaking away from one's everyday life and entering a different kind of reality. And yet, although being caught up in a book may cut readers off from their immediate milieu, it forges other kinds of ties: for example, to real or to imagined persons. Perhaps there is a sensed affinity with other readers of the same book; one feels oneself to be part of a virtual community of kindred spirits. Or readers may develop an obsession with certain authors, hunting down everything they have written, poring over the details of their biographies, having ongoing conversations with them in their heads. Or certain characters may elbow their way into readers' lives, becoming almost as real as those around them: avatars, allies, or love objects. Fictional figures, as we'll see in chapter 3, can become an integral part of an *Umwelt*—the world as it is lived from a first-person perspective.

Alternatively, a reader may be seduced by a style or by the intricate architecture of a fictional world or by the vividness of a descriptive technique. Susan Fraiman, for example, reflects on her enjoyment of literary descriptions of homemaking. Pushing back against a feminist equation of the domestic with entrapment, she traces out a counterhistory of what she calls shelter writing: looking, for example, to key passages of Lesley Feinberg's *Stone Butch Blues*, with their itemizing of domestic objects—rugs, dishes, curtains, couch—and careful accounts of sanding floors, unrolling rugs, and placing furniture.[45] Or—to toggle between media—perhaps someone who is rushing through an art galley on her way to lunch is caught up short by a Matisse, without quite knowing why (see chapter 2), or a museum visitor is entranced by the hazy penumbras of Turner's paintings, with their maelstroms of agitated water and blazes of light. "Emerging from Turner's heliocentric cathedral, I felt I had cataracts: it takes time to re-accustom your dazzled eyes to the wan, monochrome mock-up we call reality."[46] There are countless ways in which artworks can compel our attention or solicit our devotion.

It is here that ANT's flat ontology is exceptionally clarifying. In steering clear of the usual presorting mechanisms, it allows us to appreciate the many ways we can become attached. It is no longer a matter of equating ties with something called "society" while treating art as a tie-free zone. Aesthetic experiences not only break bonds but also make bonds; they separate us from some things but connect us to many others. Like the phone line linking Latour to his mother thousands of miles away, they cut across swathes of space as well as time; audiences can become hooked to texts, characters, scenarios, and ideas that originate in very different worlds; that these ties are not tangible does not mean that they are not enduring, sustaining, and important. Actors that seem far distant from each other come into intimate contact; "space and time have no absolute jurisdiction," Wai Chee Dimock remarks, "when it comes to the bond between texts and readers."[47]

It is possible, in short, to be as tightly bound to a seventeenth-century painting as to a friend seen every day, as intensely invested in *Big Little Lies* as the dramas of one's neighborhood community. The former bonds have their own solidity, salience, and force—they are not just displacements of the latter, to be waved away as escapist or apolitical. And those who are not at home in the world—who find themselves out of sync with the social or sexual norms of their milieu—may be especially reliant on such aesthetic bonds. An expression of yearning, a snarl of anguish, a shimmer of beauty can offer itself as a partial recompense or reparation. I disagree with

Ross Posnock's remark that an ANT-ish stress on relations cannot account for the "vertiginous challenge of the aesthetic." As I hope to show, especially in chapter 2, it speaks to this very question.[48]

Affect, Love, Value

To say we are attached to works of art is to say that we have feelings for them. It is also to say that they matter, that they carry weight. How are these aspects related? Lawrence Grossberg introduces the idea of "mattering maps" as a way of thinking about how affect connects to value. His concern is with the sensibility of the fan—how feeling, identifying with, and caring about take on a certain shape and coherence. For Grossberg this question pertains solely to popular culture; it makes little sense, he declares, to see someone as a fan of art.[49] And yet, that devotees of Liszt or aficionados of Proust are not usually described via the language of fandom does not mean they are not caught up in similar investments or passions.

In its most obvious sense, attachment denotes an emotional tie: whether passions and obsessions or low-key moods and lukewarm likes. Such ties are ubiquitous in academic life: critical devotion to James Joyce or Toni Morrison; a flicker of anticipation at lecturing on *Stella Dallas* or *The Maltese Falcon*; tamped-down annoyance when a favorite Maria Callas recording is met with blank faces in the classroom. Against the usual portrayal of academia as an affect-free zone, I would venture that affective ties are often *stronger* in academia than elsewhere, because more is at stake; the ties are thicker and woven out of more diverse strands. The scholar who's written several monographs on Virginia Woolf is bound to her work not just because of a longstanding love of *Mrs. Dalloway*. Literary modernism has become a defining part of a scholarly identity and professional persona, a cornerstone of a chosen life path, with its rites of initiation and its yearly rituals, its complicated blend of rewards and regrets. Affective labor, as Deidre Lynch points out, is a defining aspect of literary studies; and yet, while often on display in the classroom, it is rarely acknowledged in critical writing.

I approach the "affective turn" in an oblique rather than direct fashion. I do not elevate feeling over thought (though one or other may dominate in a specific response), nor do I attempt to offer any kind of taxonomy of affect, feeling, mood, and emotion. My starting point, rather, is curiosity about how we become attached to works of art—as calling into play an often volatile blend of sensation and reflection. And here there are several possible lines of inquiry. We can consider *representations* of affect: how a novel or a film depicts the emotional states of its characters; how song lyrics convey a mood of melancholy or a sense of yearning; how a painting—by Mary Cassatt, for example—captures the intimacy between a mother and her child. Alternatively, we may be more interested in *solicitations* of affect: looking at how an artwork encourages certain kinds of emotional response. As Carl Plantinga writes, movie audiences are "often thrilled, excited, or exhilarated; moved to tears, laughter, scorn, or disgust; made fearful, expectant, curious, or suspenseful; outraged, angered, placated, or satisfied."[50] Such affective states, he remarks, are not incidental but fundamental to meaning—emotions can be crucial, for example, to making sense of a film's narrative.

Feminist critics have often argued that affect cannot be separated from politics—while also acknowledging that they rarely line up in perfect harmony or synchrony. Analyzing her own experience of watching *Pretty Woman*, Robyn Warhol notes an accelerated pulse of excitement, alternating with a sense of mild nausea and shame at her involvement with a narrative she finds politically questionable. Tackling the tension between critical reading and what she calls implicated reading, Lynne Pearce also explores how academic commentary may be undercut by more unruly or unseemly attachments. Feminist critics, she observes, may experience a sense of anxiety or guilt about surrendering to a text, as if abandoning their intellectual and political commitments. And yet, while the text may be blamed for its seductions, Pearce remarks, the "reader is certainly more active in creating, sustaining, and negotiating her *ravissement* than it at first appears."[51]

And then there is a third question: not how art represents feeling nor how it elicits feeling, but *how we feel toward works of art*—specifically those we care for, as distinct from those that irritate us, bore us, or leave us cold. These questions are not unrelated; art is often lauded for its potential to offer nuanced or evocative portrayals of emotional states. And yet it is not uncommon to have strong feelings about works that do not involve emotion in any obvious sense. Someone can be drawn to a novel by its provocative ideas; to a painting by its austere minimalism; to a film by its tone of disenchanted irony. Conversely, it is possible to have an overpowering emotional reaction—to be scared out of one's wits by a B-grade horror movie—without feeling a strong tie to its source. The emotional content of artworks does not correspond in any straightforward way to the kinds of emotions we have about them.

How to describe this attachment, the sense of being powerfully drawn to a film or a painting: a feeling triggered by its qualities but not synonymous with them? Here theory and criticism have surprisingly little to offer, beyond an occasional reference to love. Alexander Nehamas, for example, makes love central to his account of aesthetic pleasure. Insisting that it is impossible to love someone or something without also finding them beautiful, he cites examples of paintings and novels as well as persons. "I can still remember falling in love with *In Search of Lost Time*," he remarks—as well as how wonderful it felt when he began to hate Hermann Hesse.[52] Film criticism, meanwhile, has its own history of cinephilia, a history that is invoked by Susan Sontag in an elegiac lament. "The love that cinema inspired, however, was special. It was born of the conviction that cinema was an art unlike any other: quintessentially modern; distinctively accessible; poetic and mysterious and erotic and moral—all at the same time. Cinema had apostles. (It was like religion.) Cinema was a crusade. For cinephiles, the movies encapsulated everything."[53]

Nowadays, the response to such fervent testimony is likely to be one of discomfort, if not outright embarrassment. Film scholars very rarely admit—at least in their writing—that their career path may have been motivated by a love of cinema. And any talk of loving literature seems jejune to most English professors, guaranteed to trigger a pained recoil or a moue of distaste. Such language brings academic discourse perilously close to adolescent infatuation or amateurish enthusiasm, to a treacly and treacherous cult of feeling. There is a rich history of philosophical reflection on love; and yet when the word is applied to art, it is often the case that anecdote overshadows—or even replaces—argument. Jerrold Levinson, for example, declares that it is possible to fall in love with *The Castle* but not *The Trial*; with *David Copperfield* but not *Our Mutual Friend*; with Kundera's *The Unbearable Lightness of Being* but not Houellebecq's *The Elementary Particles*. This is not because the latter are less worthy, he remarks, but because they are less lovable; they are admirable but not endearing. Here Levinson draws a distinction that greatly interests me: the difference between admiring a work of art and being affected by it. Yet individual preferences are presented without qualification or explanation as if they had the status of universal truths. (Would it really be as impossible to fall in love with *The Trial* or *Miss Lonelyhearts* as Levinson assumes?)[54]

One difficulty is that the language of love can feel descriptively thin, conveying little of the spectrum of affective responses toward art: curiosity, excitement, rivalry, infatuation, jubilation, enthusiasm, anticipation, or consolation, to name but a few. It highlights the strength of an affect but nothing of its qualities, tone, or shading. I'm inclined to agree with Ronald de Sousa's view that love is not an emotion but a condition—or perhaps a syndrome, made up of intricate patterns of thoughts, behaviors, and feelings.[55] Love talk, moreover, often triggers an impulse to personify, to treat novels or paintings as if they were friends or lovers. Here again, ANT's flat ontology seems a propos. Relations to artworks are not imitations of relations to persons; to treat them as such is to diminish rather than honor them. Moreover, the language of love and especially of "falling in love" is weighted down by scripts of male pursuit and female submission that need to be reckoned with rather than ignored. Lynne Pearce offers one of the more illuminating accounts of the "reader as lover"; in dialogue with Roland Barthes, she details her own experience of reading as lurching from one affect to another: enchantment, devotion, anxiety, jealousy, frustration, disillusionment.[56]

If talk of love can overpersonify, some recent theories of affect are eager to depersonify, rhapsodizing about flows and forces, intensities and sensations. Affect, in this line of thought, is to be sharply distinguished from emotion; it is seen as preconscious rather than conscious, linked to bodies rather than minds, depicted, in some cases, as an autonomous system that is independent of language or thought. Common reference points for such accounts are Deleuze and Spinoza, as well as Silvan Tomkins. To my mind, the most insightful work along these lines comes from scholars such as Ben Anderson: even if affective ties have little to do with cognition or conscious belief, he argues, they are shaped, synchronized, articulated; they are patterns of relation rather than a "pure unmediated realm of affective richness." Affect is never "affect as such," he writes, but "always involved with the non-affective—that is to say, it is mediated."[57]

And here we need to account for the relative solidity of actors involved in aesthetic relations—whether a painting, a person, the routines of a graduate seminar, or a habituated pattern of response—as well as the ever-present possibility of surprise. In contrast to the language of flows and forces, a stress on attachment keeps these actors squarely in view. It reminds us that there are not only relations but also things that are being related: phenomena that are equipped with distinct features, shapes, contours—and sometimes hard edges. Friction and resistance are not uncommon; we can stub our toe on an obdurate or recalcitrant object. Connections, from an ANT-ish perspective, are less a matter of fluid intensities than of translation, hesitation, blockage: Why do I fail to "get" the TV show that all my friends adore? Why is this novel a bestseller, while a virtual twin vanishes from bookstores without a trace?

Attachment, meanwhile, is a question not just of feeling but also of valuing: something matters; it carries weight. Value talk has often been cast under a cloud in recent decades: castigated for being hierarchical, exclusionary, or authoritarian. And yet to rail against values is not to float free of the field of value. Accusations of bourgeois hypocrisy or endemic sexism carry their own normative force; value judgments are unavoidably in play, even if the basis for such judgments is not spelled out. It is impossible to get outside value frameworks; we cannot help orienting ourselves to what we take to be better rather than worse.

And here the language of attachment can sharpen our sense of the multimodal nature of value relations. Values, norms, and ideals are things that act upon us but also that we act upon. Their actions are not just coercive; they also energize, galvanize, give weight to our words. We are *animated* by values, ideals, principles—as touchstones for both art and life. Certain words—such as "justice" and "freedom"—have inspired rumblings of discontent, utopian visions, manifestos, marches, sit-ins, protests large and small. These words function as actors, in ANT's sense of the term; their presence—in a conversation, a blog post, an essay—makes a difference, pitching a sentence into a different register, conjuring up a sense of gravity or urgency, soliciting certain kinds of response. They are not just clichés to be abused by cynical speechwriters but objects of intense and enduring investments.

Of course, not all attachments are equal and not all values matter equally. Charles Taylor distinguishes between weak and strong forms of evaluation. In the former, the criterion for something being good is just that I desire it; weighing up the available options, I choose what I take to be preferable or more pleasing. Here there is infinite room for variation in my own desires as well as in those of others: my enthusiasm for Thai food is not threatened by your passion for French cuisine. That tastes differ is a truism; much of the time, nothing of consequence hangs on these differences. Strong values, by contrast, carry a normative force; they imply a contrast between higher and lower, better and worse. They involve not just desires but the *worth* of these desires. Here it is a question not just of difference but of disagreement and potential conflict. And we can, of course, direct such assessments at our own desires, as being in harmony—or not—with the kind of person we take ourselves to be.[58]

Literature and art seem, at first glance, to have undergone a shift from strong to weak values. A democratizing of taste has taken place; whether one enjoys James Joyce or James Bond is nobody's business but one's own—no longer something to be adjudicated by bookish mandarins. Meanwhile, recent years have seen the rise of omnivore taste: an increased cultural eclecticism that takes the form of appreciating *Game of Thrones* as well as Jean-Luc Godard. (This shift in reception is also steered by changing forms of production; the rise of HBO, Netflix, Amazon Prime, and other forms of media streaming has blurred divisions between popular and "quality" television and between niche and mass audiences.)

Yet we should not conclude that strong values have vanished; rather, as Günter Leypoldt points out, weak and strong values coexist. On the one hand, the literary sphere often appears as a nonhierarchical space of choices: a huge bookshop in which "capital-L Literature is merely one option among many, on a par with Mystery & Crime, Romance, Science Fiction & Fantasy, Thrillers, Westerns, and Self-Help."[59] The purpose of such labels is simply to help consumers orient themselves and find what they are looking for. But, on the other hand, the literary world (and, even more, the art world) is also a sphere of strong or sacralized values. Here books are not just a matter of consumer preference but seen as having the potential to offer something higher—a "higher" that can be defined in many different ways. "The horizontal array of labeled aisles in your local bookshop then acquires a vertical tension," notes Leypoldt; "some sections suddenly strike us as closer to the higher moral-political life of the culture than others."[60] From the perspective of strong values, discriminations of worth are not incidental but fundamental.

This vertical tension does not appear out of nowhere, of course; it is tied to institutions and tastemakers: museums and galleries; art and literature departments; Nobel, Man Booker, and other prestigious prizes; the reviewing pages of the *New York Times*, the *London Review of Books*, and *Artforum*. Within these frameworks, individual works may lose or gain status, but shifts of fortune are mediated via a language of strong values. To make a case for adding an overlooked writer to a syllabus, for example, it is not enough to declare that her novels are a gripping read. Other kinds of arguments must be brought into play: testimonies to their aesthetic complexity, ethical ambiguity, or political urgency. In the realm of weak values, that a book fails to resonate testifies to the book's inadequacy; in the realm of strong values, it says something about *my* inadequacy.

While institutions mediate strong values, they do not single-handedly impose them. We are talking about a force field that radiates outward to shape canons, fashions, college curricula, and museum displays. Yet audiences may pay little attention to such pressures; in the United States, for example, the authority of cultural experts is relatively weak, especially outside metropolitan centers. The art world, meanwhile, is far from being the only arbiter of strong values. bell hooks, for example, cites a long history of African American aesthetic expression that served as a source of spiritual meaning and communal ties. She invokes her grandmother, a quilt maker, who taught her about the aesthetics of daily life. Uplifting experiences of pleasure and beauty, she writes, have been essential for those living lives of material deprivation. The performance arts of dance, music, and theater, in particular, played a vital role in black culture long before aspects of such culture were taken up and sanctified in prestige-granting institutions (courses on rap music or the aesthetics of the quilt).[61]

Attachments are, by their very nature, selective: we cannot care for everything equally. And the criteria by which we evaluate vary. In English departments, for example, literary merit has often been equated with the glitter of the meticulously chiseled sentence. Closely tied to New Criticism and the heritage of modernism, such a template is a poor fit for assessing the merits of Balzac, let alone Stephen King. Here other criteria are called for: artfully orchestrated narratives, stylized yet vividly realized characters, spine-tingling thrills of excitement or suspense, the cathartic relief of narrative closure, evocative orchestrations of mood or renditions of milieu. "Aesthetics" is a noun conjured in the plural, not just a matter of irony or artfulness but of affective intensities, spectacular effects, moments of transport or enchantment, different registers of perception and feeling.[62] These value frameworks bear the imprint of education, class, gender, race, and other variables, but there is common ground as well as unpredictable variation.

Hooked looks at examples of people getting stuck to novels and paintings and films and music in ways that matter to them. This mattering can be aesthetic, political, emotional, ethical, intellectual, or any combination of these. The issue is not just attachment, in other words, but of attachment to one's attachment—or what we can call, after Taylor, second-order evaluations. Not just pleasure but one's assessment of such pleasure: whether it is felt to be warranted, justified, worth reflecting on, deserving of being described and conveyed to others. In this sense, even the most nebulous or inarticulate reaction, in being singled out for attention, is drawn into the realm of interpretation and judgment.

This focus stems from my conviction that we need an ampler repertoire of justifications for literature and art. Instead of prescribing what kinds of responses people should have, we might start by getting a better handle on attachments they *do* have. How can we think more capaciously about differing uses of novels and films and paintings and music? As Leypoldt remarks, people want all sorts of things from literature and, I'd add, from the arts generally: "pleasure, knowledge, wisdom, catharsis, moral growth, political vision."[63] Can we do better justice to this range of motives, opening up the question of art's relation to the world beyond the preferred academic options of interrogating a work's complicity or commending its canny acts of resistance (praising it, in short, for mirroring critics' own commitments, for being just like them)? Can we find ways of talking about the world-disclosing force of art that do not sideline its social shaping? And how might this expanded repertoire reveal commonalities as well as differences between academic and lay audiences?

Of course, it's far from being guaranteed that artworks will inspire epiphanies—or even lukewarm stirrings of interest. I take it as uncontroversial that we do not care very much for much of what we read, watch, or listen to: not even the swooniest of aesthetes is enraptured by everything. New technologies, moreover, can affect our ways of paying attention. Like Latour and Hennion, I am not persuaded by Benjamin's claim that the aura or presence of an artwork is destroyed by its technological mediation (I make the case that presence *requires* mediation in chapter 2). Yet the affordances of cell phones make it easier to engage with art in a casual or distracted manner. As Jeff Nealon points out, the experience of listening reverentially to an entire album—on the analogy of reading a book—is now much less common. Instead, individually curated music lists serve as mood enhancers to "create various 'scapes' in our individual and social lives—the sleep scape, the gym scape, the study scape, the commute scape, the romance scape, the political rally scape, the shopping scape."[64] Such ambient listening— engineered to harmonize with different tasks and spaces—is less likely to stir up an intense response.

Meanwhile, teachers are well acquainted with expressions of indifference, apathy, or outright dislike. Reactions to literature in the classroom, for example, can be a matter of "hating characters, being bored, being made to feel stupid by a text, or feeling that a text is stupid."[65] Hopes that students will mirror our attachments— not just to specific works but to the painstaking deciphering of such works—are often disappointed. But seasoned critics are no less likely to harbor feelings of antipathy, irritation, or boredom, even if they are rarely brave enough to own up to them. Reflecting on his experiences of walking around the Louvre, Amit Chaudhuri lists the things that set his teeth on edge: Titian and Rubens, varieties of Renaissance oil painting, the very texture of Greek and Renaissance sculpture. Try as hard as he might, meanwhile, "I couldn't open up to a Rembrandt."[66] This impatience, he remarks, is not a question of playing the postcolonial card; rather, its causes lie elsewhere, perhaps in the murkier realm of temperament or taste. Nowadays, it seems that any objection to a novel or a film must be dignified by being presented as a critique, as grounded in a substantive form of political or philosophical disagreement. How might criticism change if we could admit that sometimes our real topic is dislike!

That art collections can inhibit the appreciation they strive to foster, meanwhile, has long been recognized. Museums sap energy and deaden consciousness, remarks Deborah Root; the combination of sensory overload and mental exhaustion can impede our best efforts to engage with a painting. She continues: "I passed out in Saint Peter's Basilica from all the bad taste, all the Berninis, the weirdness of the images, like the skeletal arm reaching out with an hourglass as a memento mori to passersby. I swooned under Saint Teresa and a woman from California whom I had never seen before had to revive me with grapes."[67] Attachments, as we've seen, depend on various things coming together; given the many contingencies at play, it is hardly surprising that all too often things fail to connect or fall apart. Fascinating books are waiting to be written about the vast graveyard of aesthetic disappointments: the misfirings, glitches, malfunctions, breakdowns of various kinds that characterize experiences of reading novels, watching movies, or looking at pictures, underwritten by feelings of irritation, boredom, anxiety, peevishness, or shame.[68]

In the following pages, I take up words that are often associated with popular art—"attachment," "engagement," "identification"— and apply them to a broader range of objects, from Joni Mitchell to Matisse, from Thomas Bernhard to Brahms, from *Thelma and Louise* to *Stalker*. Cultural studies has amply documented the passions of Star Trek and Madonna fans; but "higher" forms of art are not usually discussed in these terms—at least not by the academics who study them.[69] Meanwhile, the assumption one sometimes sees in cultural studies—that academics somehow do not count as "real" readers or viewers—seems highly questionable. They do not, of course, represent audiences as a whole, but it seems weirdly self-negating—and a potential act of bad faith—to deny the salience of one's own investments.

Hooked was originally about attachments to literature; but as I stumbled across the many parallels to music, painting, and film, it soon became clear that a broader optic was needed. We now inhabit a multimedia environment where students come to Austen or Shakespeare via their film adaptations, where works of contemporary fiction often deal with paintings or performance, and where music is an inescapable backdrop and reference point in countless lives. Isolating literary from other forms of aesthetic response felt like a missed opportunity. Of course, media differ significantly in their affordances—yet a focus on attachment can also sharpen our appreciation of salient commonalities. Because the argument ranges widely in terms of media and also method (drawing not only on ANT but on cultural studies, sociology, the philosophy of art, and literary, art, music, and film criticism), I restrict its historical focus to the present. Much has been written, and remains to be written, about attachment in the past and attachment to the past, but they are not my concern here.

What counts as evidence of people's reactions to movies or music or novels? That no source can be definitive or unimpeachable inclines me toward a variety of examples: memoirs, works of fiction, critical essays, reflections on my own attachments, audience ethnographies, and online reviews. Several decades ago, cultural studies made a pitch for ethnographies of audience response as a way of reining in wilder flights of academic fancy. As a result, it's become harder for critics to deploy a casual or unthinking "we"—to assume that all readers or viewers or listeners react to the same works in the same way. Such empirical studies can be exceptionally useful in pushing back against entrenched academic assumptions. That film viewers identify unpredictably in terms of both difference and sameness (Stacey) challenges established axioms of film theory;

that many readers of literary fiction are interested in experiences rather than interpretations (Miall) contravenes certain premises of literary criticism; that music fans describe their attachments in the language of religion rather than politics (Cavicchi) speaks back to cultural critics who are eager to frame everything in terms of ideological complicity or resistance.[70]

Yet there is also a sense in which these responses often do not go very deep—whether because of the large size of an audience sample; conversational norms that encourage a reliance on ready-to-hand phrases (one cannot press "pause" on an interview in order to search for exactly the right word); "hesitancies and inarticulacies" among fans who struggle to explain their own feelings; or a reluctance, perhaps, to reveal one's innermost thoughts to a stranger. In implicit acknowledgment of this fact, direct quotations occupy a surprisingly modest space in most ethnographies—small islands in a sea of prose that surrounds, processes, analyzes, interprets, and extends them.[71]

It is here that memoirs, novels, and first-person essays have built-in advantages. Afforded ample time to reflect on the textures of their response, as well as a much broader repertoire of stylistic and expressive options, writers can convey far more vividly what it feels like to be lost in a book or brought up short by a painting. Such accounts are better able to capture the phenomenological "feel" of aesthetic response—those affective shimmerings or nascent stirrings of thought that are exceptionally hard to convey in words.[72] To be sure, such descriptions are mediated in countless ways: shaped by the conventions of genre as well as the assumptions, tastes, and styles of thought of those who belong to the "writing class." While conscious of these differences, I want, as noted earlier, to question the assumption that aesthetic experiences are incommensurable: that a "popular aesthetic" consists of a desire for entertainment and immediate satisfaction that has nothing in common with the "pure gaze" of educated audiences. Interweaving the musical conversion of Zadie Smith with the self-reportage of Brisbane clubgoers, Amazon book reviews with examples of academic identification, I strive to honor connections as well as differences.

We often come to realize the strength of our attachments, Hennion remarks, only when they are tested or threatened in some way.

Several decades ago, Foucauldian critiques of the welfare state were all the rage; now that free dental care and unemployment benefits are being dismantled across much of the Western world, many of us look back on this same state and its benefits with nostalgia and gratitude. When I headed off to college in the 1970s, literature and art were still widely sacralized, at least in the undergraduate curriculum, and seen as beyond serious criticism. In such a context, it was imperative to drive home that aesthetic relations were also power relations; to reckon with the imprint of class, gender, racial, and sexual inequality; to read against the grain and between the lines.

We now find ourselves in a different moment. Departments of German and classics are threatened with closure; funding for the humanities and public arts is being slashed; far from being naive worshipers at the altar of Matisse or Mozart, many of our students have never heard of them. Meanwhile, scholars in the humanities are highly fluent in a rhetoric of skepticism but struggle to formulate frameworks of value beyond the usual homilies to critical thinking. The assumption that art's value lies in its power to negate—to interrogate ideology or subvert the status quo—is not false, but it offers a very partial account of what art can do. Such a line of argument, moreover, resonates only with the converted: those who are already on board with one's own political convictions. We need to step back and once again ask some fundamental questions. Why are music and literature and novels and paintings worth bothering with? Why should anyone *care*? The wager of *Hooked* is that something can be learned, as William James might have said, from attending to the varieties of aesthetic experience.

CHAPTER **2**

Art and Attunement

Why are we drawn to a certain painting or novel or piece of music while being unmoved by others that seem, on the face of it, not so very different? Can we do justice to what such a response feels like and why it matters—yet without overlooking the various prompts and pressures (a college syllabus, an over-the-top review, a parent's approving look or raised eyebrow) that incline us toward some works rather than others? Perhaps *attunement* will give us a fresh slant on such questions. To become attuned is to be drawn into a responsive relation—to experience an affinity that is impossible to ignore yet often hard to categorize. Being attuned is not primarily an issue of representation, of the "aboutness" of the work of art, but its presence, in a sense that will need to be clarified.

Attunement is relevant to more than just art; we can be attuned—or not—to persons, a milieu, a style of thought, a way of life. Its salience for criticism lies in addressing art's palpable force and vividness: how it can affect us in ways we struggle to verbalize or explain. And here I draw less on Heidegger or Cavell than on a remarkable essay by Zadie Smith, which I interweave with other accounts—both autobiographical and analytical—of expected or surprising affinities. Novels and music and paintings do things; they intervene in the world; they inspire and energize, seduce or repel. David Freedberg writes: "the picture is reality; it is not bad, or deceiving, or misleading, or even weak copy."[1] Art history has lost its way, Freedberg suggests, in placing all its bets on acts of historicizing, contextualizing, and criticizing. Amid this flurry of activity, something quite fundamental is being lost: the presence and force of images. Why do critics turn away from the obvious, and at what cost?

Attunement is not a specific affect but a state of affectedness—referring, as Erik Wallrup writes, to the relations between persons and musical (or visual or literary) worlds.[2] It is not a feeling-about but a feeling-with: a relation that is more than the sum of its parts. In contrast to what we might call container theories of the emotions—a person having an inner feeling about an external object—attunement is about things resonating, aligning, coming together. Reading the opening lines of a novel, hearing a song on the radio, we may be gripped by the strength of a felt connection. At other times, we duly appreciate the skill or sophistication of a piece of art but without feeling ourselves to be touched or moved. Why are we hooked in one case and not in another?

In tackling this question, James English distinguishes between two scales of aesthetic value: prestige and pleasure. At the end of the semester, he invites the students in his survey classes to rank the works on the syllabus according to two sets of criteria: the greatest and their favorite (both categories are intentionally left undefined). While the two lists are not complete inversions of each other, they often diverge: *Lord Jim* is ranked as the greatest but the least favorite, for example, while Ishiguro's *Never Let Me Go* rises to the top of the favorite list while being ranked as least great. English remarks that his students have no problem operating with different scales of value, differentiating between those works that afford them the most pleasure and those that are reputationally weighty or prestigious. And yet literary studies has paid little attention to these differences, assuming that education will cause them to vanish: students become good readers by learning to enjoy those works that are held to have the highest merit.[3] This assumption is not entirely mistaken—education, as we'll see in the final chapter, can be a process of coming to care for things one did not previously care for—and yet the differences between admiring a work and being affected by a work call for more attention.

"Pleasure," however, is rather too thin a word for my purposes. As I argued in the last chapter, we are drawn to certain works because they matter to us—a mattering that involves more than a hedonistic calculus. And while these ties, as English points out, are socially shaped, they are also varied and sometimes unpredictable—requiring close-up attention to both the response and the work. The language of "attunement" allows us to honor the distinctiveness of a novel, a film, or a painting as well as the textures of response. Instead of an object being dissected by a critic, phenomena are resonating with each other. Something strikes a chord, or it doesn't. (We are often *not* attuned, of course; if attunement implies an openness, a receptivity, we can tune out rather than tune in. There can be friction, awkwardness, a lack of fit.)

Referring, in a literal sense, to tuning an instrument to create the appropriate pitch, "attunement" might seem especially well suited to what Michael Gallope calls the "befuddling, vague, and untranslatable specificity" of musical experience.[4] The philosophy of music has often claimed the ineffable as its own, in the writings of Adorno, Bloch, Jankélévitch, and others. Invocations of attunement and *Stimmung* orient us toward the nonsemantic nature of music: to what Gallope describes as its unique blend of sensory immediacy and formal coherence. These qualities have often inspired claims for music's exceptional status: its difference from reading-as-interpretation as well as from the distanced gaze that is trained upon images. And yet, as we'll see, people can also be drawn to novels, paintings, or films in ways they find exceptionally hard to articulate, finding themselves captivated by a singular mood or a contagious atmosphere. With regard to images, for example, W. J. T. Mitchell remarks that they possess magical qualities that do not disappear as we grow up, become modern, or acquire critical consciousness.[5] All art, in this sense, has a noninterpretive aspect. Conversely, experiences of music are never entirely outside the ambit of language: what we happen to know about a singer or composer; an album's liner notes; a friend's eloquent endorsement; memories of music lessons in elementary school. In this sense, as Nicholas Cooke remarks, all music is a form of multimedia.[6]

In recent years, we've seen the emergence of a vibrant strand of post- or neophenomenology in cultural criticism, architecture, geography, and other fields that blends a philosophical language of mood and attunement with attention to historical and empirical detail. Sara Ahmed, for example, weaves phenomenology and queer theory together in illuminating ways to elucidate the politics of orientation, alignment, and habituation. And there is Steven Connor's rallying call for a "cultural phenomenology" that is geared to mundane realities and rituals: table manners, doing the laundry, humming along to the radio. My own thinking runs along roughly similar lines. The wager of this chapter is that the fuzzy word clouds of phenomenology—its language of attunement and affinity, mood and world—can be blended with the empirical, thing-oriented, trail-sniffing emphases of actor-network theory, and that this mash-up can enrich our understanding of what art does and why it matters.[7]

While on vacation in Konstanz a decade ago, I idly pick up a paperback with a dark-blue and yellow cover in an English-language bookstore. I've appreciated most of Kazuo Ishiguro's novels without really being affected by them, but this particular title—*The Unconsoled*—is not familiar to me. Reading the opening lines, I find myself drawn, abruptly and without recourse, into a maze-like narrative set in an unnamed Central European city. A concert pianist named Ryder has arrived to perform a major concert, yet he finds himself oddly paralyzed, sapped of will, all his attempts at rehearsal or preparation coming to naught. We are squarely in Kafka territory—diffuse anxiety, strange portents, conversations at cross-purposes, enigmatic or eccentric figures appearing out of nowhere against a Habsburg backdrop—though the novel also brings to mind the writings of the Swiss recluse Robert Walser. As Ryder takes the elevator up to his hotel room, the porter's fussy-pedantic monologue on his personal rules of service (a good porter will never put down a guest's bags, not even for a moment!) could easily be an outtake from Walser's *Jakob von Gunten*, with its strange school for servants and hymns to subservience. But how could this meandering speech—extending over five pages—be spoken during an elevator ride that could have lasted only a few seconds? And how, during all this time, can Ryder have failed to notice the young woman pressed into the elevator's corner?

I give myself up completely to *The Unconsoled*: its warping of time and space and its pointless encounters and bungled rendezvous make perfect intuitive sense. "Aboutness" is not entirely irrelevant to my reading experience—literature cannot help but represent—but the novel's draw has much to do with its stylistic conjuring of a certain mood. A sense of low-grade anxiety hovers over a restrained, even stately prose; an oddly alluring flatness of tone is garnished with fillips of foreboding and unease. I cannot *not* read until the book is done, at which point I switch on my laptop, eager to find my fascination validated, to find out that others have admired what I admire. My hopes are quickly crushed: pitilessly, the critics pile on the barbs. "Ishiguro's new novel has the virtue of being unlike anything else," snarls James Wood; "it invents its own category of badness." On TV, the British journalist Tony Parsons recommends that *The Unconsoled* be consigned to the flames. Meanwhile, in the *New York Times* Michiko Kakutani speaks of a "dogged, shaggy-dog narrative" that "sorely tries the reader's patience."[8]

Who has not been taken unawares by their reaction to a novel, a film, or a piece of music? We are enthralled by what we did not think we would care for; we are left cold by what we were eagerly anticipating. Meanwhile, it is not at all uncommon to discover that others do not share our enthusiasm; that what strikes us as remarkable they find unexceptional, even trite. We are often confounded by ourselves, in short, as well as being confounded by others. And yet neither aesthetic theories nor social theories leave much room for surprise. As Steven Connor remarks, the stance of much contemporary scholarship has a Boy Scout quality: be *prepared*.[9]

That responses to artworks can be unpredictable or contentious is not something that formalist approaches are likely to address.

To engage in a meticulous and fine-grained analysis of a poem or a painting, after all, is to take for granted that it is worthy of attention. And yet, writes Antoine Hennion, these "famous works themselves, those absolutes of beauty, have constantly changed meaning, shape, place, and direction throughout history, along with the judgements on them."[10] Borrowing from the language of science studies, we can say that artistic value is black-boxed. That is to say, the many trials that art and literature have undergone are lost from sight; their value is slowly stabilized and becomes self-evident. No work, after all, is fated to be great; it must attract supporters, allies, enthusiasts, compete against rivals, counter the voices of naysayers and skeptics. Yet these acts of squabbling and disputation are soon forgotten and coactors fade away into the shadows. A few especially memorable cases are enshrined in literary history and marveled at: those dunderheads who trashed the first edition of *Moby-Dick*! Yet for the most part, the rough terrain of disagreement is patched over; we perceive the work, in its numinous glory, not the grubby penumbra of hesitations, demurrals, and disputations that once encircled it. It is only in the present—faced with the mortifying clash between what we know to be exceptional and the vigorous rebuttals of reviewers, colleagues, or friends—that the volatility of value becomes visible.

Other scholars, meanwhile, are only too eager to underscore the contingent nature of aesthetic value—in order to explain art as a form of politics by other means. This ambition connects sociologies of culture indebted to Bourdieu with demystifying critiques in the humanities. "Any account of artistic experience in terms of beauty, sensation, emotion, or aesthetic feeling is thus considered misleading," Hennion remarks, insofar as it merely reflects the illusions of everyday actors.[11] The truth of social structure not only trumps the status of first-person experience but pulverizes it into irrelevance. Here again, an ultimate cause is nailed down: no longer in the work but in the social field or social system, which determines what we like and the reasons (power, status, ideological bewitchment, fear of being shamed) we like it. Uncertainties are smoothed over and explanations are delivered.

Yet cultural sociology includes far more than such acts of critique and demystification; we might think of Howard Becker's thick descriptions of art worlds, Claudio Benzecry on the passionate affiliations of Argentine opera fans, Tia DeNora's reckoning with the many uses of music in everyday life, or Maria Olave's highlighting of self-understanding, ethical reflection, and self-care as motives of the female readers she surveys. All these writers dispute the view that attachments to artworks can be reduced to a single logic of distinction and domination or to metaphors of capital.[12] Further questions arise around the predictability and generalizability of taste. It's undeniable that a fondness for Bach or Beuys is neither universal nor purely idiosyncratic but shaped by pressures of class and culture. This point needs to be insisted upon, against those who believe that aesthetic appreciation requires nothing more than personal sensitivity or a refined mind. We are always pre-oriented by the milieu into which we are thrown; not all of art and literature is equally available to all persons. And yet the results of Bourdieu's own surveys do not always support his arguments as strongly as he claims. While the preference for classical music is influenced by social class, for example, only 20 percent of professionals identify it as their preferred form, and almost half have never been to a classical music concert.[13]

Such a line of argument, moreover, cannot explain why some texts *within* a general category (whether we are talking about avant-garde art or middlebrow fiction) can resonate far more powerfully with a reader or viewer than others. Why I am captivated by *The Unconsoled* rather than Ishiguro's other works, for example, though they offer similar amounts of cultural capital. Nor can such an approach account for the change of heart or the volte-face, those times when our social circumstances remain unchanged and yet we radically revise or reverse our aesthetic judgments. How—face-palm—could we have failed to see the obvious?!

Both aesthetic and social theories of art, in short, struggle to account for the unforeseen. Appealing to either the work itself or to theories of the social structure or social field, they presume regularities that do not always exist, foundations that are less stable than they assume.

How, asks Janice Radway, can we more fully engage the vitality and ongoingness, the forward trajectory and the unsecured nature, of social processes?[14] Styles of thinking are needed that can be fine-tuned to the puzzle of particulars, reckoning with the surprising as well as the scripted yet without pitching aesthetic experience outside the social world. Actor-network theory, meanwhile, is premised on contingency. (Latour's *Reassembling the Social*, we might remember, is organized around five sources of uncertainty.) It is this mutability that makes change possible—that allows us to be caught off guard, to revise or reverse an opinion. As constellations come together or fall apart, as actors turn into allies or antagonists, as meanings are remediated and translated, new realities come into view—and new attachments to artworks are forged.

Zadie Smith's Attunement

"The first time I heard her I didn't hear her at all," writes Zadie Smith, in an essay reflecting on her changing response to Joni Mitchell.[15] During her twenties, she remembers, Mitchell's music seemed tuneless, discordant, a white girl's warbling that was little more than noise. At a certain moment, without being fully conscious of it, her perspective underwent a dramatic shift. Nowadays, Smith writes, listening to Mitchell brings "uncontrollable tears. An emotional overcoming, disconcertingly distant from happiness, more like joy—if joy is the recognition of an almost intolerable beauty" (105). A quite ordinary album, *Blue*—owned by millions—now unleashes extraordinary emotions, an almost unbearable intensity of feeling. How, she wonders, did she hate something so completely and then come to love it so unreasonably? "In a sense," she writes, "it took no time. Instantaneous. Involving no progressive change but, instead, a leap of faith. A sudden unexpected attunement" (110).

How are we to explain such intense affinities that have little to do with conscious commitments? As a writer, Smith has made deliberate efforts to expand her knowledge, to immerse herself in diverse traditions of writing. "By forcing myself to reread *Crime and Punishment*," she remarks, "I now admire and appreciate Dostoyévsky, a writer whom, well into my late twenties, I was certain I disliked" (105). Literature, after all, is Smith's area of expertise; through a steady accumulation of examples and exposure to the unfamiliar, she trains her perception, educates her taste, and comes to value what once seemed impenetrable or dreary or trifling. (She even learns to appreciate Anaïs Nin, a writer once alien to her sensibility.) Here we have an example of what Hennion calls taste formation as a reflexive activity: preferences that are purposefully pursued, that are based on techniques and trials.[16] And yet not all commitments are of this kind; not all attachments arise out of effort or education. "I didn't come to love Joni Mitchell," Smith writes, "by knowing anything more about her, or understanding what an open-tuned guitar is or even by sitting down and forcing myself to listen and re-listen to her songs. I hated Joni Mitchell—and then I loved her. Her voice did nothing for me—until the day it undid me completely" (106). A transformation, then, that seems unrelated to will or intent, one that arrives as if out of nowhere.

Taste is, of course, the preferred way of characterizing our aesthetic preferences: those affinities—for certain films, fashions, foods, even fonts—that possess a social aspect and yet that often operate at a semiconscious or nonrational level. Taste can have a visceral force, as we are magnetically drawn to certain objects while recoiling with disgust or irritation from others. Yet the word does not quite capture those aspects of attachment that interest me here. Its connotations seem, on the one hand, too snobbish, linked to condescending or fussy distinctions between good and bad taste, and, on the other hand, too superficial, hinting at a whimsical preference for vanilla versus strawberry ice cream: "there's no accounting for taste."

Another word is needed for the issue at hand: that the artwork creates a world and makes its own demands, to which we may or may not measure up. The idea of attunement has a respectable philosophical legacy. It crops up, for example, in Stanley Cavell's discussion of how we come to agree about criteria: as being not just a matter of reason but of attunement in words and in forms of life. For Cavell, language is always bound up with relations between persons, and attunement is a real, if fragile, achievement: a testimony to our connections with others. "Attunement" is also a standard translation for the Heideggerian term *Befindlichkeit*—for how one finds oneself in relation to the world, an overall orientation or disposition. And here it overlaps with his account of mood, or *Stimmung*, a notion I've found helpful in describing the dispositions of contemporary scholarship. I share Heidegger's view that analytical detachment is not an absence of mood but one kind of mood that reveals the world in a specific—and partial—way. As a word that spans thought and feeling, subject and object, "mood" alerts us to the ways in which we are always predisposed.

Yet this line of thought does not quite get at what interests me: how we attune, or become.attuned, to works of art. Moods are for Heidegger intentionless; that is to say, they are not directed at specific objects. Rather, they embody an overall orientation to the world; they are background rather than foreground; they embody a shared or collective state. "Mood is *primordial*," writes Matthew Ratcliffe, "a precondition for any form of intelligibility or sense-making."[17] My concern here, however, is how persons "get" (or fail to get) a work of art, as a process of adjusting, recalibrating, fine-tuning. Attunement, in this sense, involves a distinct *other*: there is a directed response and a vector of attention. It also implies a *process* and a series of gradations (in contrast to the steady state implied by *Befindlichkeit*: how one finds oneself); one can be, after all, more or less attuned. And finally, while this process of acclimatizing can hum away quietly in the background, it can also burst into consciousness with unbidden force. On these questions, Smith's essay turns out to be more revelatory than much of philosophy and aesthetic theory.

In looking back at her earlier self, at that stranger who disdained Joni Mitchell, Smith is mystified: "I truly cannot understand the language of my former heart. Who *was* that person?" (104). Deploying a harsh word—"philistinism"—that has fallen from favor in recent decades, Smith wields it in order to voice a severe self-judgment at her own failure to measure up to Mitchell's music, her inability to hear its claim upon her. Her reproach to her younger self echoes that of her irritated husband: "It's *Joni Mitchell*. What is *wrong* with you? Listen to it—it's beautiful. Can't you hear that?" (102). Here we are squarely in the Kantian realm of aesthetic judgment as being subjective yet normative: when we are drawn to a piece of music or a painting, we cannot help wanting others to share our perception. It does not seem beautiful just to us but embodies a beauty that should be unmistakable to others.

The issue, of course, is how such shared perception comes about.

As Cavell reminds us, argument will take us only so far in trying to persuade others. I can point to features that inspire or excite me, provide reasons, and justify my judgment; perhaps my fervor or my eloquence will have an effect. But there is also an inescapably subjective dimension to aesthetic response, a point at which disagreements cannot be resolved and intellectual justifications falter. In an often-cited passage, Cavell sketches the scenario of a conversation about art, with one person finally saying in exasperation: "don't you see, don't you hear, don't you dig? . . . Because if you do not see *something*, without explanation, there is nothing further to discuss."[18]

This same question—how one shifts from not seeing to seeing, from not hearing to hearing—lies at the heart of Smith's meditation on Mitchell. "The first time I heard her," to cite her words once more, "I didn't hear her at all." She continues: "My parents did not prepare me. (The natural thing in these situations is to blame the parents)" (100). Here Smith acknowledges the role of nurture in shaping taste, while interjecting a mild note of irony—how tempting, after all, to ascribe all our failings to our upbringing! The sounds of her youth were those of Burning Spear and the Beatles, Bob Marley and Bob Dylan, Aretha Franklin and Ella Fitzgerald: the tastes, she writes, of the young black woman and the older white man who raised her. There was, by contrast, no demographic for white women's music. Later, at university, her friends pressed Joni Mitchell upon her, fervently, zealously, to little avail. "*You don't like Joni?* My friends had pity in their eyes. The same look the faithful tend to give you as you hand them back their 'literature' and close the door in their faces" (102). She steadily resists the cajolery of the true believers, is unwilling to be made over in their image.

It is in her thirties that something shifts. Smith is on her way to a wedding in Wales; her husband, a poet, suggests they make a brief stop at Tintern Abbey. Smith, intent on chasing down a sausage roll at the next motorway service station, is reluctant; her mood is sour, not least because of the enervating sounds emanating from the car's music system: "that bloody piping again, ranging over octaves, ignoring the natural divisions between musical bars, and generally annoying the hell out of me, like a bee caught in a wing mirror" (102). As she wanders among flagstones bordered with thistles, looking out through ruins on to green hills, her mind is still preoccupied with the prospect of microwaved snacks. "And then what? As I remember it, sun flooded the area; my husband quoted a line from one of the Lucy poems; I began humming a strange piece of music" (103), "humming Joni, not yet conscious of the transformation" (104). A change has been brought about: an attunement has imperceptibly occurred. Did a unique config- uration of actors—a ruin, a landscape, a husband, some lines of Wordsworth—come together to effect a shift in perception? Or did the process start much earlier, with the fervent testimony of friends that had no impact until, combining in mysterious alchemy with an afternoon at Tintern Abbey, a defense was suddenly breached? Did the music act alone—or did it resonate only because the ground was prepared, the viewer already receptive?

If you want to effect a breach in the edifice of the human per- sonality, Smith writes, it helps to cultivate a Kierkegaardian sense of defenselessness. Shaped by the sounds of her childhood, she had long resisted a different style of singing—distrustful of music in a way that she had never been distrustful of words. Receptivity was a more difficult state to attain. "I don't think it is a coincidence," she continues, "that my Joni epiphany came through the back door, while my critical mind lay undefended, focused on a quite other form of beauty" (113). Attunement cannot occur without a nascent state of readiness; aesthetics cannot forgo or dispense with the first-person response. No one, after all, can listen or read or look for you; no one else can have your aesthetic experience. And yet, in contrast to a traditional phenomenology of art—a stage stripped bare of all but a solitary self facing a self-contained work—Smith conjures up a cavalcade of friendly coactors and active mediators: the friends, the landscape, the sun, the voice of the husband, the resplendent ruin, even the longed-for sausage roll.

Meanwhile, Smith reminds us that experiences of attunement are also indebted to the past words and work of others, to the laying down of a history of response. Artworks that once seemed scan- dalous or vacuous are now unconditionally admired. If she had paid a call on Picasso at his studio in 1907 and caught sight of *Les Demoiselles d'Avignon*, she would have been "nonplussed, maybe even a little scandalized. If, in my real life of 2012, I stand before this painting in the Museum of Modern Art, in New York, it seems obviously beautiful to me. All the difficult work of attunement and acceptance has already been done by others. Smart critics, other painters, appreciative amateurs. They kicked the door open almost a century ago—all I need do is walk through it" (113). Do we perceive the beauty of a Picasso because it is there or because others have inspired us to see the artwork in this way? ANT would suggest that the antithesis is false, the question not only unanswerable but uninteresting.

And yet friends also disagree with friends and critics with critics. Even museums and galleries will squabble over the merits of specific works. And while we are oriented to find some texts more resonant than others—by education and class background, by pressures of gender, race, religion, sexuality, or nationality—glitches are common; expected and actual affinities may not smoothly coincide. It is these disjunctures that are likely to be missed by the academic's questionnaires. As the French sociologist Robert Escarpit wrote many years ago, the "cultured man" who knows Racine will never be so foolhardy as to admit that what he really loves is Tintin.[19] Our consciously held beliefs about literary or cultural value do not line up perfectly with our attachments (those works that captivate and change us). Such attachments are not found but forged: neither purely self-created nor epiphenomena of social systems, they are cocomposed. And they are made and unmade over time.

Smith's essay thus alerts us to several aspects of attunement. There is, first of all, the question of its duration. Is it immediate or protracted? A sudden infatuation or a steady acclimatization? And what of the time lag that can occur: a work of art that has no discernible impact on a first encounter, only to unexpectedly resonate a week, a month, a year later? Smith, it seems, could hear Joni Mitchell only when she was ready to hear her, when the ground was prepared, the listener receptive. Second, there is the status of the artwork as an active force in the world. To what extent can a painting or a novel make us feel things? Who acts and who is acted upon; who possesses and who is possessed—or dispossessed? And finally, there is the "ineffability" of a certain aesthetic relation: those aspects of experience that we struggle to articulate. Is such talk nothing more than Romantic bluster and mystification, the last gasp of the ideology of the aesthetic—or does it point to something real that needs to be grappled with?

Aesthetic Time

How aesthetic response unfolds over time is exceptionally hard to pin down. This is one reason why trying to measure the impact of art in laboratory conditions—using questionnaires to assess whether people have become more empathetic after reading a few pages of Jane Austen—can seem counterintuitive or absurd. (As if literary prose were injected directly into the bloodstream, to work its effects on the brain cells a few minutes later!) Did that painting affect me as I stood in front of it—or was it an alteration that took place over days or weeks, as it worked its way into my memory and my thoughts? At what moment does an alteration of perception or sensibility come about?

Smith's essay tells a captivating story of conversion, one that links up to a long history of spiritual or secular transformations. These epiphanies share certain qualities: they are sudden and transformative; they resist being accounted for in rational terms; they feel authoritative to those who experience them (their force does not lend itself to doubt).[20] An epiphany has ethical force: it is about the revelation of what truly matters. But it also has an aesthetic aspect: it is dramatic, contrast filled, anchored in a sense of crisis. And yet, while Joni Mitchell's music may be extraordinary, it is also utterly ordinary; listened to by millions, endlessly streamed through headphones and speakers, it is an integral part of commodity culture. And while Smith's conversion takes place at Tintern Abbey, it does so within a mundane drama of summer weddings, motorway snacks, low-grade irritation, and marital squabbles.

The language of epiphanies is often dismissed by present-day critics, who see it as a holdover from the era of Romanticism and its swooning poets. And yet the experience it points to has a much broader purchase. In a fascinating ethnography, Ben Green interviewed club-goers and music fans in Brisbane about their "peak experiences"—encounters with popular or alternative music that stood out to them as especially meaningful and memorable. Their stories, he remarks, sounded very similar to George Gershwin's description of hearing his first recitation of Dvořák's *Humoresque*: in both cases there is a sense of experiential intensity and heightened affect that seems impossible to capture fully in words. Pushing back against the tendency to slot the study of high and popular culture into separate silos, Green draws out striking similarities. As he remarks, there is a fundamental doubleness about such aesthetic encounters. The epiphany is a narrative trope, a way of making sense of experience—even as it also points to an affective intensity that is felt to be beyond language. The realness of music's effects cannot be disentangled from what people hold these effects to be. And yet a famous artist may be resisted or scorned, may be heard but not really listened to; until, for whatever reason and without any warning, a barrier is suddenly breached and a certain song, as one person put it, "completely broke me to pieces." Having paid no attention to Bruce Springsteen for two decades—too obvious, too mainstream—this interviewee was suddenly, inexplicably, moved to tears.[21]

Not all attunement, however, arrives as a bolt from the blue. Beyond the drama of her Mitchell conversion, Smith's essay is an essential guide to the differing rhythms and varying time frames of how we become attuned. There is, to begin with, the pressure of upbringing and milieu. To be born is to be thrown into a form of life, with its preferences and prohibitions, its idioms and its silences. Becoming attuned, in this sense, is a precondition of any form of being and living with others—whether we think of the young child's attuning to the gestures and facial expressions of a parent, as described by psychologist Daniel Stern, or the later attuning to what counts and what matters in the world within which one must make one's way. In Cavell's words, attunement is "a matter of our sharing of routes and feelings, modes of response, senses of humor and significance and fulfilment, of what is outrageous, what is similar to all else, what a rebuke, what forgiveness."[22] Some of these responses are widely shared, while others are closely tied to certain milieus: ways of talking or laughing, of mourning or failing to mourn; the foods that are consumed or—in Smith's case—the music that is loved. It is through a history of such collective attunements that we become the persons that we are.

Second, there is a remaking of taste through education, as a matter not just of thought but of perception and feeling; a matter of getting to know and of coming to like; of learning to distinguish and discriminate; of experiencing what lies beyond the bounds of previous experience. Such a remaking can be both formal and informal, institutional or self-taught. Smith's essay describes her willingness to apprentice herself in a literary tradition, to learn the complexities of a craft. Education can shake up preferences and remake perception; one becomes attuned to what once seemed opaque or irrelevant, and one comes to admire what once seemed unworthy of affection. And so *Les Demoiselles d'Avignon* may come to seem beautiful, thanks to others—smart critics, other painters, appreciative amateurs—who paved the way. But education can also involve estrangement and shame, as Smith well knows: a sense of embarrassment at one's own lack of knowledge or "bad taste," disorientation at a failure to grasp what seems self-evident to one's peers, or a growing alienation from a family of origin whose world one no longer shares. (We might think here of Smith's 2012 novel *NW* and its working-class heroine Leah, entirely at sea in her philosophy classes at Edinburgh, "listening to warbling posh boys" and "being more bored than you have ever been in your life.")[23]

And there are, finally, those flashes that come as if out of nowhere, unexpected and unprepared for. The language in such cases is often that of being arrested, transfixed, frozen in place. Here, for example, is the writer Patricia Hampl hurrying through the rooms of the Art Institute of Chicago on her way to meet a friend at the cafeteria:

> I didn't halt, didn't stop. I was stopped. Apprehended, even. That's how it felt. I stood before the painting a long minute. I couldn't move away. I couldn't have said why. I was simply fastened there.
>
> I wasn't in the habit of being moved by art. I wasn't much of a museum goer. I'd never even taken an art history class, and I thought of myself as a person almost uniquely ungifted in the visual arts. . . . Maybe only someone so innocent of art history could be riveted by a picture as I was that day by Matisse's gazing woman . . . with her no-nonsense post–Great War bob, chin resting on crossed hands, elbows

propped on the peachy table where, slightly to the left, a pedestal fishbowl stands. . . . I wasn't thinking in words; I was hammered by the image.[24]

Indifferent to art, Hampl is brought up short by a painting: as she says, "hammered by the image." Such accounts (for there are many others to be found) would appear to give the lie to the claim that a love of art is always tied to appropriate schooling. Unfamiliar with Matisse's oeuvre, Hampl does not approach it through the usual categories of art history: she is unaware, until one of her friends informs her, that *Woman before an Aquarium* is classified as a minor work. As in Smith's case, the lack of insider knowledge seems not to impede attachment but to intensify it. (Curious about the painting that had inspired Hampl's book, I chased it up in the Art Institute of Chicago last summer, to be disappointed by a glum, pasty-faced woman trapped inside a drab canvas, with no trace of the sun-bright colors or bold outlines that I associate with Matisse. Did we react differently to the same painting—or in some sense see a different painting?)

While a sudden revelation is, by definition, unexpected and unprepared for, there are differences in how it relates to a prior history of exposure. Like virtually every Westerner of a certain age, Zadie Smith had heard Joni Mitchell's music long before her change of heart at Tintern Abbey; there was a delayed reception, a time lag. For Hampl, meanwhile, the first sighting of *Woman before an Aquarium* was also the moment of conversion: seeing and being struck by Matisse's painting occurred in one fell swoop. Here differences of medium also come into play: paintings afford the possibility of instantaneous apprehension, of seeing something all at once. Music, however, can be experienced only over time; it is intrinsically tied, through its form, to process, sequence, and continuation. Pictures, as a result, would seem to have a greater potential to trigger a sense of surprise or astonishment.[25]

An intriguing example that falls somewhere between long-term exposure and love at first sight is offered by Geoff Dyer in his account of his obsession with *Stalker*. What prompted this obsession, Dyer wonders, and why did he latch on to this specific film? How could the agonizing slowness of Tarkovsky's takes come to affect him so strongly? After describing a scene in Tarkovsky's film involving a bird, Dyer writes this:

> It was not a case of love at first sight—the first time I saw *Stalker* I was slightly bored and unmoved. I wasn't overwhelmed . . . but it was an experience I couldn't shake off. Something about it stayed with me. I was living in Putney at the time and one day my then-girlfriend and I went walking in Richmond Park. It was autumn and a bird flew over the sloping ground toward a clump of trees, flapped and flew in a way that was strangely reminiscent of the way that second bird had flown into this vast room of sand. I wanted to see the film again immediately after that, and since then, the desire to see it again—and again and again—has never gone away.[26]

The film, at first, has no appeal; there is no immediate hook; Dyer remains unmoved, even bored. And yet some scrap or residue lingers in his mind, waiting to be activated. At some point (a month later? a year later?), as he is strolling through the park, the flapping wings of a bird bring back the memory of a scene in *Stalker* and an enduring tie is forged. A period of *incubation* was necessary, it seems, before the film could take hold. The pathway is created not by words—although Dyer has much to say about Tarkovsky's dialogue—but by a pattern of movement that sets up a reverberation, a kinesthetic resonance. (Just as Smith did not fall for Mitchell by learning about open-stringed guitars, Dyer did not become obsessed with Tarkovsky by reading commentaries on his films.) The book that transpires is a scene-by-scene description of the film and also, Dyer writes, an account of watchings, rememberings, misrememberings, and forgettings. "I do know," he remarks, "that if I had not seen *Stalker* in my early twenties my responsiveness to the world would have been radically diminished."[27]

As we see from even this handful of examples, the time span between encountering a work and experiencing its effects is unpredictable. We can be hooked immediately, or after a week, a month, or a year has passed. Delay, deferral, time lag are not uncommon; aesthetic experience is aslant of clock time and pursues its own rhythms. Virginia Woolf writes of reading a book and waiting for "the dust of reading to settle; for the conflict and the questioning to die down; walk, talk, pull the dead petals from a rose, or fall asleep."[28] Later the book will return, she remarks, but it will do so differently. An affinity can be registered suddenly or slowly; an attraction can be instantaneous or build over time.

Perhaps we may be tempted to allot the sudden attraction—arriving out of nowhere, unbidden and unprepared for—a greater weight. Whether its object is a person or a painting, the *coup de foudre* claims a certain authority; fracturing familiar schemas and assumptions, it promises a liberation from routine. In the art of modernism, for example, we often see a visceral distrust of story and sequence, a conviction that truth can be found only in the flare-up of a sudden illumination: what Karl Heinz Bohrer refers to as the annihilation of continuity by the ecstatic moment.[29] It is in the glimmer of the transitory experience that a shard of authenticity can be found. Similar themes often crop up in French critical theory, as in Jean-François Lyotard's reflections on Barnett Newman's massive red painting *Vir Heroicus Sublimis*. What renders this work sublime, Lyotard insists, is its emphasis on the "now," as that which dismantles or disarms the viewer's consciousness. Newman's painting is the quintessential instance of presence without meaning, of a monumental *thereness* that is shorn of any representational content or narrative coherence. The work of art is extraordinary because it assails the continuity of time.[30]

Not all instances of attunement, however, are as dramatic as those of Smith or Hampl. T. J. Clark's *The Sight of Death* is an exercise in slow and sustained looking, as Clark returns over a period of months to look at two paintings by Poussin hanging in the Getty Museum in Los Angeles. His text is a painstakingly precise record of what he sees: shimmering birch leaves; the curls on the head of a goatherd; tonalities of blueness; the smudge of sun on a horse's backside; patterns of cubes and parallelograms; the balancing of background and foreground and shaping of space; how the mood of a painting can be transformed by changes in natural light. Poussin, he remarks, is a painter of the unnoticeable—of a hillside with no significance, of marsh grass and winding dirt roads. Slowness, here, does not negate or annihilate surprise but makes it possible. "Coming to terms with pictures is slow work," writes Clark. "But astonishing things happen if one gives oneself over to the process."[31] Such slowness can be a process of unlearning, not the drip-drip of habituation but the coming into view of something new.

Little has been written, Clark continues, on the practice of repeated looking; we believe, somehow, that images happen all at once. Of course, art historians and critics *do* look at paintings for extended periods; but they have written little about what it means to do so, about the experience of returning to an image over and over again, at different moments, under varying conditions, with shifting feelings and expectations. We need, Clark writes, "to throw the image back into the flow of time"—where time means not the history of its making but the period during which viewers look away and then look back, shrug their shoulders, move closer to look at a dog peeking out from behind a chair in the painting's corner, stand back to appraise a larger pattern. "Paintings are capable of getting in the way of our framing of them," Clark remarks; they do not always do what we expect.[32] While he does not invoke the word, *The Sight of Death* is unmistakably a record of an attunement: one that is premised on slowness rather than speed.

As Clark would be the first to admit, being able to gaze at paintings for hours requires a certain privilege and freedom from temporal constraints: punching the clock, lengthy commutes from the suburbs, the fractious demands of children. And yet slowness might also have a broader relevance. For Jean-Marie Schaeffer, what defines aesthetic experience is *delayed categorization*. It is only when we suspend our rush to analyze and summarize, to judge and to justify, that a work of art can begin to reveal itself. Attunement, in this light, becomes a slow and often stumbling process, a gradual coming into view of what we would otherwise fail to see. Yet this is not a matter, Schaeffer insists, of valuing difficulty for its own sake. Our encounters with art are not cut off from the world but are infused with thoughts and feelings that shape other aspects of our lives. What art does offer, though, is a training in modes of paying attention. Through its relentless curiosity about detail and nuance, its fierce concentration on the qualities of its own medium, it invites us to look closely at what we might otherwise overlook. Patience and slowness are mandated, not the greedy and indiscriminate gulp.[33]

Much of Schaeffer's argument seems entirely plausible—until it collides with the problem of counterexamples. The claim that delay is a necessary condition of aesthetic experience cannot account for the bolt from the blue: Hampl's experience of being hammered by the image; Smith's unanticipated conversion. In such cases, there is no tentative process of feeling one's way but an abrupt swerve into commitment. And yet one would be hard-pressed to claim that these do not qualify as aesthetic responses. Perhaps, then, there is no formula for specifying the "right" rhythm and speed of attunement, no general model that we can pin down, whether one of suddenness or one of slowness. Bence Nanay, for example, contrasts Richard Wollheim, who needed to look at a painting for at least an hour in order to have an aesthetic experience, to Clement Greenberg, who was known for instantaneous appreciation and split-second judgment.[34] We are left, simply, with the variability of how people become attuned to works of art.

Agency

Let's return to Hampl's phrase "hammered by the image." Clearly, Matisse's painting is doing something—though of course most viewers will not react in the same way as Hampl. How, then, are we to understand this doing? In what way can we think of an artwork as being an actor? What is interacting with what? And in what sense does a work's agency either afford or undercut our own?

Hampl's book belongs to a distinct genre: memoirs reflecting on what it means to be obsessed or possessed by a painting. Other recent examples include Mark Doty's *Still Life with Oysters and Lemon*, a meditation on the author's affinity with a seventeenth-century canvas by the Dutch artist Jan Davidsz de Heem, and Michael White's *Travels in Vermeer*, in which the author decides, in the aftermath of a divorce, to see as many of the world's Vermeer paintings as he can track down. Tying these works together is an emphasis on a painting's power of address: its ability to engage and take the measure of the viewer. In Doty's words: "I have felt the energy and life of a painting's will; I have been held there, instructed."[35] Meanwhile, countless memoirs testify to literature's impact and influence on a life. In *My Life in Middlemarch*, for example, Rebecca Mead invokes "the strange potency of a great book: the way a book can insert itself into a reader's own history, a reader's own life story, until it is hard to know what one would be without it."[36] In all this talk of the energy of paintings or the potency of novels there is an insistent theme: that art can *do* things to people, that it can make things happen.

Until recently, there was a chasm between such autobiographical reflection and academic criticism: not just in style but in their underlying premises. It is not only the casual mixing of art and life that jars with the protocols of scholarship but the belief that one can be transformed for the better by an aesthetic encounter. The New Critics brushed aside the question of literature's impact on its readers—such talk was a matter for psychologists, not literary critics. And later historical and political approaches waved the banner of "context" and "structural conditions" in a way that left little room for reflection on how art affects *persons*.

Yet countercurrents have always existed. The midcentury philosopher and musicologist Vladimir Jankélévitch gently mocks the "stalwart spirit who focuses on musical form in order to demonstrate that they have not been duped." "Everyone knows the type," he remarks, "the cool cerebral people who affect interest in how the piece is 'put together' after the concert." For Jankélévitch—who has been called the anti-Adorno—this "fear of being bewitched, the coquetry of refusal, the resolve not to 'submit'" are symptoms of modern alienation rather than any form of resistance to it.[37] And the contemporary scholar Carolyn Abbaté pursues a similar questioning of formalism and historicism in music; both approaches, she remarks, rely on a critical distance that is supposed to shore up liberal credentials. And yet "it is in the irreversible experience of playing, singing, or listening," she writes, "that any meanings summoned by music come into being. Retreating to the work displaces that experience, and dissecting the work's technical features or saying what it represents reflects the wish not to be transported by the state that the performance has engendered in us."[38] Musicology, she suggests, has been exceptionally adept at avoiding the fundaments of musical experience.

Meanwhile, in his 1989 book *The Power of Images*, David Freedberg questions the phantom of pure response (the disinterested and disembodied aesthetic gaze) as well as art history's preoccupation with large-scale history and context. Instead, he conjures up a dazzling spectrum of reactions to artworks over hundreds of years: "People are sexually aroused by pictures and sculptures; they break pictures and sculptures; they mutilate them, kiss them, cry before them, and go on journeys to them; they are calmed by them, stirred by them, and incited to revolt. They give thanks by means of them, expect to be elevated by them, and are moved to the highest levels of empathy and fear. They have always responded in these ways; they still do."[39] Paintings are powerful, Freedberg argues: they inspire devotion, anger, consternation, and love; they make things happen.

While Freedberg's book was widely reviewed, its immediate impact was modest. Art history continued to trundle along well-worn paths: critical analysis of the social construction of art and taste, close attention to the formal composition of paintings—or, in some cases, a blending of both. Yet the question of what art *does* is once again being broached, thanks to the intellectual excitement generated by Alfred Gell's *Art and Agency*. Approaching art as an anthropologist rather than an art historian, Gell is deeply interested in the question of art's influence and impact on the world. "I view art as a system of action," he writes, "intended to change the world rather than encode symbolic propositions about it."[40] Arguing against semiotic approaches that treat art as a visual sign to be deciphered, Gell focuses not on what artworks mean but on what they do, how they captivate, fascinate, and entrap spectators, their associations with magic and power. This means, Gell contends, turning away from aesthetic questions in order to define art objects as actors that sustain social relations. *Art and Agency* is a pivotal text in its stress on the relational dynamics of art, and its impact is being felt in art history, visual studies, and cultural sociology.

And yet Gell's counterposing of agency and aesthetics—his assumption that art as social action has nothing to do with aesthetic experience—should give us pause. Surely the reverse is true: the perception of phenomena as aesthetic phenomena, rather than destroying their impact, accentuates their impact. The "specialness" of art—as shaped by social institutions, shared yet idiosyncratic responses, and the works themselves—is not an airtight chamber cut off from the world but a dynamic and agitated force field of action and transformation. It is *because* art is held to have special qualities that it can have such intense effects. And here Gell fudges somewhat on the issue of agency: art objects, after all, do not act in the same way as the other examples he cites of mantraps or poisoned arrows; rather, they depend on the consent and participation of humans. As Caroline Van Eck points out, reacting to artworks as if they were alive has nothing to do with cognitive confusion or delusion, but with *experiencing* them as living.[41]

Here we might look to James Elkins's *Pictures and Tears*: a compendium of people crying in front of paintings. Elkins is interested in strong emotional responses that contravene art's association with detachment or disinterestedness. One of his respondents writes: "I cried at a museum in front of a Gauguin painting—because somehow he had managed to paint a transparent pink dress. I could almost see the dress wafting in the hot breeze."[42] What kind of causal relations are at work here? Even if this particular viewer is highly sensitive or sentimental and is primed to respond in certain ways, it is nevertheless this painting and not another—it is how *this* pink dress is painted, the delicacy of its flimsy fabric, afloat in the air—that triggers a physiological as well as emotional reaction. The picture is doing something; it makes a difference. And yet the object does not contain its own effects: whether a viewer responds with tears or a smile of delight or turns away in indifference cannot be predicted by analyzing the painting, even though these responses define its impact for that viewer. Meanwhile, other factors also play their part in wetting the viewer's cheeks: the framing space of the museum; the proper name Gauguin; the knowledge that the thing to do in an art gallery is to stand in front of a painting and look with rapt attention. Not a zero-sum game, then, but a coming together of multiple factors: what we have called *distributed agency*.

To explore what art does, in short, is not to bracket its distinctiveness as a work of art—these questions are interconnected rather than opposed. It is precisely these qualities—these affordances— that allow a work to reattune us in ways we do not expect and may not be able to predict. Whether she is listening to Bach rather than Beethoven, or Mötley Crüe rather than Metallica, matters enormously to a music lover; these names not only connect to large-scale patterns of taste, prestige, or cultural hierarchy but are also attached to different objects. And yet, as Hennion remarks, "we have to actively make the objects of our pleasure emerge in all their differences, and make ourselves aware of those differences."[43] Art's specialness can be realized only through practices of discrimination.

Hennion and Latour draw on the language of "instauration," taken from the French philosopher Etienne Souriau, to talk about how things are realized—that is to say, how they are made real. And here art has its own modes of instauration—its particular ways of having an impact. What is the difference between being carried away by a story and by a subway train? It is not that one experience is false or illusory while the other is real, remarks Latour. Rather, the former requires our attention and participation in a way that the latter does not. The effects of paintings, novels, and plays depend on their being taken up by readers or viewers, as intermediaries through which they must pass. Without their input, a painting is reduced to nothing more than daubs of pigment on a stretched canvas; a novel dissolves into endless black squiggles on glued-together sheets of paper.

We are confronted with what looks like a puzzle: an acknowledgment of the agency of artworks, yet these works act only insofar as readers or viewers or listeners allow themselves to be acted upon. This puzzle speaks to the irresolvable ambiguities of agency: we make works of art even as they make us. If we find ourselves transfixed by a Rembrandt painting or feel compelled to listen to Mitchell's "California" for the fiftieth time, the division between doer and done-to is hard to pin down. Who is setting what in motion? Phrases such as "active dispossession" or "consensual self-abandonment" are used by Hennion and Emilie Gomart to capture the swirl of active and passive, the ways in which music or art or film lovers seek to abandon themselves, how people strive to be overcome by the objects of their passion. The double verb *faire faire*—meaning "to be made to do"—conveys the uncertainties of agency, as we allow ourselves to be acted upon. We are made to do something by the song that moves us, but our letting ourselves be moved is no less active than the song's making.[44]

Here again we need to attend to variations in experience: even if aesthetic response is cocreated, the balance of power is not always the same. One does not like wine or music just by chance, Hennion remarks; rather, one enters into an "activity which has a past and a space marked by its objects, other participants, ways of doing things, places, and moments, and institutions."[45] This observation makes perfect sense for the groups that Hennion studies: music fans, wine lovers, film buffs. To define yourself along these lines is to enter into an existing field of practices, to make a conscious decision to pursue certain interests or passions. One is initiated—into certain ways of talking, modes of being, collective attunements—but one also initiates, choosing to define oneself as a certain kind of person. And yet, as we've seen, not all attachments are formed in this way. This does not mean they are inherently inexplicable, but their causes are likely to be heterogeneous, dispersed over time, and exceptionally difficult to trace. And experientially, such an attunement may feel very different—like an overcoming rather than an embrace.

George Steiner has some interesting things to say about how works of art can affect us, seemingly against our will. While often seen as the most mandarin of critics, Steiner is perfectly willing to admit that aesthetic quality, however we choose to define it, may have little to do with the affective force of art. In a memorable passage he reflects on Edith Piaf's "Je ne regrette rien" and the puzzle of his own response. "The text is infantile, the tune stentorious, and the politics which enlisted the song unattractive," Steiner begins stonily, yet "the opening bars, the hammer-beat *accelerando* . . . tempt every nerve in me, touch the bone with a cold burn and draw me after into God knows what infidelities to reason, each time I hear the song and hear it, uncalled for, recurrent inside me."[46] The phrasing is a tad overheated, but it is to Steiner's credit that he is willing to own up to the intensities of his response: how a popular tune is able to seize command of his mind and body. While he begins with the defensive jabs that intellectuals are so fond of—sentimental, manipulative, melodramatic—he ends in a different register.

"Manipulative," especially, strikes me as an unhelpful word that shuts down thinking about art and agency before it has even begun. To dub something manipulative is to assume that there is something false or dishonest about being moved by art—that a lump in the throat testifies to the shallowness of the work rather than our own vulnerability. We find ourselves only a hair's breadth away from the perorations that rained down on the "cheap emotions" in the middle of the twentieth century (Clement Greenberg, Milan Kundera, Dwight McDonald). And here Steiner is more open-minded: while "accredited monumentalities pass us by," he writes, "the ephemeral can be addictive. It is the sheer force of the experience, its insertion into the quick of our being, which challenge understanding and clear phrasing."[47] Like myself, he's curious as to why certain works of art stick, bond, have an impact, whereas others disappear without leaving a trace. As Steiner notes, there are certain attunements that knit together those of similar milieu and educational background. And yet there are others that are irreducibly particular—"as if the honeycomb of each individual receptivity, of each individual psychic indwelling, [was] intricately specific."[48] Such affinities are distinctive, yet not necessarily chosen; a certain work grafts on to our psyche whereas another does not even begin to take hold.

Presence

We come, finally, to the question of presence, meaning not just that artworks exist but that their existence seems exceptionally vivid: they embody some kind of overwhelming *thereness* that cannot be bracketed or overlooked. As we've seen, such perceptions are not uncommon—but how do we honor and make sense of them? At one point in the history of criticism, such perceptions could not be honored but could only be condescended to; the most damning thing one could say about other critics was that they unwittingly subscribed to a metaphysics of presence. These prohibitions have now loosened somewhat, but squabbles and standoffs are still frequent. In one corner, those convinced that aesthetic experience exceeds linguistic and conceptual framing; in the other, those adamant that any such talk can only be Romantic blather or reactionary bluster.

Hans Ulrich Gumbrecht has recently offered a vigorous defense of aesthetic presence. As he defines it, such presence is spatial rather than temporal; it appeals exclusively to the senses; it involves moments of intensity (epiphany); and it arises from the "thingness," or materiality, of the work of art, as something that *is* rather than represents. Gumbrecht is at pains to insist that he does not see presence as destroying or negating meaning; aesthetic experience is an oscillation (and sometimes an interference) between presence effects and meaning effects. He is not, he stresses, against interpretation, but the current bias toward hermeneutic approaches calls for a correction. We urgently need to consider, he writes, how art can generate a sense of *"being in sync with the things of this world."*[49]

Gumbrecht cites the pushback he received from friends and colleagues when he started down this track: raised eyebrows and skeptical looks, accusations of mysticism and religiosity, concerns that he was taking a rightward turn. What lies behind this response? A sense of the vividness of a work is, after all, a common experience that—as we've seen—crosses boundaries of class and ideology. We are not moved by the same works or in the same way, but most people can point to novels or songs or films that they consider special, that affect them strongly in ways they find hard to articulate. Why, then, should talk of presence be seen as risible or reactionary? Janet Wolff, for example, takes issue with Gumbrecht's line of thought and the implication that we can have a visceral encounter with a work of art, worrying that this kind of thinking is leading in a conservative, even a protofascist direction. What bothers her, she writes, is the abandonment of mediation as a category.[50]

This worry that a stress on presence will result in a bracketing of the social aspects of art does not seem entirely unjustified. In a book called *Art Matters*, for example, Peter de Bolla sets himself the task of arriving at "a better understanding of what it means to be moved profoundly by a work of art."[51] A very worthy task; yet the possibility that such experiences might vary—that people are moved by different things and in different ways—is something he seems reluctant to address. Rather, de Bolla's account of his own reactions to Barnett Newman, Glenn Gould, and Wordsworth come to stand for aesthetic experience tout court. Any concerns that these works or his own response might not be representative are waved away as symptoms of a desire to be politically correct or appear fashionable. Instead—and there is a parallel tendency in Gumbrecht—art's presence is treated as a purely individual and strangely asocial matter. One of the potential pitfalls of phenomenology, Annemarie Mol remarks, is that one person's self-ethnography can be elevated to grandiose proportions.[52]

I've proposed, meanwhile, that art's presence is not attenuated by its relations but made possible by its relations. That we find a piece of art to be extraordinary, radiant, sublime—that it fills up our consciousness, crowding out awareness of other things, such that the rest of the world dissolves into nothingness—does not mean other actors were not involved. It is not a sign that we have vaulted into the stratosphere, far removed from the things of this world. Rather than subtracting from art's presence, these things help to bring it into view. Mediation does not block access to phenomena but makes it possible. As the philosopher Alva Noë puts it, we *achieve* presence; it arises out of interaction, engagement, involvement. Noë discusses the experience of listening to an album of music or of looking at paintings in a gallery, where at first the songs or the pictures all seem pretty much the same—undifferentiated, uninteresting:

> But suppose you don't give up. You listen to the record again and again; you begin to notice different qualities in the different songs. As you familiarize yourself with them, they begin to engage your attention and offer you comfort, or excitement, or stimulation, or pleasure. Perhaps you discuss the music, or the paintings in the gallery, with a friend, and she draws your attention to patterns or devices or lyrics. Whereas before the works—the songs, the paintings—were flat, opaque, undifferentiated—now they reveal themselves to you as structured and meaningful, as deep and involving.[53]

This description holds not just for classical music or museum paintings but for forms that carry less prestige. To the uninitiated, Nadine Hubbs remarks, country music "all sounds the same"; unable to distinguish or discriminate among those features that matter to its fans and often prejudiced by class bias, they focus only on unfamiliar elements or apply incongruous criteria.[54] Conversely, if we delve more deeply into a particular genre or form, are exposed to the force of more examples, and mull over them with friends, the work becomes more present, more solid, more real. To be sure, the deliberation that Noë sketches out here is not always in play—as we've seen, it is possible to be brought up short, to be taken off guard by one's own response. What his description drives home, however, is that presence is *co-made* rather than simply found.

In one sense, the point might seem obvious, even commonsensical. Why, then, is it so hard to take it on board? Perhaps because of the hold of a certain philosophical picture: language as a screen or veil separating us from a reality that we can never know "in itself." To invoke presence, in this line of thought, is to deny that the language-screen exists and to believe—with a touching naivete—that we can gain access to the plenitude of things as they really are. (Here I'm invoking, of course, the premises of the linguistic turn, which has cast its long shadow over the humanities in recent decades.) The response of the skeptic, then, is to flip things around and to insist that what we take to be real is its antithesis. Presence is a projection, a flimsy fiction imposed on an unknowable and unreachable world. We see only what our system of language allows us to see, or what it dictates that we see.

Increasingly, scholars are becoming restive with this picture of how language works. Language, they point out, is far from being a closed and self-contained system; words are intertwined with our ways of engaging with the world. Because these engagements are so infinitely varied, it makes no sense to speak of language as such; all we can do is assess the merits of language in use. Language, in short, is more like an interface than a firewall, an array of devices that connect us to other things, including those that matter to us. Toril Moi, for example, offers a forceful challenge to the theories of language that have shaped literary studies over the last few decades. Drawing especially on Wittgenstein, she questions the assumption of a gap between language and meaning, or between words and the world. Language neither represents nor fails to represent. Instead of constructing general theories of language, she remarks, we would do better to attend to the richness of examples and the extraordinary variations of language in use.[55]

If we think of language in this way, we are no longer crestfallen to discover that it does not match up exactly to the things to which it relates, any more than a hammer need resemble a nail. Some devices—some ways of talking or writing—are better suited to our purposes than others, some will sustain us while others are likely to lead us astray, but we are no longer held captive by a certain philosophical picture. There is no yawning gap between two spheres of "language" and "reality" but multiple relations of likeness and difference, as heterogeneous phenomena jostle, collide, and connect. There are countless contact zones. And that we can be surprised, discomfited, or changed in ways that we did not anticipate reveals the flimsiness of the "projection" thesis: things live their own lives; they can resist or evade our framing; they are not just servile minions of linguistic schemes.

Words and the world, remarks Latour, are not two hostile kingdoms at war with each other, such that we must pledge our fealty to the former or the latter. Language, rather, is one salient actor in our multimodal involvement with reality. Images, for example, have a rather different impact than words do. When someone says that their experience of a painting is hard to articulate, there is no need to reproach them for buying into a metaphysical wholeness beyond language. We need not wring our hands about resorting to the language of the ineffable, Clark remarks; some things—such as experiences of painting or music—are far harder to verbalize than others.[56] The point is not that such experiences are unmediated; one of the ways we learn to look at paintings is by looking at other paintings. But what we see does not translate perfectly into what we say. Reading Clark on Poussin is not like looking at a Poussin painting, even though the two experiences can certainly affect each other.

Mediation, in other words, is tied to the affordances of different media and cannot be fully captured via notions of reading or text. When we watch a film, many aspects of the sensorium are engaged: lighting, color, camera angles, facial expressiveness, music, and sound combine to conjure up a certain atmosphere long before a word of dialogue has been spoken. Perhaps we are caught up in a sense of elation or gripped by a sense of dread; a cinematic world is created that causes things to show up in certain ways. The resort to language may come belatedly, as a way of trying to verbalize or make sense of the experience; it is not the only or even the primary medium in play. Vivian Sobchack writes beautifully on this question in describing her embodied response to Jane Campion's film *The Piano*, which sensitized the surfaces of her skin, such that her fingers responded to its opening shots before her mind was able to make sense of them. We do more than interpret a film or even *see* a film, Sobchack writes:

> My experience of *The Piano* was a heightened instance of our common sensuous experience of the movies: the way we are in some carnal modality able to touch and be touched by the substance and texture of images; to feel a visual atmosphere envelop us; to experience weight, suffocation, and the need for air; to take flight in kinetic exhilaration and freedom even as we are relatively bound to our theater seats; to be knocked backward by a sound; to sometimes even smell and taste the world we see on the screen.[57]

The issue here is not just sensory and embodied forms of awareness but the crucial addendum that these forms act and react. Far from being neutral recording devices like cameras or cassette recorders, our sensory capacities distinguish and discriminate, carve out grooves of response. An unfamiliar genre of music sounds perplexing, grating, discordant; yet if I hear it over and over, it may start to resonate, to echo insistently in my mind. Moving to a big city, I am dazzled by the confusion of gaudy neon signs, flashing lights, video advertising screens; as days pass by, this confusion slowly dissipates and the kaleidoscope of color comes to seem comforting rather than chaotic. This, precisely, is what it means to become attuned: forms of alignment, a coordinating of senses, affects, bodies, and objects that can happen with or without linguistic support. Academics have a tendency to overintellectualize knowledge, which can also be a matter of practice, habituation, flair, or "feel." For the experienced chess player or omelet maker, Gilbert Ryle writes, it is less a matter of thinking than of doing.[58] In like fashion, engaging with art may involve modes of apprehension and sensation that have little to do with ideas.

Once we realize there are many kinds of mediation—which need not be conceptual or even linguistic—the dichotomy of the social versus the aesthetic/affective loosens its grip. It is no longer a matter of contrasting a "social" response with a "pure" response (whether to side with the former or the latter) but a matter of tracing out the various ties that bind readers and viewers to works they

CHAPTER 2

care about. These ties, as we've seen, can be longstanding or newly fashioned; they can be consciously embraced or linger below the radar of consciousness; they can be unmade and remade, as old loves give way to new passions.

In *Pictures and Tears*, James Elkins has some harsh things to say about art history and theory: that it is dry, alienating, self-involved, overly abstract, and oblivious to the beauty of images. Not only is it qualitatively different from the affective force of personal response—Elkins writes movingly about his own fascination, as a fourteen-year-old boy, with Bellini's *The Ecstasy of St. Francis* at the Frick—but it destroys it. (Other critics, as we'll see in chapter 4, take a rather different view.) Reading books about the history of Bellini's painting, he writes, "took my own experience away and substituted a different kind of understanding. The one didn't correct the other, it swamped it. My historical knowledge dulled my encounter with the image, deflected my attention onto other things . . . and finally extinguished the emotion I had once felt."[59]

Yet this difference is not a division between a purely subjective experience and the cultural baggage later imposed upon it. As Elkins concedes, the love of lonely woods that drew his teenage self to Bellini's painting was also influenced by various sources, including the ideas of nineteenth-century writers like Ruskin; Elkins was the unconscious heir of a tradition. "The things I loved about the woods—the thorns, the swamps, the slanting light from the winter sun—were all the stocks-in-trade of Romantic poetry and art criticism."[60] His early response to Bellini may have been more intense or enraptured than his later perspective as a scholar of art, but it was not, therefore, unmediated. And, of course, other prompts and pressures were also in play. Consider how many actors had to be assembled—art museums, techniques of display, conventions of looking at paintings, exposure to linguistic and iconographic traditions, encouragement from family or friends or books—so that his younger self could have a glorious epiphany at the Frick!

The language of presence, then, points to a real experience, yet one that cannot be understood simply by looking inward. Such a view, to put it simply, overlooks the many other actors that are involved. Hennion writes: "music is not simply a matter of a particular piece; it passes through a multitude of mediators beginning with the present (the sound of an instrument, the atmosphere of a hall, the grain of a record, the tone of a voice, the body of a musician) and the duration of a history (scores, repertoires and styles, genres and more or less stable forms), as well as for each individual—a past, works heard, moments lost, desires unfulfilled, roads travelled with others, and so on."[61] Things, persons, events, and spaces come together—not to diminish or undercut the presence of the artwork but to help disclose it and bring it into view.

A New Constellation

"Attunement" is one of a cluster of terms—"affinity," "atmosphere," "*Stimmung*," "mood"—that share certain resemblances. Isabelle Stengers describes how "affinity" is carried over from medieval alchemy into eighteenth-century science, where it comes to denote the chemical bonds between substances. Later, its meanings will expand to those forms of interpersonal chemistry—emotional, erotic, or spiritual—that may elude explanation or rational thought. (The parallels between chemical and personal bonds are a guiding thread of Goethe's *Elective Affinities*.) An affinity is akin to an inclination, according to the *Oxford English Dictionary*; it involves a turning or bending toward something. We may be reminded of Nathalie Sarraute's novel *Tropisms*, which documents the infinitesimal and imperceptible movements that take place at the threshold of consciousness. Without being aware of what they are doing, persons incline toward or away from each other, like plants turning slowly toward the light.[62]

Meanwhile, "atmosphere" has been championed by Gernot Böhme as the central term of a new aesthetics. The etymology of *atmos*—the Greek word for steam—refers to what is nebulous and diffuse: lacking contours, boundaries, or clear demarcations. As an aesthetic category, it has less to do with judgment or meaning than with modes of perception and spatially extended qualities of feeling. An atmosphere envelops, surrounds, and radiates. It is not inside the head, nor can it be imposed by an individual will. Rather, atmosphere speaks to how we find ourselves immersed in a world that shows up in certain ways, encompassing both perceiver and perceived. Picking up on the same term, Dora Zhang expands on its political and public, as well as aesthetic, entailments. "Created by a myriad of interacting elements—objects, bodies, relations, affects, colors, sounds, smells, speech"—atmosphere is, by its very nature, difficult to pin down. Invoking the term may court charges of irrationalism or mysticism. Yet becoming attuned to atmosphere—what it allows for and what it precludes—is a vital skill, one that might usher in new ways of doing politics, or what Zhang calls an "affective climate change."[63]

And then there is "*Stimmung*," which can be translated as both "mood" and "attunement," with the German word having philosophical, metaphysical, and auditory resonances that are not carried over into English. The idea of *Stimmung* stretches back to classical and medieval notions of cosmic harmony, as in the heavenly music of the spheres, and is embraced by the German Romantics, especially Schiller, Herder, and Kant. Tracing its history, David Wellbery describes the association of *Stimmung* with vibrations, tonal variations, and echoes. Even as it retains this hint of musicality, the word has gradually drifted free from its original meaning—the tuning of an instrument—to become increasingly subjectivized, hailed as a defining feature of aesthetic experience.[64]

Thanks to this history, *Stimmung* was excoriated by Adorno and other critical theorists as a regressive idea. How could one speak of concord or reconciliation in a world that was so profoundly out of joint? Harmony could only be a deeply ideological concept in the harsh light of modern alienation and political catastrophe.[65] Increasingly, however, these Romantic connotations (always less evident in English than in German) have started to fade, and the critique of *Stimmung* and its correlates can now seem overwrought. While "attunement," for example, refers to a "tuning in" among two or more actors, it brings with it no larger moral message and involves no metaphysical guarantees. Indeed, as shown by my example of *The Unconsoled*, it is not uncommon to be drawn to what is disorienting, discordant, uncanny: to find oneself attuned with what is out of tune. (This phenomenon would play a starring role in a work that cries out to be written: an affective history of criticism.)

"Mood," meanwhile, is rapidly becoming a key term of affect studies. Critics have expanded on its most striking elements: that moods are ubiquitous (there is no mood-free relation to the world) and that they circumvent oppositions of subject and object (we do not have a mood but find ourselves in a mood, such that "mood" implies and involves milieu). In this respect, mood resonates with the arguments of my first chapter; we cannot extricate ourselves from attachments, because we are already pre-oriented by the world into which we are thrown. The world never presents itself as valueless, observes Jonathan Flatley: things always appear to us as mattering or not mattering in some way. And here mood serves as the "affective atmosphere in which intentions are formed, projects are pursued, and particular affects can attach to particular objects."[66] Moods are modes of existence that form and inform relations to the world.

My preference for the language of attunement stems, as I noted earlier, from my interest in relations *between* persons and artworks. As a noun-verb, it captures better than "mood" or "atmosphere" the act of synchronization or modulation, how phenomena are changed over time by resonating or aligning. "Every attunement," writes Kathleen Stewart, is "a tuning up to something, an accretion chosen or unwillingly shouldered."[67] Yet all these terms—mood, atmosphere, affinity—offer vital resources for criticism, combatting the intellectualism of recent theory without falling back into notions of pure, unmediated feeling or the picture of a self cut off from the world.

It is not especially surprising that music and painting promote talk of attunement, and yet forms of literature—as well as ways of reading literature—are also amenable to such an approach. Poetry is an obvious candidate, given its ties to the sonorous and the resonant, but attunement has a wider relevance for drawing out relations between mood and style. W. G. Sebald's abiding concerns, for example, include questions of spatial orientation and of a person's attunement, or lack of attunement, to place. Yet his writing also strives to reattune the reader, deploying language to cast a pervasive mood. What David James calls the solace of Sebald's style—its slowly unfurling sentences and stately phrasing, its subdued, aloof, and melancholic tone—works both with and against the bleakness of works such as *Austerlitz*. Style can have a compensatory as well as expressive force, as a tentative and temporary counterforce to the historical catastrophes it records.[68]

And here Anna Jones Abramson captures well the salience of literary forms of attunement: a text is not a sequence of signs to be decoded but a structure that we come to inhabit. "Reading atmospherically, our bodies become instruments—what is the tone, the pacing, the mood; what feels impending, what feels hauntingly persistent?"[69] Rather than clearing the fog away, attunement alerts us to the messy co-implication of text and reader. Meanwhile, Robert Sinnerbrink expands on how mood reveals a cinematic world, with *Stimmung* encompassing both the expressiveness of a film and the affective responsiveness of viewers. It has less to do with narrative (the "aboutness" of character identification will be considered in the next chapter) than with setting a scene: via visual framing; the blending of music and sound, or silence; the rhythms of glances and gestures. The aesthetics of mood informs experiences of being caught up in a film.[70]

Attunement can also manifest itself in rather different ways. We might think of shared attachments that are fleeting and ephemeral: a catchy hit song, a new gadget, a summer movie, or a style of wearing one's hair that at a certain moment seems vital, urgent, indispensable, only to fade into oblivion a few weeks later. There is a mystery about such waves of collective enthusiasm and the ways in which affinities are sparked. While capitalism plays an obvious part in promoting fashions and fads, economics can tell us nothing about why certain things "catch on" while countless others are met with collective indifference. Meanwhile, references to mood, ambience, and atmosphere are now ubiquitous in everyday life as well as criticism—shaping everything from the design of department stores and coffee shops to contemporary fiction, music, and experimental video art.[71]

In thinking about attunement, I've tried to do justice to the stakes of the word: to describe modes of alignment that are affectively powerful yet hard to clarify or pin down. Attunement, in this sense, can work within yet also against the pressures of education, class, and culture; aesthetic attachments may or may not form along expected lines. And here I've considered differing rhythms of attunement as well as variations of scale: that it can be a matter of stability but also surprise, that it can be collectively shaped but also idiosyncratic. Rather than presenting a general theory, I have tried to build up a picture by looking at examples and seeing where they lead us.

At the same time, I have also argued a thesis: that attunement is the result, not of a break with the social—a flight into otherness, a withdrawal into interiority—but of things "coming together" in expected or unexpected ways. We often give art an exceptional credit for ushering newness into the world—as if it were the sole agent of change in a world of sameness, monotony, and soul-crushing predictability. That art can invigorate or astonish is not in dispute. Yet I have argued—with the help of Zadie Smith, Antoine Hennion, and others—that the artwork cannot act by itself; it needs allies, supporters, helpers. And crucially, that our experience of art as coproduced does not "take away" from the value of the work but makes it possible. Mediation does not detract from the magic of art but creates it. Hennion puts it beautifully in one of his eloquent descriptions: the "musician sitting down to the keyboard . . . knows there are his scales, his score, his touch, and the skills he has acquired, that without them he is nothing, and yet, even if he starts with these mediations, nothing is settled, the music will have to emerge; there is nothing that is automatic or guaranteed. . . . The surprise that peels away from the flux of things is the most ordinary of experiences."[72] What Hennion says here about playing the piano holds equally for the experience of listening to music, reading a novel, or looking at a painting. "The surprise that peels away from the flux of things"—could there be a better way of describing the puzzle of our attunements?

Identification

A Defense

Many of us have felt a tug of connection with a character in a novel or a film: a sense of affinity or shared response. We explain this tie by saying we are *identifying*. But how, exactly, are we drawn in? What kinds of ties are being forged? There is often a carelessness when critics talk about identification: the experience is judged before it is fully seen. It is often held to be slightly shameful—something that other people do (the naive, the unschooled, the sentimental). Yet identifying is a default rather than an option; a feature, not a bug. Two forms of confusion have led critics astray. Identification is often equated with *empathy*, or co-feeling—though empathy is just one of the ways in which readers and viewers identify. And it is also conflated with the question of *identity*, with a fixing or circumscribing of the parameters of selfhood.

Both assumptions are ripe for reassessment. Audiences become attached to fiction in an abundance of ways; these ties can be ironic as well as sentimental, ethical as well as emotional. Identifying involves ideas and values as well as persons; may confound or remake a sense of self as well as confirming it; and is practiced by skeptical scholars as well as wide-eyed enthusiasts. Tackling the academic disdain for identification as a naive or "bad" reading practice, Faye Halpern points out that "sophisticated literary critics read to identify as well. The difference comes not from the practice of identification but from the differing *grounds* of identification."[1] What, then, are these differing grounds? What are the beliefs, hopes, habits, or obsessions that lead readers or viewers to identify in specific ways? What part is played by a text and what kind of intermediaries are involved? Why audiences care about fictional figures, how they treat them as matters of concern—such questions deserve closer scrutiny.

To rethink identification is also to rethink character. We can think of characters as being like persons without scanting or short-changing their aesthetic qualities. Neither do we need "the illusion of reality" to identify—an assumption that fails to account for attachments to Bugs Bunny, Cinderella, or Vladimir and Estragon. Characters do not have to be deep, well-rounded, psychologically complex, or unified to count as characters; nor, of course, do they need to be human. They need only to be *animated*: to act and react, to will and intend.[2] Why do critics so often equate character with the genre of realism—whether they come to bury or to praise it? Audiences can identify with figures from fairy tales, comic strips, melodramas, parables, and superhero movies, not to mention *Star Trek*, *The Texas Chain Saw Massacre*, or *Blood and Guts in High School*. The draw of character has far less to do with realism than with qualities of vividness and distinctiveness. As any cartoonist knows, a few well-chosen strokes can be far more effective than a detailed rendering; stylization is a powerful tool. In "Notes on 'Camp,'" for example, Susan Sontag writes: "character is understood as a state of continual incandescence—a person being one very intense thing."[3] Identification proves to be as relevant to *Malone Dies* as to *Middlemarch*, to *Tom and Jerry* as to *Doctor Zhivago*—though the *mechanisms* of identification will certainly vary.

The messiness of how we identify runs up against two intellectual temptations: overpoliticizing and overpsychologizing. At a certain moment in film studies, for example, the first tendency ran rampant; a gamut of aesthetic experiences was boiled down into a single story line. Mixing up potent cocktails of Freud, Marx, and Mulvey, critics excoriated any form of identification as a trap: a means by which viewers were seduced into the acceptance of fixed identities and a complicity with the status quo. Identification had to be "broken down" in order to make critical thinking possible. (The intensity of their own identifications with critical theory and theorists, meanwhile, went entirely unremarked.) The recent turn to cognitive psychology has led to much more fine-grained accounts of the mental processes that bind us to works of art. And yet the connections to a larger world and agencies beyond the self are often lost. Reading these accounts, one gets the impression that identifying is a drama played out in the cloistered cells of individual minds.[4] Can an ANT-ish approach allow us to do any better?

I've learned a great deal, nonetheless, from cognitive film scholars such as Murray Smith and Carl Plantinga. They both point out—with some justification—that "identifying" is a slippery and confusing word and opt instead to speak of "engaging." Yet this strikes me as a case where the cure is worse than the disease. Engagement covers an even broader and more diffuse range of reactions: being turned on by, disgusted by, possessed by, or falling in love with characters, for example, as well as identifying with them. My own interest lies squarely with "identification" as used in everyday speech: to describe an affinity that is based on some sense of similarity. This commonsense usage does not exclude complexity; to be like a character is not synonymous with *liking* a character: a felt affinity can be underwritten by diverse, conflicting, or ambivalent affects. Meanwhile, these shared qualities may motivate or inspire identification (as when we are drawn to a work of fiction that captures something already known); or they may be produced *by* identification (as when we temporarily "take on" or assume aspects of fictional figures).

By contrast, when a group of British women interviewed by Jackie Stacey reflected on their love of moviegoing in the 1940s, some of them stressed the utter remoteness and unattainable glamor of an actress such as Rita Hayworth; she was "out of this world," "the most perfect woman I had ever seen," someone to be admired from afar. Parallels between aesthetic and religious experience came to the fore, as they spoke of worship, goddesses, and films that transformed them. Devotion was tied to the frisson of difference: to a perceived chasm between viewer and Hollywood star. "I adored Ava Gardner's dark magnetism," commented one interviewee, "but knew I wasn't like that."[5] The experience of engagement was intense but had very little to do with identification.

Identifying, then, implies something shared, but this does not mean obliterating or overriding differences. There is no Vulcan mindmeld, no fusion of viewer and character where we lose all sense of self or capacity for independent thought. Here philosopher Berys Gaut is on the right track in pointing out that identification is aspectual—a matter of which *aspects* of a character one relates to. One can identify with a character's perceptions, emotions, motivations, beliefs, self-understanding, physical characteristics, experiences, or situation, for example—none of which necessarily implies the others.[6] To identify with something is not to be identical with it; we are talking about the rough ground of resemblance rather than pure sameness. There is a rich vein in cultural studies—especially its feminist variant—that has traced the empirical complexities of how audiences identify. As Stacey shows in her detailed description of viewer response, such a process can involve complex and often unpredictable processes of negotiation between, say, a star persona and a viewer's sense of self. My argument builds on these ideas rather than recapitulating them, but I want to underscore my debt to the groundbreaking work of Jackie Stacey, Ien Ang, Janice Radway, Judith Mayne, Kim Chabot Davis, and others. (That this work is so rarely acknowledged in literary theory, film theory, and philosophical aesthetics continues to astonish me.)

The existence of queer studies, meanwhile, pivots on the possibility of identifying across identities (Douglas Crimp), on a view of identifications as mobile, elastic, and volatile (Diana Fuss).[7] And here aesthetic identifications—to characters, stars, authors—are selective, speaking to an affinity with certain qualities rather than with the whole person: "I never wanted to be her," writes Jim Elledge of Tina Turner; "I just wanted her strength, her self-assuredness and a body I wasn't ashamed of." They can be empathic, involving a shared sense of pain or abjection: Christopher Murray ponders the phenomenon of gay attachment to "tragic figures of ridicule" such as Margaret Dumont, the comic foil of the Marx Brothers movies. They can be a matter of comeuppance: Edward Field writes of larger-than-life movie stars who represent "yearnings for vindication, in which we see ourselves transcending the difficulties a gay man faces in the world." They can be as much about style as about selfhood: "it's in the shape of my sentences and the trajectory my thinking follows that I find her lambent voice and habits of mind limning my own" (Brian Teare on Virginia Woolf).[8]

Identifying, moreover, does not simply entrench a prior self but may enrich, expand, or amend it. Perhaps we glimpse aspects of ourselves in a character, but in a way that causes us to revise our sense of who we are. The phrase "shock of recognition" is not just a cliché. We can be sustained, but also disconcerted, by a felt kinship with a fictional figure. In an analysis of amazon.com reviews of *The Kite Runner*, for example, Timothy Aubry quotes the following remark: "While reading this book I wished to scream at the characters in the book, wished to tell them that they were making the wrong decision. But then I looked into myself and realized that I would have made the same wrong decision. At that point my hatred was toward myself."[9] As we see here—and as I argue in more detail in chapter 4—identification is not the opposite of critical or reflective thought: in the act of identifying, we may come to reassess or question our previous views. Meanwhile, it is not at all uncommon to sense the alien or unappealing aspects of a character one is also drawn to.[10]

And while something shared is key, the nature of this "something" cannot be predicted ahead of time. Is it temperament or social situation; feelings, histories, or values; who one is or who one would like to be? That audiences can identify with a hobbit or a rabbit is a sign that semblances are often metaphorical rather than literal. Affinities experienced while reading a book or watching a film can cut across divisions of gender, race, sexuality, class, or even, in certain genres, species. It is a matter not just of finding oneself but of leaving oneself. In her autobiography, Jeanette Winterson speaks of "reading herself" in the mode of fiction as well as fact, as the only way of keeping her story open. She is transported into alternate worlds, even as these worlds turn out to be remarkably close. "And so I read on, past my own geography and history. . . . The great writers were not remote. They were in Accrington."[11]

Why Be Happy When You Could Be Normal?—the title of Winterson's memoir—is the bewildered question asked by her adoptive mother on learning that her daughter is a lesbian. Neither happiness nor normality turns out to be on the cards. The book is a record of woundedness: the scars inflicted by the abusive and eccentric Mrs. Winterson; by having been given up for adoption; by never quite knowing who one is. It is also an account of how stories help make things bearable. As a teenager, Winterson leaves home, sleeps in a Mini, and makes her home in the Accrington public library, reading her way through English literature from A to Z. Allies are at hand: a solicitous librarian; the Dewey decimal system; the comical but informative Mrs. Ratlow (head of English). Through books she forges ties to real and fictional lives, to authors who write and to characters who are written. Personal stories speak to others, she observes, when they become paradigms or parables. "The intensity of a story . . . releases into a bigger space than the one it occupied in time and place. The story crosses the threshold from my world into yours."[12] A transpersonal crossing or connection is achieved. Central to Winterson's text are two forms of aesthetic relation that I'll consider in more detail: *allegiance* (a felt affiliation or solidarity with certain others) and *recognition* (the struggle to know oneself and to be known). "I have always been interested in stories of disguise and mistaken identity, of naming and knowing. How are you recognised? How do you recognise yourself?"[13]

It is hardly surprising that a novelist testifies to the salvific power of stories. Not everyone, of course, will respond along the same lines as Winterson, or in the same way. And glitches and misfirings are all too common; there can be a failure to identify (being bored, distracted, apathetic, irritated, turned off) or a conscious refusal to identify, for political, ethical, or other reasons. Countless contingencies are in play. My aim is neither to prescribe nor to prohibit but to redescribe a form of attachment that is often caricatured or poorly understood and to tackle some canards: that identifying is synonymous with sameness; that it involves a naive view of character; that it can only be sappy, sentimental, or unreflective.

Character as *Umwelt*

A second aspect of identification is its relation to persons: what readers and viewers identify with, above all, are *characters*. (Though, as we'll see, this attachment may bleed into a felt affinity with an author, an actor, a situation, a style: audiences are promiscuous in their affections.) There has been much hand-wringing over the status of character in literary and film studies. The antihumanist orientation of the last few decades inspired a default skepticism about the status of fictional persons; critics insisted that characters were nothing but signifiers: textual holograms, verbal phantasms, or visual illusions. As such, they bore no relation to persons; to treat them as such was the epitome of naivete or philistinism. Yet the case is hardly compelling; after all, characters do share qualities with people, while interactions with others often draw on insights gleaned from novels or films. We translate between fiction and life without blinking. Meanwhile, in one sense, fictional characters *are* real; they have effects in the world; they inspire emulation and adaptation, irritation and dislike; their existence makes a difference.

More recently, critics have taken a different tack, appealing to ideas from evolutionary psychology. Humans, they point out, have an intrinsic bias toward sociability: we are primed to be curious about the thoughts, feelings, and actions of other persons. The draw of fiction is akin to the pleasures of gossip and other forms of bonding. We have evolved to be curious about the motives of others—being able to distinguish between friend and enemy is a competitive advantage that promotes survival—and are drawn to stories that stimulate deep features of our social brains. Such stories teach us to mind-read, to make sense of other people, to hone our interpersonal intelligence. Fiction, for Blakey Vermeule, offers large doses of social information and cognitive stimulation that it would be too costly, dangerous, and difficult for us to extract from the world on our own.[14]

Yet the act of leveling here is perhaps a little too vigorous. Is there such a close correlation between interest in real persons and in fictional persons? Is the latter just a shadow or spin-off of the former? After all, the lack of reciprocity in how we relate to characters is nothing like real-world interactions: rather than teaching us how to interact, obsessive book reading might conceivably go along with a *lack* of sociability or social intelligence.[15] Meanwhile, there are other ways in which attachments to characters differ. We can be drawn to fictional figures (de Sade's Juliette, Roquentin, the Underground Man) whose real-world equivalents we would run miles to avoid. Moreover, the affordances of fiction—sneaking into the minds of strangers to capture fragile wisps of thought and feeling; stoking suspense and choreographing crisis—can make fictional figures more vivid, more intensely present, than many of the people around us. They are fascinating not just as prototypes or models for real-world interaction but because of their difference— their aesthetic difference. "A handful of fictional characters," writes Mario Vargas Llosa in his engaging meditation on *Madame Bovary*, "have marked my life more profoundly than a great number of the flesh-and-blood beings I have known."[16]

Emma Bovary is an especially striking case of such fictional attachments. She has been endlessly deciphered by critics; adopted, translated, and reimagined by film directors and artists; invoked by pundits and commentators and absorbed into the French language (*bovarysme*). Her creation is tied to Flaubert's fastidious concern with literary technique; for some critics, she serves as little more than an alibi for parsing the formal features of *indirect style libre*. Yet this technique raises intriguing questions: does its blend of emotion and distance encourage identification or undercut it? Literary critics have typically stressed distance, vaunting the famed impersonality and detachment of Flaubert's prose. And yet there are also murmuring acknowledgments—and not only from women—of intense affinity and identification. Here is Vargas Llosa again, drawing out commonalities between himself and Emma: "our incurable materialism, our greater predilection for the pleasures of the body than for those of the soul, our respect for the senses and instinct, our preference for this earthly life over any other."[17]

Neither of the above options fits the bill: hammering home the fictionality of characters in order to render them shadowy and insubstantial; or minimizing their fictionality by treating imaginary persons as nothing more than evolutionary spin-offs. Another possibility presents itself: it is their fictional qualities that make characters real. Characters are not real persons; they are real fictional beings. Art is frequently feted, Latour remarks, while being denied any objectivity or ultimate importance; it is seen as significant, yet not really serious. We are in need of ontological fattening therapies, he suggests, so as to endow fictional beings with more substance. These beings "offer us an imagination that we would not have had without them. Don Juan exists as surely as the characters in *Friends*; President Bartlett occupied the White House for some time with more reality than his pale double George W. Bush."[18] Certain figures encountered in novels and films are vivid, memorable, arresting, alive, not despite their aesthetic qualities but because of them. They possess a kind of reality that we should cherish and respect; that they are made up does not mean that they do not matter.

That they are fictional, meanwhile, means both more and less than their fictionality is often taken to mean. *More*, in the sense that characters cannot be separated from their mediations: identifying with a character can also be a matter of cathecting onto a plot, a situation, a mise-en-scène, a setting, a style. In narratology, character is often treated as a distinct unit; when we consider the phenomenology of response, things become much messier. To what extent can an impulse to identify with Thelma and Louise be disassociated from the sublime landscape that surrounds and enframes them? In what sense is affinity with the hectoring narrator of a Thomas Bernhard novel a matter of identifying with a style as well as a person? Flipping things around, however, characters can also merge into real-world persons; they are *less* than fictional insofar as identifying with a character, as we'll see, may bleed into an attachment to an author or a movie star. Divisions between what is inside and outside the text are often transgressed, overlooked, or ignored.

Fictional characters, moreover, are not stuck fast to the works in which they first appear. Like Emma Bovary, characters may refuse to stay put; they survive adaptation, hopping from literature to film to graphic novel, wresting themselves free of the words out of which they were first made. A figure with a walk-on part in one novel may pop up as the central protagonist of another. *Wide Sargasso Sea* is the most well-known example of this "minor-character genre," but recent years have seen a slew of new novels recounting the fate of Ahab's wife or Mr. Dalloway.[19] The proliferation of fan fictions in recent decades, meanwhile, testifies to the translatable aspects of characters, their potential to be reborn in new contexts. Such fiction, Francesca Coppa remarks, poses "what if" questions about characters: What if Sherlock Holmes were a Harlem crime fighter? What if Bilbo Baggins were queer? Characters are not just transposed but transformed: kitted out with new traits, moved into alternate worlds.[20] It is not only boundaries between texts that are porous but boundaries between texts and everyday life. Joyce's portly protagonist is resurrected in literary festivities on June 16; young people around the world don striped scarves and metamorphose into Harry Potter or Hermione Granger; Carrie Bradshaw beckons from a magazine or beams from the cosmetics counter. Sherlock Holmes, the object of countless biographies and histories, has recently been reincarnated in the TV series *Sherlock*, and we can now, courtesy of Daniel Mallory Ortberg, read phone texts from Jane Eyre.[21]

Characters are movable, teleporting into new media and milieus, times and places. They swarm among us, populating the world with their idiosyncrasies, trademarks, sidekicks, and sayings. They are not just inside books, awaiting our attention to spring to life, but also outside books, beings we may bump into without expecting it. They differ from persons yet are easily recognizable as akin to persons, objects of widespread devotion (or dislike). In short, they form part of an *Umwelt*. In contrast to the mechanistic associations of a "context" that bears down on us, the idea of *Umwelt* seeks to convey the dynamic and open-ended nature of a being's relation to its surroundings, which it customizes in particular ways. We act on this *Umwelt*—that is, surrounding world—in interacting with it; the environment as it concerns us is a networked array of phenomena. Characters matter to *us* and yet are not simply "in our minds"; they come to us as if from elsewhere; they possess a degree of solidity, permanence, and force.[22]

It is here that formalist theories of character come up short, in their failure to account for the felt vitality of fictional beings. The world would look very different without Jekyll and Hyde, Faust, Antigone, Mary Poppins, Norman Bates, Dracula, Nancy Drew, Don Juan, Spock, Hedda Gabler, Oedipus, Winnie the Pooh, Scrooge, Darth Vader, Hercule Poirot, HAL, Mickey Mouse, the Simpsons, Alice, Medea, Scrooge, Gandalf, Sam Spade, Anna Karenina. These figures are not just bundles of signifiers; they are worldly actors haloed with affective and existential force. Historical theories, meanwhile, often strive to rein in character by restricting its reach: defining it as a literary device tied to the genre conventions of eighteenth- and nineteenth-century European novels. Yet the reality that radiates from fictional beings does not depend on the requirements of realism: some of the most vivid exemplars come from fantasy, science fiction, stories for children, Greek and Renaissance tragedy, and tales of divinities. Of course, the sense of what it means to be a person fluctuates over time: philosophies of individualism, changing religious and political ideas, legal categories, the rise of human sciences such as psychology and psychoanalysis all play their part. Fictional persons evolve accordingly, as new forms and genres grapple with these changes. Yet characters can also cut across such historical and cultural boundaries: that Medea has survived the long trek from a Greek amphitheater to a Pasolini film set suggests the limits of a certain kind of contextual explanation.

Another important thing to be kept in mind: although characters are fictional beings, they cannot be quarantined from historical persons who make claims on our attention. In *The Bell Jar*, for example, it is virtually impossible to separate the protagonist from the long shadow cast by Sylvia Plath. And here second-wave feminism played a decisive role, as a social movement linked to literature from the start. Feminist novels often strengthened ties between female characters, authors, and readers by deliberately blurring distinctions between fiction and autobiography. Many of these ties are still sustained in women-only book clubs, college courses devoted to women's writing, and the marketing of female-centered genres ranging from chick lit to feminist fantasy. They are woven out of the passions and obsessions of readers, the diffuse yet still powerful aftershocks of a social movement, and the calculations and guesses of publishers, which may hit the jackpot or entirely miss the mark.

Yet we should not conclude that "identity politics" motivates all author-character confusions. Elena Ferrante has attracted a passionate cohort of feminist readers drawn to her Naples trilogy and its portrayal of female friendship across class differences. Yet when she was outed in 2016—her cover blown by a zealous Italian journalist—many of these same feminist readers responded with outrage and a sense of violation. Here was a case where the author's separation from her writings—her refusal to give credence to autobiographical readings—was to be respected. Meanwhile, Karl Ove Knausgård is a writer who moves fluidly in and out of the pages of his own text, such that the distinction between fiction and autobiography no longer makes sense. The seven volumes of *My Struggle* include numerous feedback loops between work and life; aggrieved reactions to Knausgård's no-holds-barred account are folded back into the work being written and trigger a new wave of commentary and reaction; the author's celebrity, nationally and internationally, affects the way in which his first-person narrator is perceived. *My Struggle* is widely acclaimed as a work of literature rather than just a well-written autobiography—and yet author and protagonist blur into one, such that standard genre distinctions no longer make much sense.[23] The "death of the author" thesis— a ubiquitous slogan in literary studies for several decades—has come to seem increasingly outdated, as authors become ever more visible, voluble, and inescapable. They give interviews, hold forth on blogs or Twitter, opine on the latest political events, talk back to prize committees, appear in full or half-empty auditoriums—not titans to be worshiped but promoters of their work and participants in numerous networks.

A crossover of another kind occurs when viewing a film: responses to fictional figures are often mixed up with reactions to the persons who play them. (One of the 1940s film fans interviewed by Jackie Stacey remarked: "I was completely lost; it wasn't Ginger Rogers dancing with Fred Astaire, it was me.")[24] In the theater, actors are physically present yet are subsumed by their characters; in the movie theater, actors are physically absent, yet they subsume their characters (someone decides to see the new Tilda Swinton film). "The character in a film," remarks Erwin Panofsky, "lives and dies with the actor."[25] Not invariably, of course—experimental and avant-garde films often strive to block such forms of identification. Yet the claim commonly holds true, with the entanglement of character and actor being carried over into multiple venues— any high school performance of *The Sound of Music* will call up the specter of Julie Andrews. Meanwhile, images encountered on the cinema screen are haloed with factoids, BuzzFeed interviews, magazine articles, and other films in which a star has appeared. This spillover creates a many-layered text, in which character and star image may harmonize, overlap, or conflict. (As an instance of the latter, Richard Dyer cites *Gentlemen Prefer Blondes*, where the cynical gold-digger persona of Lorelei clashes with the guileless sexuality radiating from Marilyn Monroe.)[26] Viewers cannot revert to a state of ignorance or innocence; the penumbra of associations around Nicole Kidman or Gérard Depardieu can markedly affect the textures of response.

Characters, in short, are portmanteau creatures, assembled out of disparate materials drawn from fiction and life. Rather than being restricted to a single text, they often serve as nodes in many networks. They are distributed, adapted, and mediated. Their presence can be exceptionally vivid, yet it is painstakingly composed. We might say, drawing from Hélène Mialet's ANT analysis of the public persona of Stephen Hawking, that characters are *incorporated*.[27] They are fabricated out of many things working together: the texts that house them; random scraps of knowledge about authors or actors; acculturation into ways of reading and habits of response; the diligence and devotion of publishers, producers, agents, reviewers, fans; the fictional objects with which they are associated (Sherlock Holmes's pipe; Jane Eyre's gray dress) and the real objects they bring into the world, from Harry Potter wands to Don Quixote prints.

And in identifying with characters, we connect *through* them to other persons as well as to other things. As Jon Najarian points out, "from film-screenings and book-releases to comic-cons and quidditch matches, characters can encourage us to form social ties with other, non-fictional human beings." In some instances, as we'll see in the case of *Thelma and Louise*, such group identifications can have a dramatic impact, fanning out into the public sphere to shape attitudes and ideas. Characters also mediate our relations to stuff, most obviously in the case of commercial spin-offs (*Thelma and Louise* T-shirts) but also in relation to mementos, fetishes, totems, tokens, love objects. When the house of Leopold and Molly Bloom was demolished in 1967, Joyceans rushed to preserve it but could salvage only the front door, which is now displayed in the James Joyce Center in Dublin. It has become part of a network of Joycean entanglements. Looking at it implants a vague sense of melancholy, Najarian writes. "You may realize that this never was a door of ingress or of egress for Leopold Bloom: neither he, nor Molly, nor Stephen, nor the pussens, ever walked through this door, ever listened to it creak. Bloom never remembered, standing in front of *this* door, that he had forgotten to remember his keys and found himself locked out. . . . And yet, although Leopold Bloom never walked through the door that is housed currently at 35 North Great George's Street, that does not mean that he never lived."[28]

To live in this fashion, characters must rely on the kindness of strangers; without the input of readers or viewers, they are naught. Yet the latter are also obligated to the fictional beings that take possession of them, infiltrate them, speak through them. Stripped of the sediments of the novels I've read, the films and TV shows I've watched, I would be another person entirely. Fictional beings serve as alter egos, ideal types, negative exempla, moral guides, objects of desire, imaginary friends. They depend on us yet also engender us. Characters encountered in fiction often cross over into other contexts; they can linger in the mind after a book is finished, readers have reported, interacting with them in daily life in a vivid, even hallucinatory fashion.[29] Here again, we see how characters are taken up into an *Umwelt*. As Latour writes, fictional beings "have this peculiarity, then; their objectivity depends on their being reprised, taken up again by subjectivities that would not exist themselves if these beings had not given them to us."[30]

An objection, meanwhile, has been gathering force: surely such talk about identifying is far more relevant to some texts than to others. Does it make any sense in relation to the milestones of modernism? These works, after all, dealt a death blow to character—that is to say, the creation of well-rounded fictional persons, kitted out with extended families, parlors, mustaches, and hats, who marched through the endless detours and byways of Victorian novels to a satisfying finale. We might think of the celebrated modernist counterexamples: Musil's "man without qualities," the multivoiced ebb and flow of Woolf's *The Waves*, the blank-faced ciphers that populate the writings of Kafka and Beckett. For Adorno, the import of modernism lay in its exposure of the anachronism of character. Individuality, he declared, had been liquidated by the historical and political upheavals of the twentieth century. To cling to notions of the person in a world of standardization and commodification was nothing more than sentimental illusion, the stuff of cheap biographical literature.[31] Bolstered in recent years by poststructuralist skepticism about selfhood, this view of modernism as dissolving character is a persistent thread in literary studies.

Julian Murphet has recently restated the case with vigor, elaborating on the ties between modernism and multiplicity. Not just the instability but the impossibility of character, he argues, are vividly actualized in the architecture of modernist form. In the works of Joyce, Proust, and Woolf the very idea of character is shredded, dissolved, and washed away, as unity gives way to a multiplicity of shifting and unstable identities. Adamant that modernist fiction is a break with everything that came before, Murphet is unwilling to acknowledge any continuities between modernism and its precursors. He also waves away—as merely pragmatic—questions of how readers engage with fictional persons.[32] Yet such questions cannot so peremptorily be pushed aside; works come into being only insofar as they are actualized by readers or viewers. Here Hans-Robert Jauss's response to Adorno seems apropos: "interpretation that bypasses this primary aesthetic experience is the arrogance of a philologist who subscribes to the error that the text was not created for readers, but for him."[33] No one would dispute that fictional figures look different in *Mrs. Dalloway* than in *Middlemarch*—a difference marked in the unspooling of plot, the rendering of dialogue, the fracturing of time, the capturing of mental states. Yet it does not follow that person schemas drop out of sight or that readers do not form ties to figures in modernist fiction. The twofoldedness of character—as both person and aesthetic device—is manifest in both Eliot and Woolf, though in differing ways. And if we keep in mind the other ties we've looked at—to authors, film actors, etc.—we might want to make a case not just for the twofold-edness of character but for its *multifoldedness.*[34]

Rebecca Solnit has written about her difficulties appreciating *Lolita* in the light of her empathy for the heroine. One of her readers responded with a testy reprimand: "To read Lolita and 'identify' with one of the characters is to entirely misunderstand Nabokov."[35] What to make of this interchange? As this reader suggests, Nabokov was notoriously dismissive of any desire to identify; his verbal pyrotechnics and layers of irony sought to school readers in a different kind of literary response. And yet the claim that the works of Nabokov—or other examples of stylized, ironic, or rebarbative fiction, whether by Kafka or Kathy Acker—have abolished or done away with identification might give us pause. The claim only holds, I am suggesting, if we adhere to an overly schematic idea of what it means to identify. After all, the indignant reader who responded to Solnit by rallying to Nabokov's defense is hardly free of attachment—perhaps he does not identify with one of *Lolita*'s characters, but he is certainly identifying with *something*. An author? A work? A style? A text-person composite? The gap between himself and Solnit may not be as wide as he thinks.

Strands of Identification

A sharpening of terms is overdue. What exactly is going on when we identify? What kinds of attachments are being forged? I share the view of film scholar Murray Smith that identifying is not one thing but differing things that occur in varying combinations. In the following pages, I draw on some of his ideas—while also revising and reformatting them in ways he might not sanction—in order to disentangle four strands of identification: alignment, allegiance, recognition, and empathy.[36] Less exhaustive than they are suggestive, these terms can give us a better handle on how films and novels reel in audiences—how they solicit our devotion and care.

Alignment refers to the formal means by which texts shape a reader's or viewer's access to character: the part played by the work rather than its audience. (It is, in this sense, akin to the idea of "focalization" in narrative theory.) It points to the directive force of narrative, description, and point of view: whose decisions or desires drive a plot; which figures are depicted in scrupulous detail; whose perspective we are invited to adopt. Some characters bask in the ambient warmth of the novel's attention, while other are relegated to a Siberian wasteland; we are made privy to every rueful reflection or flutter of desire in the mind of X, while the inner life of Y remains utterly beyond reach. Alignment thus resonates with familiar ways of talking about fiction: major and minor characters, round and flat. How a work directs its focus can strongly affect its power to resonate with particular audiences—or fail to do so. It can also hook up to larger patterns of amplified attention or neglect; that attention to character is striated by social inequality and sanctioned ignorance is by now a familiar point within criticism.

Of course, to center a novel or a film on a character's perspective is not to endorse that perspective, as an unruly throng of unreliable narrators makes clear. In responding to characters, we draw on various sources: accounts of their actions or motivations; the judgments of other characters; textual cues, whether implicit (hinting at a character's mental state by panning across a disorderly room; using chiaroscuro lighting to conjure up feelings of dread) or explicit (naming a figure Cruella De Vil). A piling up of discrepancies and evasions often indicates that a character is misrepresenting, misreading, or misevaluating, that their words are not to be taken at face value. Scholars of narratology have expended much energy on this question; *The Remains of the Day*, especially, has been pored over by critics eager to parse the various techniques used by Ishiguro to cast doubt on the first-person account of his self-deceiving butler. Alignment may or may not encourage identification: narratives offer varying blends of reliability and unreliability, intimacy and distance.

Yet we must also keep in mind that films and novels are not tyrants commanding their subjects on pain of death. Other forces are also in play, creating distractions, offering countersuggestions, running interference. Alignment is only one aspect of the puzzle of identification; while the formal features of a work invite audiences to respond in certain ways, they cannot impel them to do so. A dislike of a particular film star; a critical essay read in college; a felt affinity with a minor character or a villain; the impact of a trenchant or excoriating review—there are numerous reasons why audiences do not fall into line and may identify in a haphazard or unpredictable fashion. It is entirely possible to see oneself as Casaubon rather than Dorothea, to identify with and admire Archie Bunker rather than seeing him as a satiric foil. "Bad fans" are all too frequent—audiences who fail to honor a work's intent, whether willfully or unknowingly.[37] It is here that film theory, at a certain moment, went down the wrong path, not in highlighting recurring formal patterns in movies (such as the asymmetry between who looks and who is looked at) but in seizing on such patterns as clinching evidence of how audiences identify or—even worse—of their overall psychological makeup or political beliefs. The text, in short, was hailed as the sole actor; all other actors and intermediaries, mishaps and serendipities, were airbrushed out of the scene.

Allegiance speaks to the question of how ethical or political values—that is, acts of evaluating—draw audiences closer to some figures rather than others. It is a familiar idea that art, in modernity, has sought to wrest itself free from moral prescriptions; a distinguished roll call of censored writers, from the marquis de Sade to Henry Miller, have lobbed hand grenades at religious and social pieties. Thanks to this history, no critic nowadays would praise a novel or a film by dubbing it "moral"—a language now used only by the Christian Right. And yet, that art provokes established values does not mean it floats free of value; excoriations of bourgeois hypocrisy or endemic racism carry their own normative force; ethical as well as political judgments are in play. In experiences of both art and life, it is impossible to escape frameworks of value, to orient ourselves to what we take to be the better rather than the worse.[38] The "is" cannot be disentangled from the "ought"; matters of fact are mixed up with matters of concern. And here there are countless crossings between the modes of aesthetics, ethics, and politics; attempts to purify these modes by keeping them entirely separate are an exercise in futility.

Allegiance, then, is in play whenever we find ourselves siding with a character and what we take that character to stand for—an allegiance that can, of course, be partial, qualified, or ambivalent. Such acts of evaluating affect what audiences perceive and how they respond, shaping assessments of character and situation. An attachment may be brief—lasting only the length of a novel or film—or it may have a lasting effect on our perception of how things are. Such ethical engagement does not rule out critical estrangement, as Carl Plantinga points out—but is often tied to an experience of immersion in a fictional world that film theory has failed to seriously engage.[39]

Here we might look to *Thelma and Louise*: a film that inspired passionate arguments and became a touchstone of public debate. The film serves as a striking example of collective identification: where individual reactions were heavily mediated by larger patterns of response. To express an opinion on *Thelma and Louise* was to take up a position in an extended network of relations, a heavily trafficked zone of analysis, argument, and conflicts about values. The film triggered strong responses and partisan commentary; it did not simply speak to preexisting groups but called these groups into being. Via their responses, viewers defined themselves as fans or skeptics, as antifeminist or as subscribing to differing kinds of feminism. In their reactions to *Thelma and Louise*, many viewers came to see themselves as part of a "we": a virtual feminist community founded in devotion to a film and what it stood for. They became attached to a film that in turn connected them to others and to shared passions and convictions.

Why did this film about a waitress and a housewife on the lam forge such enduring ties? Surely because these ties were woven out of multiple strands: the mythic resonance of classic film genres (the road movie, the female friendship film, the Western) blended in unprecedented ways; a widespread hunger for new female character types and the film industry's willingness to capitalize on this demand; the dazzle of Hollywood names with both artistic credibility and wide appeal (Ridley Scott, Susan Sarandon); and, not least, the forging of ties between aesthetic and political representation. It is only at certain moments—thanks to the rise of new social movements and what came to be known as "cultural politics"—that fictional portrayals of women and minorities are scrutinized as a revealing index of their overall status in society.[40] A film is no longer either enjoyed or else dismissed without further thought; rather, it is painstakingly *deciphered*—not only by academics but also by audiences at the Cineplex—for what it conveys about equality or inequality, inclusion or exclusion. The 1970s saw the emergence of what I've called a feminist counter–public sphere, a space of public debate about newly compelling and contentious topics: women in the workplace, sexuality, motherhood, harassment, sexist images.[41] This sphere inspired fresh ways of interpreting and also cathecting onto works of art: practices of critique, along with a widespread yearning for new female-centered narratives. And in this context, *Thelma and Louise* became a flashpoint for strong attachments and heated arguments; as was repeatedly said, the film "struck a nerve."

The impulse to identify—or not—with Susan Sarandon and Geena Davis was thoroughly entangled with questions of value. What was the ethical import of a story line in which women were transformed into outlaws after shooting a rapist? Did it matter that most of the male characters were portrayed as buffoons or scoundrels? What was the film saying about female camaraderie and love between women? Its heroines were widely seen as icons of female rebellion, and yet responses did not always fall along predictable lines. Sheila Benson, writing in the *Los Angeles Times*, declared *Thelma and Louise* a betrayal of feminism in espousing revenge rather than "responsibility, equality, sensitivity, and understanding." Echoing similar sentiments, Margaret Carlson in *Time* underscored the difficulties of allegiance: "it becomes harder and harder to root for the heroines, who make the wrong choice at every turn and act more like Clint Eastwood than Katherine Hepburn."[42] Conversely, while male viewers often dismissed or disparaged the film, others saw it several times, claiming that it had galvanized and transformed them.[43]

The messy realities of such responses contravene what were once axioms of film theory. Women do not always identify with women; meanwhile, some men connect with female figures across gender lines, finding points of affinity or relation. Moreover, acts of identifying, while they can be emotional, even passionate, are also *reflective*: they are informed by beliefs, ideals, and values. It is a matter not just of feeling but of thinking. As Kim Chabot Davis points out in an illuminating reception study of Jane Campion's art-house melodrama *The Piano*, identifying is not just an unconscious or subliminal activity, as psychoanalytical film theory assumed. Rather, it is shaped by how audiences assess characters and evaluate situations, by their core commitments and their consciously held beliefs. And here ethical and political affiliations can inspire wildly variant reactions. In the case of both *The Piano* and *Thelma and Louise*, conflicting views of feminism—not just whether viewers saw themselves as feminist but what they took feminism to *mean*—had a decisive impact on whether and how viewers identified. Was feminism a matter of equality or freedom, of reclaiming femaleness or rejecting it, of real-world goals or utopian dreams? Political ideas and beliefs served as key mediators, shaping what audiences cared about, their affective reactions, and the texture of their response.[44]

Of course, other kinds of values and frameworks were also in play. Some of the above-cited objections to *Thelma and Louise* may sound overly literal, assessing characters as moral exemplars rather than fictional beings. The draw of the film had much to do with a comeuppance that was fundamentally aesthetic in nature. *Thelma and Louise* was a riposte to a history of impoverished plotlines, a corrective to a restricted repertoire of roles for women. That audiences delighted in its narrative reversals and appropriation of masculine symbols (cars, guns) spoke to a sharpening public realization of how severely gender norms had constrained possibilities of character and plot. The film helped forge a new tonal repertoire for women's films: a mood of defiance, rebellion, and exuberance that is underscored by the physical as well as mental metamorphosis of the main characters, including the shedding of restrictive feminine clothing and a freer, more forceful body language. Now that female action heroes are commonplace, it is hard to realize the audaciousness of such a tonal shift—and the riskiness of a screenplay that fell outside the marketing templates of its time and almost didn't get filmed.[45] When critics worried that audience identification with Thelma and Louise would trigger direct imitation—acts of real-world violence by women against men—they were relying on an overly simple notion of what it means to identify.

Meanwhile, another kind of complaint—that the film was antifeminist in portraying female independence as leading to death—also seems a tad overliteral. The film ends with the heroines driving their turquoise Thunderbird off the edge of a cliff and soaring over the Grand Canyon: are they committing suicide or taking flight? Screenwriter Callie Khouri drily notes: "We left them in mid-air. That wasn't because they ran out of film."[46] Here, as elsewhere, *Thelma and Louise* meshes the political with the existential-symbolic: Ridley Scott's spectacular shots of desert landscapes and canyons tie his characters to a visual language of the sublime—a sense of overpowering awe and magnitude—that has traditionally been the province of men. This visual backdrop endows their condition as women on the run with a metaphysical weight and substance; soaring into the sky, they join a mythological cohort of airborne women. As Louise pushes down on the accelerator and the women grip hands, the film's final moments convey their sheer undauntedness—an unflinching facing-up-to-death—and solidarity.

That some critics chose to assess the film as a blueprint for real-world behavior rather than a flight of the imagination, meanwhile, is not an argument against allegiance as such. After all, those who passionately defended *Thelma and Louise* were also taking a stand; siding with it against one-sided interpretations, reaching for another critical language that was based on fantasy rather than mimesis; defending the flawed complexities of its heroines against attempts to flatten them into man-haters or feminist role models. A pushback against reductive readings is also an ethical position: defending a work of art against those who would cram it into a preexisting box. Allegiances, in short, are always in play. Poetics borrows from ethics, writes Paul Ricoeur, even when calling for a suspension or ironic inversion of ethical judgments; fiction serves as an ethical laboratory that allows for all kinds of experimentation with values.[47] *Thelma and Louise* serves as a striking example of such a value experiment, its effects still traceable a quarter of a century later.

Murray Smith introduces the idea of *recognition* to account for the apprehension of a gestalt: how we come to see pixels on a screen (or black marks on a page) as adding up to human figures. Viewers rely on perceptual cues (especially body, face, and voice) to distinguish human agents from other aspects of a film and to understand them as being individuated and continuous. Recognition is thus, Smith proposes, the most basic level of engagement with a film; it is a precondition for the audience's ability to follow and make sense of a narrative—though one that can be flouted by avant-garde film—and to respond emotionally to characters. Smith does not tackle, however, what strikes me as a more interesting question: recognition as an aspect of identification. In contrast to a base-level ability to recognize all characters *as* characters, such a response is fundamentally selective; one recognizes oneself in certain characters rather than in others. On what grounds? And what does it mean to see aspects of oneself in a film or a novel? Whereas allegiance involves ethical or political values and empathy is about co-feeling, recognition names an experience of *coming to know*: of being struck by some kind of insight about the self (which may, of course, have an ethical, political, or emotional spin-off).

And here the forms of self-knowing afforded by aesthetic recognition are more unpredictable and multifaceted than they are often taken to be. Critical theorists have often dismissed experiences of recognition in art, equating them with a sense of complacency and an endorsement of the commonplace. And yet "recognition is not repetition: it denotes not just the previously known, but the becoming known. . . . In a mobile play of interiority and exteriority, something that exists outside of me inspires a revised or altered sense of who I am."[48] Glimpsing aspects of oneself in fictional beings involves a volatile mix of the familiar and the different; to recognize is to know again but also to see afresh. As I recognize myself in another, I may also see something new in myself, and I may be startled or discomfited by what I see.

In a previous book I discussed how experiences of self-recognition can link up to struggles for social recognition: that Ibsen's female audience identified with the repressed rage of Hedda Gabler, for example, was not just a matter of individual response but helped fan the sparks of the early suffragette movement. Self-knowledge (a woman seeing aspects of her own life or situation in Hedda's) linked up to a call for public acknowledgment (women demanding to be recognized as equal agents in the world). I now want to consider a different kind of self-recognition—one that is harder to leverage in terms of any discernible political use value—as it relates to the work of Austrian novelist Thomas Bernhard, acknowledged master of the tirade, the diatribe, the rant. A typical Bernhard novel consists of a single unbroken paragraph of insults, invectives, and exaggerations spewing from the mouth of a monomaniac narrator. Its language is repetitive, relentless, incantatory, spiraling obsessively around the same ideas and phrases. Bernhard's writing is often described as absolutist, dogmatic, solipsistic, and hyperbolic; he is hailed as an exaggeration artist, a madman of exasperated orality.

Bernhard is an illuminating case for rethinking certain commonplaces about identification. There is, first of all, the relentless negativity of his writing: an oceanic heave of venom, disgust, bitterness, and loathing. If readers are identifying with something, this "something" has little to do with affection or positive emotions. The lure of the rant lies in its destructive and self-destructive qualities, its hectoring and haranguing, its push toward extremity—what Robert Cohen calls its bilious, scorched-earth quality. Cohen writes beautifully of "the giddy drunken music of obsession, that agitated, overstated letting-go, which pushes us viscerally to the edge of our conditioned responses, and then asks us to follow our deepest, most self-annihilating instincts and plunge with it over that edge, into god knows what."[49]

As these words suggest, one effect of the Bernhardian rant is to batter the edifice of individuality. Sound takes precedence over sense; selfhood sags and sways under the torrential force of words gone wild; the reader is bludgeoned by repetition heaped on repetition, by a flood of verbal tics and manic twitches. Language churns relentlessly, as if without human intervention; readers find themselves trapped in what feels like an automatic writing machine. Bernhard's famous nested sentences—one character recounts the words of another in stylistically indistinguishable prose—have the effect of confusing frames of narration, such that it is often difficult to discern who is speaking: "Glenn locked himself up in his North American cage, I in my Upper Austrian one, Wertheimer said, I thought. He with his alomania, I with my desperation. All three with our desperation, he said, I thought."[50] The typical scenario of a Bernhard novel is a trio of figures who reflect and refract each other's obsessions: the logic is spatial rather than temporal, a closed field of repetition rather than an open-ended plot.

And yet, despite its disdain for character development and literary realism, its aggression and misanthropy, Bernhard's work inspires ardent identification. (There is even talk of a Bernhard cult.) His influence on the work of W. G. Sebald is frequently noted, but there are many other disciples. Geoff Dyer's *Out of Sheer Rage,* a meditation on writing—or failing to write—a book about D. H. Lawrence, is thoroughly Bernhardian in its prose style, as is much of the work of novelist Tim Parks. There is the explicit homage—or is it pastiche?—of *Revulsion: Thomas Bernhard in San Salvador*, whose vituperative narrator spews indiscriminate insults at every aspect of Salvadoran life, from its corrupt universities to its revolting cuisine. (Its author, Horacio Castellanos Moya, received death threats after the book's publication.) Even Bernhard's reviewers become infected, as in this *Village Voice* commentary by Gary Indiana:

> In those years when Bernhard was writing *The Loser*, *Old Masters*, *Woodcutters*, and finally *Extinction*, I lived in a country where the obvious truth of Bernhard's writing was intolerable, a country where a writer like Bernhard or Sartre or Gombrowicz would only be reviled as a nest-fouler, a raging disease of a country bent on becoming Disney World, a country of advanced senility, a malignant nation of putrid happy endings, a country ruled by malevolent dwarfs, a country intoxicated by technology, a country crawling with desperate hypocrites, spiritually no different than Austria.[51]

For Indiana, Bernhard's excoriations of Austria call to mind the United States, a country equally well stocked with "desperate hypocrites." The two writers share a loathing for putrid happy endings; the baffled and impotent rage of the Bernhardian narrator echoes Indiana's own. As we see here, identification does not depend on literary realism or mimetic accuracy; truth can also lie in excess and exaggeration; affiliations can form around kernels of antisocial venom and apoplectic spleen.

I admit to being infected by the same virus and only narrowly escaped the fate of a Bernhard dissertation; returning to his work feels like picking a scab, the characters' obsessions rubbing in my own. What should we call this form of attachment? Empathy, with its associations of care, concern, and tolerance, seems like entirely the wrong word here. (Tolerance! A laughable idea in the Thomas Bernhard universe.) Identification-as-recognition, then, but not via any kind of obvious matching. I am not an Austrian man, share little of the background of Bernhard or his characters, and am, if anything, rather conflict averse. And yet there is something in Bernhard that resonates, that feels familiar. "Affective situation" is a phrase coined by Ethan Reed to capture the diffuseness of certain affects as they splay across self and world, transpersonal patterns of response forged out of various things working together.[52]

What I share with Bernhard, I want to say, is an *irritation situation*. By temperament I am something of a malcontent, prone to brooding and seething. There is something exceptionally gratifying about Bernhard's channeling of this irritation: the relief of seeing it acknowledged, cranked up a hundredfold, and vomited out into the world. Recognition meets up with a pleasure in vicarious expression. And yet, in its sheer hyperbole and lack of discrimination, its flagrant contradictions and digressions, the Bernhardian rant teeters on the edge of absurdity. To rave about the stupidity and self-righteousness of others is inevitably to reveal the extent of one's own stupidity and self-righteousness. The manic energy of Bernhard's prose is exhilarating yet also estranging; the mirror it offers conspicuously does not flatter. In recognizing my rage against idiocy, I am confronted with the idiocy of my own rage.

Meanwhile, what exactly am I identifying with? Bernhard? Bernhard's first-person narrator? The characters? The seductive-coercive pull of his incantatory sentences? It seems impossible to nail down any definitive answer. A certain kind of critical response would focus on language alone, yet the force of this language lies in conveying a certain attitude. Excessive feelings and categorical judgments are constantly in play, pointing back to a recognizable—if luridly magnified—disposition. What is a Bernhard protagonist if not the quintessential *bad-mouther* and *faultfinder*? Person schemas, even if stylized, exaggerated, and caricatured, are very much in play. And here the characters echo the compulsions of the narrator; the narrator brings to mind the author, with his notorious and vitriolic attacks on the Austrian establishment ("this tiny state is a gigantic dunghill"); meanwhile, neither Bernhard nor his characters can be disentangled from the remorseless rhythms of his unmistakable prose. Author, characters, and words blur together to form a composite site of attachment. We are dealing, once again, with hybrids, with text-person combinations. Identifying involves a response not only to fictional figures but also to the overall atmosphere of a text as created by its style. Recognition in Bernhard is both personal (character based) *and* transpersonal (a linguistic-aesthetic relation).

I turn, finally, to *empathy:* sharing someone's feelings and responding with concern to these feelings. As we can see, this definition splits into two parts—feeling *with* someone and feeling *for* someone—that are not automatically connected. Analytical philosophers like to cite the example of a torturer getting inside his victim's psyche in order to apply pain-inducing techniques more effectively; he is feeling with, they argue, but certainly not feeling for. Conversely, we can care or feel for a character without experiencing their emotions or mimicking their affective state. (When the hardworking Boxer is carted off to the slaughterhouse in *Animal Farm*, the horse's joyful expectation of retirement is not echoed by the book's readers but only heightens the pathos of his fate.) Yet I find the solution that is sometimes proposed—a strict separation of empathy from sympathy—to be unsatisfying, given their entanglement in everyday usage. To refer to someone as empathic is to imply not just that they are aware of others' feelings but also that they respond to these feelings in a compassionate manner. (More than other strands of identification, empathy is tied to the acknowledgment of suffering: responding to the pain of others.)[53]

It is here that literature—with its ability to stick us inside the minds of strangers—is hailed as a force for the greater good. Empathy has received far more attention than other aspects of identification. "There is a surprising level of agreement," Ann Jurecic writes, "from educators to politicians and philosophers, and even talk show hosts, that *reading literature* makes us more empathic."[54] Feeling a sense of empathy with fictional persons, according to Richard Rorty and Martha Nussbaum, can expand the limits of experience, engender a sense of solidarity with distant others, and do valuable civic and political work. Since the eighteenth century, literary empathy has been hailed as a means of encouraging altruism and of binding readers into a community—working against strong social and economic pressures toward egoism and self-interest. Empathy is also a gendered term: that women are more empathic than men is taken for granted in daily life, popular commentary, and much psychology and neuroscience.

Critical theorists have taken a rather different view, arguing that empathy is soaked through with power and privilege; reading a novel may delude affluent Westerners that they know what it's like to be a slum dweller in Mumbai. Meanwhile, in stressing the role of emotion—I feel, therefore I am—empathy promotes a sentimental and overly simplified understanding of social relations. Jurecic references a number of arguments along these lines, including a feminist critique of *Reading Lolita in Tehran* that accuses the best-selling memoir of divorcing affect from analysis and thus promoting "neoliberal feminism and U.S. imperialism."[55] Here we see echoes of the Brechtian distrust of identification: the conviction that emotions—or at least softer emotions such as empathy—block critical thinking and are complicit with inequality and injustice.

This pushback carries a certain force: the claim that reading literature engenders empathy, which in turn promotes social solidarity, teeters on a shaky platform of assumptions. As we've seen, empathy is not always a motive for reading or the most salient aspect of reading. It proves more pertinent to some genres and some readers than others; meanwhile, it remains an open question whether empathy with fictional characters has any long-term effects on behavior. And yet denouncing empathy seems no better than idealizing it: no less closed off to the variability and messiness of reader response. And while empathy has its limits, a lack of empathy—a turning away from the perspectives and the pain of others—hardly seems like a preferable alternative. My former student Kiley Garrett offers another take: "reading a book from another person's perspective may not prompt readers to act altruistically, but it might cause them to think more openly."[56] Repeated exposure to differing forms of life may have a gradual, subtle, or inadvertent effect—even if readers can't point to a specific text that changed their way of thinking. Lines of causality are hard to pin down, and the "impact factor" of literature is exceptionally difficult to measure—yet a world without imaginative fiction would surely be a very different world.

Here we might look to a review of Mohsin Hamid's *Exit West* by fellow novelist Viet Thanh Nguyen. Published in 2017, *Exit West* follows the lives of a couple, Saeed and Nadia, as their country—unnamed, sketched only in the broadest strokes—descends into civil war and chaos. Electricity and water are cut off; bombs explode on the streets; public executions become routine. Saeed and Nadia struggle to sustain some shreds of their familiar routines, until normality is no longer possible and survival becomes their only goal: "for one minute we are pottering about our normal existence and the next minute we are dying."[57] Doors mysteriously begin to appear in apartment buildings and parking lots: magic portals that allow Saeed, Nadia, and their compatriots to step into other countries and start new lives in London or Mykonos or Marin County. Hailed as intruders, they must grapple with hostility and contempt, with the deployment of troops and tanks. Parallels with the Syrian refugee crisis are evident but not belabored. The novel focuses less on geopolitical realities than on conditions of displacement ("that summer it seemed to Saeed and Nadia that the whole planet was on the move") and on how such displacement alters the bond between Nadia and Saeed, forcing them into proximity yet also rendering them strangers to one another.[58]

As Nguyen notes, *Exit West* engages in a delicate balancing act between sameness and difference. Its main characters are educated city dwellers; the textures of their everyday lives—smartphones, recreational drugs, dinners in Chinese restaurants, seminars on "corporate identity and product branding"—connect them to the novel's most likely readers. And yet in other respects—Saeed's insistence on sexual abstinence and devotion to prayer, Nadia's donning of a long black robe to ward off advances from strangers—differences are made manifest. Portraying catastrophe at a slight remove, the text refuses to linger on the spectacle of suffering. (The magic-portal device deflects attention away from the all-too-familiar stories of deadly refugee journeys that permeate the media.) Meanwhile, the crystalline simplicity of Hamid's prose and the quasi-allegorical portrayal of his characters' travails invite readers to place themselves in a related position. Such a stretching of experience, Nguyen suggests, can alter how people feel about refugees. "The reader, of course, must think about what would happen if her own normal life was suddenly, unexpectedly upended by war." In this scenario, empathy with characters does not rule out critical reflection but makes it possible. In bringing home what it feels like to be a refugee, *Exit West* makes ethical and political claims upon the reader. "The novel asks readers why doors should be closed to refugees when the readers of the novel might become refugees one day."[59]

Online comments include examples of readers engaging seriously with these concerns. An Amazon reviewer, for example, writes that "*Exit West* challenges you to think in new ways about a familiar issue, to question what you understand when you see generic terms like refugee or migrant applied to millions of individuals, who each has their home, their emotional life, their door, and has to make the decision to take that chance, or not, while they can."[60] Such observations get to the heart of the novel's choices: its turn away from exoticism and sensationalism; its emphasis on emotional and existential, as well as political, dilemmas; its portrayal of migration as a shared experience, albeit one inflected in very different ways. Nguyen's own review adopts a similar tactic: buttonholing its readers, putting them in the position of refugees, and emphasizing the ordinariness of a way of life:

> You wake in the morning and drink your coffee or tea. You drive a car or a motorbike, or perhaps you take the bus. You go to work and turn on your computer. You go out at night and flirt and date. . . . [Y]ou keep believing you are human even when the catastrophe arrives and renders you homeless. Your town or city or countryside is in ruins. You try to make it to the border. Only then, hoping to leave, or making it across the border, do you understand that those who live on the other side do not see you as human at all.[61]

Whether such attempts to create empathy will result in changes in action or long-term behavior remains, of course, an open question. But we might query the expectation that a novel trigger some kind of radical change—and that if it fails to do so, it must therefore be mired in ideological complicity. "That people may feel empathy or sympathy without becoming political actors," Kim Chabot Davis remarks in her study of cross-racial identification, "is not a fault inherent in the emotions."[62] Davis goes on: "many other individual circumstances—political ideologies, an ability to be self-critical, witnessing of discrimination, previous encounters with people of color, other cross-cultural encounters, and innate variations in empathic ability—all play a role in making empathetic responses possible."[63] Change is brought about by many things coming together—not by a single, almighty, agent acting alone.

As we have come to see, there are different ways of getting close to characters, though these strands are often intertwined in various combinations. In *Jane Eyre*, for example, there is a formal *alignment* with the heroine's first-person perspective; the novel orients readers toward *allegiance* with Jane as the novel's moral center; it invites female readers to *recognize* gender-based barriers they have encountered; finally, it encourages *empathy* by dwelling on the heroine's impassioned responses to hardship and misrecognition. Thanks to this thick rope of connection, Brontë's novel has been highly effective in promoting identification. Yet here again, there are no guarantees. In Michelle Cliff's *No Telephone to Heaven*, for example, the heroine struggles against identifying in a manner that has been echoed by numerous postcolonial critics: "The fiction had tricked her. Drawn her in so that she became Jane. . . . With a sharpness of mind, she reprimanded herself. No, she told herself, she could not be Jane."[64] Since Brontë's novel is part of a colonial education and since the Caribbean heroine of Cliff's novel has acquired an anticolonial consciousness, any sense of commonality can feel only like a fraught capitulation. The ties between Brontë's protagonist and female readers have considerable durability and strength; but there is nothing inevitable about them.

The affordances of other texts, meanwhile, may pan out quite differently. In the Sherlock Holmes stories, we are *aligned* with Watson's perspective; but any allegiance is likely to be to Holmes. First-person narration often encourages identification with the narrator—but not when he is utterly subordinate to his charismatic companion. Who cares about, dreams about, wants to be Watson? (A plausible riposte from one of *Hooked*'s reviewers: "everyone who wants to sleep with Sherlock Holmes!") Meanwhile, in reading an Ian Fleming novel, we are formally aligned with Bond and also invited to root for him (an allegiance that need not reflect any real-world commitments—caught up in *Goldfinger*, I feel a flicker of delight as Bond outwits his villainous opponent, even though I have no interest in saving the free world from Soviet conspiracies). But what about empathy? As Umberto Eco pointed out decades ago, 007 is a magnificent machine who lacks interiority and is voided of any complex emotions; he neither feels empathy nor inspires it. Similar issues arise in the very different literary world of Camus's *The Stranger*; Meursault's famous opening lines on his mother's death advertise his lack of empathy and are likely to block the reader's own. There are notable parallels, in this respect, between action-driven genre fiction and some canonical works of modernist literature in terms of a shared, often strenuous avoidance of co-feeling (though readers may experience a form of "kinesthetic empathy" that is anchored in bodily sensations rather than emotional depth: sensing the harsh assault of the blazing sun with Meursault; flinching with Bond as he receives a hard kick in the ribs from Goldfinger).

We are now in a position to question the frequent conflation of identification with empathy—as if the former always implied or required the latter. In her very useful book on empathy, for example, Suzanne Keen frequently switches between the two terms in claiming that audiences are primed to identify even with cartoon or fairy-tale characters: Little Red Riding Hood, Garfield, or Charlie Brown.[65] While endorsing the overall point, I'd argue that attachment to such schematic figures has far more to do with alignment, allegiance, and recognition than with empathy—which *is* tied to interiority and the sympathetic rendering of emotional states. This distinction also explains the pushback from critics against attempts to make empathy a catchall term for justifying the value of literature. Such a word—with its connotations of concern, fellow feeling, and altruism—seems exceptionally ill-suited to the demented, destructive, antinomian, and asocial heroes of much modern and postmodern fiction, from *Notes from Underground* to *American Psycho*. These figures are often fascinating, without a doubt—but their draw has little to do with empathy.

I should perhaps clarify that I am not "against empathy," which strikes me as a fundament of pro-social interaction and the public good. Attempts to pitch empathy as the main form of aesthetic engagement, however, quickly fall afoul of numerous counterexamples. Let us consider a few such instances in more detail. Our baseline definition still holds—identification implies a sense of something shared; it often relies on person schemas—but we are now conscious of the differing ways in which this relation can unfold. And we can take on board what might seem like a counterintuitive claim: that the readings carried out by literary scholars—however erudite, ironic, skeptical, or critical—are not outside identification but premised upon it.

Ironic Identification

In a recent book on the writing of *The Stranger*, Alice Kaplan ponders the paradoxical draw of its protagonist. How, she wonders, can indifference be so fascinating? (The original reader's report for French publisher Gallimard referred to Meursault as "inhuman" in his indifference.) Camus fashioned a character who is incapable of empathy—and who seems, in turn, to inspire little or no empathy in readers. And yet the fascination exerted by *The Stranger* is incontrovertible. "How," Kaplan writes, "can such a distant and empty narrator capture so much attention, and how can a disturbing book elicit so much loyalty?"[66] Peeling identification away from empathy makes such attachment less puzzling than it would otherwise be.

Beyond alignment—the novel's centering on the thoughts and sensations of Meursault—allegiance and recognition thus offer themselves as relevant concepts in clarifying the allure of *The Stranger*. But what kind of allegiance? And what is being recognized? "Allegiance" might seem an odd word for a character who seems so asocial and disengaged. How can readers ally themselves with someone so impervious to any bid for connection? Any sense of recognition, meanwhile, is likely to be partial and qualified, not a point-by-point matching but rather a sense that Camus's hero captures aspects of a reader's sense of being in the world.

In introducing the idea of ironic identification, I do not mean the same thing as Hans-Robert Jauss: that identifying can be interrupted or broken by moments of ironic distancing.[67] Rather, I want to highlight a style of response that has received virtually no attention: an identification that is *premised or based on irony*. That is to say, a sense of estrangement and disassociation is the connecting tissue that binds character and reader. What is held in common is an experience of having nothing in common with others, of feeling at odds with the mainstream of social life. Quite a few protagonists of modern fiction—solitary, adrift, and sardonic or melancholic—solicit such forms of affiliation: *The Immoralist, Nausea, Invisible Man, The Piano Teacher.* And here the vectors of causality are hard to pin down. Are readers drawn to fictional figures who crystallize their own feelings of anomie, or are they schooled in estrangement and ennui by reading works of modernist literature? The result, in either case, is what we might call an alliance of strangers: fictional and real persons linked by a shared sense of disassociation. It is often assumed that identifying and irony are mutually exclusive: where one is, the other cannot be. And yet irony turns out to be a surprisingly common means of identification.

We see such a tie in both academic and popular responses to Camus's novel. A lay reader remarks of Meursault: "he wasn't a character meant to sympathize with, or relate to. He wasn't even much of a character until the last chapter. He was a montage of existentialism: an indifferent symbol robotic in attitude. . . . What *The Stranger* said about God and what little time we have to dwell on such uncertainties is beautiful. And I completely agree."[68] Acknowledging the irrelevance of an empathic bond, this reader allies himself with Meursault's railing against religion; he points to philosophical themes ("montage of existentialism") rather than psychological affinities. Here again, ideas serve as mediators between works and readers. Such a response, of course, is prompted not just by the novel but by its framing; *The Stranger* is often encountered in the classroom, paired with explications of theories of the absurd. And yet this is not at all to imply that philosophical themes cannot have affective force. In a memorable anecdote, the British philosopher R. M. Hare captures the effect of Camus's novel on his young Swiss houseguest, whose behavior and attitudes changed markedly after reading *The Stranger* and becoming persuaded that "nothing matters." He took up smoking, skulked in his bedroom, was taciturn at dinner, and went for long, aimless walks around the outskirts of Oxford. There was no doubt at all, Hare remarks, "about the violence with which he had been affected by what he had read."[69]

Meanwhile, *The Stranger* is not a "novel of ideas" in the usual sense: the absurd, for Camus, has far more to do with sensation than with thought. Neither subjective (housed in the mind) nor objective (a systematic philosophy), it is a nose-to-nose encounter with the sheer senselessness of phenomena. And here, for some readers, a sense of recognition comes into play: as less a matter of what is said than *how* it is said. Reflecting on his early fascination with *The Stranger*, novelist Aaron Gwyn writes: "It was the voice I connected with first, antihero Meursault's poker-faced assessment of a world that makes as little sense to him as mine did to me." An affinity is registered; Meursault's flatness of tone resonates with Gwyn's own sense of disassociation; there is a shared sense of being unmoored, out of sync with one's milieu. And yet identification is partial, not total: "It was comforting to consider the ways the two of us were alike, more comforting to consider all the ways we were different."[70] Along similar lines, Neal Oxenhandler speaks of a negative identification: what connects him to Meursault—along an axis of recognition—is a shared lack of affect, a common inability to feel the appropriate, socially sanctioned emotions.[71]

Is the draw of Camus's protagonist—detached, distant, emotionally avoidant—limited to male readers? Some commentators have suggested as much. "If one reads as a woman or as an Arab," one critic remarks, ". . . one's tendency to identify with Meursault or to cast him in a sympathetic light will thereby be reduced if not altogether stifled."[72] Yet experiences of estrangement or disassociation are hardly limited to white men. In a fascinating book, Deborah Nelson describes the ethos of unsentimentality—being tough, impersonal, nonempathic, even coldhearted—that defined a cohort of midcentury female intellectuals, including Mary McCarthy, Hannah Arendt, Susan Sontag, and Simone Weil.[73] Meanwhile, the publication of Kamel Daoud's *The Meursault Investigation* pulverizes any generalities about reading "as an Arab." Told from the viewpoint of Harun, the imagined brother of the man murdered by Meursault, the novel is a sustained reckoning with the racial politics of literary alignment. It reflects at length on how *The Stranger* erases, in its indifference, the name and the personhood of the Arab killed by Meursault, and how this erasure is conveyed to and registered by the work's readers.

Yet the novel is also an extended homage to Camus's work, in its laconic and pared-back prose as well as in its narrative technique.

The narrator seeks exculpation for his own murderous act by recounting his story to a stranger in a bar, in a manner reminiscent of another work by Camus, *The Fall*. And like *The Fall*, Daoud's novel is a brilliant exercise in unreliable narration: Harun's evasions and silences become increasingly evident, troubling the sense of solidarity that the novel solicits. The reader is bound to the main character, yet also estranged from him.[74] And the work concludes with a fierce blast of recognition: a tie between Harun and Meursault, an acknowledgment of similarity across no-less-real racial and cultural differences. "I was looking for traces of my brother in the book," writes Harun of *The Stranger*, "and what I found there instead was my own reflection, I discovered I was practically the murderer's double."[75]

The import of ironic identification, moreover, reaches well beyond *The Stranger* and literary modernism into the intellectual culture of the present-day humanities—as one of the ways in which critical personae are formed and alliances are created. Camus's existential irony differs philosophically from the poststructuralist irony that succeeded it, yet there are notable similarities at the level of sensibility and disposition. Lee Konstantinou summarizes the present-day variant in his survey of contemporary criticism: "the ironist debunks rigid ideologies, unweaves foundationalist 'master narratives' and deconstructs every conceptual or philosophical description of the world through the close investigation of language. To be an ironist is to have the power and inclination to reveal the gaps and holes in hegemonic conceptions that pass themselves off as common sense."[76] Such an ethos of disassociation serves—paradoxically—as a form of glue, binding critics to other like-minded critics as well as to works of art that are held to embrace a similar distrust of the commonsensical and commonplace. It is via the presumption of shared estrangement that intellectual, interpersonal, and institutional ties are forged.

Faye Halpern traces out such bonds as they are manifested in American studies, looking closely at the history of commentaries on *Benito Cereno* and *Uncle Tom's Cabin*. Stowe's novel is often censured for inspiring identification and sentimental responses that gloss over the structural realities of slavery. *Benito Cereno*, by contrast, is widely admired as a self-undermining text that leaves few footholds for interpretation. Deploying irony as both a trope and a structural device, it seems to thwart any desire for attachment. And yet, as Halpern points out, critical testimonies to these ironic or self-qualifying aspects of Melville's text reveal ample evidence of identification on the part of critics: with *Benito Cereno*, with Melville, with what they perceive as the work's subversive aims.[77] In short, while identification-as-empathy may attract censure from American studies scholars, other kinds of attachments are very much in force. Recognizing traces of her own intellectual or political commitments in the work she is reading, the critic allies herself with its techniques of estrangement and critical distancing.

The term "thought collective" was coined by Ludwik Fleck in his account of how scholarship sustains itself. New styles of thinking are taken up, he observes, not just because they offer better arguments but because they succeed in gaining support: inspiring disciples and opponents, becoming fodder for keynotes, being assigned in classes. It is via such institutional practices that forms of thought are transmitted. As Fleck puts it, "a set of findings meanders throughout the community, becoming polished, transformed, reinforced, or attenuated, while influencing other findings, concept formations, opinions, and habits of thought."[78] Scholarship, in short, is a relational activity that involves forms of solidarity, rivalry, and authority; that is not just a matter of content but also mood, tone, and intellectual style. Any form of knowledge—whether affirmative or critical—depends on the forging of pathways and the coming together of multiple actors. And in the contemporary humanities, ironic identification often shapes how intellectual ties are forged and thought collectives are formed.

Amber Jamilla Musser, for example, offers a rereading of *The Story of O*, arguing that O's embrace of her sexual objectification serves as a critical commentary on women's lack of agency. "What the text reveals . . . is the ambiguity of femininity in the modern era and the difficulties that arise from that constraint."[79] A favored method of interpretation in literary and cultural studies involves drawing out hidden signs of dissent. Musser discovers in Réage's novel a protofeminist perspective that is akin to her own: that is, she *recognizes* a shared stance of dissent. This recognition in turn inspires a sense of *allegiance* with *The Story of O* and against another portrayal of female masochism, *Fifty Shades of Grey*; the latter novel is taken to task for serving up a regressive romantic fantasy and purveying a neoliberal vision of sexuality. As in Halpern's example, the issue is not one of identification versus its absence but of the value allotted to different *kinds* of identification: empathy versus recognition and allegiance; ties to fictional persons versus ties to a critical, subversive, or ironic stance that is attributed to the overall "project" of a text.

Literary authors, meanwhile, continue to inspire countless acts of scholarly identification, which drives much of the day-to-day work of literary studies: cropping up in courses and syllabi, conferences and journal titles (the Melville Society; the James Joyce Facebook page; special issues of journals devoted to Toni Morrison; Dickens Universe). While monographs on single authors have fallen from fashion, dissertations and books are still commonly organized around a handful of writers, each serving as the linchpin of a single chapter. And what we might call literary-critical fandom—crushes on specific writers, avid consumption of new biographies or criticism of their work, curiosity about details of their lives, from lover's quarrels to bedroom décor—flourishes unabated inside as well as outside the academy. Yet these attachments can vary markedly in style and tone. Think, for example, of the contrast between critical devotion to Jane Austen and to J. M. Coetzee—as shaped not just by the features of their writing but by differing critical schools (the dominance of feminist criticism in the former, deconstruction in the latter), as well as by perceptions of the author's persona (Austen as intimate friend; Coetzee's famed aloofness).

What critics care about, in short, is not just a historical author or a self-contained work but an "author-text" composite made up of disparate parts: the cadences of a literary style; the feel of a fictional world; snippets of knowledge about an author's life; critical essays or biographies; half-remembered interviews or public remarks; perhaps—in the case of a living author—a fleeting exchange of looks at a bookstore signing. The texts cocompose the author; the author is disseminated across the pages of his or her works. Mikaella Clements, for example, reflects on her ambivalent identification-as-recognition, as a queer teenager, with *Moby-Dick*—a text, she remarks, that displays no interest in women yet whose depictions of fury and bitterness resonated with her own emotions. "I met Melville, and he already knew me inside and out and sympathized, badly and with frequent misogyny, and in a way that wasn't at all comforting—except in the way that it is always comforting to meet someone who is made of the same stuff as you."[80] "Melville" here would seem to denote not just the historical person or the novel *Moby-Dick* but a hybrid of the two. Striving for a strict demarcation of writer from work proves to be yet another exercise in futility; as we engage with fiction, categories blend and blur. (Recall the indignant reader rallying in defense of Nabokov!) All of which is to say that identifying with characters is part of a continuum of text-person entanglements.

Meanwhile, person schemas do not vanish from even the most ardently antihumanist styles of scholarship—shaping relations to other scholars if not to fictional figures. Scholars may profess skepticism about the status of characters, yet they cannot entirely circumvent the matrix of character. Individual thinkers and theorists assume a field-defining importance and are endowed with a surplus of charismatic authority. Influential figures—Lacan, Derrida, Foucault, Spivak, Butler, Fish—have inspired identification among critics, writes David Shumway, in much the same way as stars of the studio era once commanded the identification of movie audiences.[81] Such writers serve as objects of affective, as well as intellectual, investments; critics cathect not only onto ideas but also onto the imagined personae behind these ideas and the attitudes, sensibilities, and ways of being in the world that they are held to embody.

Conclusion

In an often-cited book, José Esteban Muñoz invokes the language of "disidentification" to describe the creation and reception of queer performance art, especially by racial minorities. As he uses the term, it signals not a refusal to identify but rather a scrambling and recoding of received meanings. He cites James Baldwin's account of seeing aspects of himself in Bette Davis; being drawn to what Muñoz calls her "freakish beauty," sensing a tug of likeness as well as difference. Baldwin, he writes, "transforms the raw material of identification . . . while simultaneously positioning himself within and outside the image of the movie star."[82] The queer black man identifying with a white woman scrambles the cultural codes through which persons are usually classed and understood. He attaches, but he attaches *differently*.

Muñoz calls this experience one of "disidentification" to underscore its difference from the idea of identification as a matter of being interpellated by a dominant ideology. And yet, as he acknowledges, what he calls disidentifying overlaps at key points with how critics such as Eve Sedgwick, Miriam Hansen, and Wayne Koestenbaum have sought to redefine the act of identifying—as having the potential to cut across and confuse social categories rather than entrenching them. Miriam Hansen, for example, seizes on the example of Rudolf Valentino's ecstatic fans to show how the reception of his films confounded conventional assumptions about how women were expected to behave.[83] Pursuing a similar line of thought, I've suggested that variety and unpredictability are built into practices of identification—commonplace rather than exceptional.

This is not to glorify such identifications as inherently "progressive." When closely tied to a subculture (Muñoz) or the coalescing of a social movement (*Thelma and Louise*), their political salience can, perhaps, be parsed with a degree of confidence. Yet for the most part, the larger import of the countless flickering attachments that are felt to a novel or a favorite Netflix show seems impossible to adjudicate. (How exactly could their impact be determined, and by what measure?) What should be questioned, rather, is the assumption that aesthetic attachments—whether they affirm identities or thwart them—can be justified only by claiming, however implausibly, clear-cut political effects. In a generative essay, Summer Kim Lee reflects on her relation to Sandra Oh—the Asian American female figure in popular culture whom she "overidentified with, aspired to be, and unabashedly loved." In graduate school, meanwhile, she was being trained to engage in critiques of such identity-based affinities—as nothing more than a liberal pandering to minority differences that concealed structural inequalities. There was no available language, it seemed, in which she could express her attachment without exposing herself as a bad political subject. And yet, Lee suggests, other ways of thinking about identification are needed: as a relation that "remains private, close, and intimately entangled with the ways we desire to get closer to what and who we love, without having to compulsively share it so that it might have a public, properly useful political shelf life."[84] Aesthetic attachments *can* spill out into the political sphere: but to judge them solely in such terms is to submit them to a narrow and impoverished calculus.

Acts of identifying, I've argued, drive various kinds of engagement with fiction. Connections are forged across differences; expected or surprising affinities come to light that may be self-transformative or that may, occasionally, eddy out into larger social currents. Such ties may involve empathy—and yet it is not at all uncommon to identify with fictional figures who block empathy rather than foster it. It is here that ideas of recognition or allegiance prove more pertinent—keeping firmly in mind that these ties may be ambivalent, qualified, partial, or ironic.

I've also questioned certain beliefs about character—for example, that it is synonymous with a well-rounded, deep, yet unified personage. This view coincides with the stress on empathy and the dominance of realist examples in many literary-critical accounts of character. How many theses about character—whether positive or critical—have been built on a handful of novels by Dickens, Eliot, or James! To grapple with character in its richness and variety, the net must be cast more broadly. This means factoring in popular genres, where character may function rather differently: that James Bond is a "man without qualities," as Kingsley Amis points out, serves to facilitate identification rather than to block it.[85] Meanwhile, that figures in modernist literature differ—formally, thematically, philosophically—from those of nineteenth-century novels does not mean they no longer "count" as characters. Some of the most memorable figures of fiction would surely include Clarissa Dalloway, Leopold Bloom, Mrs. Ramsay, Joseph K, Mother Courage, the duchesse de Guermantes, Gregor Samsa—their degree of roundness or flatness is beside the point.[86]

Ties to fiction and to fictional beings are forged in a variety of genres, from the hermetic to the formulaic. It is not that naive readers or viewers identify and that dispassionate critics don't, but that they find different points of connection—affective, ethical, political, philosophical, or some mix of all these. Our students' search for relevance and affinity, in this light, turns out to be not so radically different from our own. Here I do not minimize the "value-added" aspects of education, as a way of acquiring new analytical and interpretive skills—the topic of my next chapter. Yet in both "critical" and "uncritical" reading, affinities are being forged and identifications are being made.

Interpreting as Relating

Yet even if the claims of previous chapters hold any water, what difference do they make? How do they affect the work of scholars and teachers and students? Studying literature or film or music is a matter of honing new skills; grappling with recalcitrant works and counterintuitive ideas; acquiring more subtle or capacious forms of understanding. It is an often arduous process of learning *not* to trust gut feelings and first impressions. Someone might well agree with the claim that art can realign perception or ignite emotion, while failing to grasp its relevance to the protocols of a graduate seminar or a grant proposal. Aesthetic experiences are available in movie theaters, art galleries, reading in bed, or while traipsing around Tintern Abbey—but how are they relevant to the library or the classroom?

Any answer to this question must be twofold. Commentary, first of all, *is* connection; we go astray if we think that analyzing is just a matter of detaching or disengaging. Critics forge ties to the works they explicate, the methods they deploy, the disciplinary identities they inhabit. Being attached is not something to be outgrown—the index of a naive or woefully underdeveloped sensibility—but a condition of any conceivable form of intellectual life. Yet attending to attachment—folding the word into our idioms, exploring its entailments—can also affect *how* we interpret. My argument, in this sense, has both a descriptive and a normative aspect. Could identifying or attuning, for example, be repurposed in the classroom? Is being receptive at odds with being reflective? Can a stress on stance and disposition be squared with a concern for method? And is the empirical at odds with the interpretive? Instead of dichotomies of affect versus analysis, we might engage the spectrum of what James Jasper calls "thinking-feeling processes"—the recursive relations between affect and argument, motivation and interpretation—as they shape what we know and how we come to know it.[1]

"Reading as Relating" would have been a more euphonious title for this chapter, but I'm not entirely at ease with how "reading" is invoked in literary studies. The phrase "doing a reading" has a faux-amateurish cast that glosses over its status as a tightly scripted form of academic *writing* that has very little to do with reading a book on the subway. (While I'll be drawing connections between professional and amateur readers, we also need to reckon with obvious differences.) "Interpretation" is a more apt umbrella term for the various genres of academic commentary that characterize the humanities—including engagements with paintings, sculptures, or music that have very little to do with text-centric notions of reading.

There is, to be sure, a longstanding wariness of interpretation in Anglo-American literary studies—from the New Critical mantra that "poems should not mean / But be" to deconstructive portrayals of interpretation as a form of violence wreaked on hapless works of literature. In *The Limits of Critique* I argued that such criticisms miss the mark in their portrayal of interpretation as a dogged hunt for a single, simple meaning. Hermes is a crafty trickster-god, and hermeneutics has often conceived of meaning as oblique, mediated, enigmatic, layered, and multiform.[2] While there is a growing weariness with the practice of browbeating works into confessing their noxious motives, such approaches hardly exhaust the possibilities of hermeneutic engagement.

"Interpreting as Relating" pushes back against a picture of scholars as dispassionate observers who diagram formal patterns or decipher symptoms. In drawing connections—between words, images, sounds, genres, and worlds—they cannot avoid getting stuck to their objects and methods of study. The language of relations—whether poetic, discursive, or historical—is well established in the humanities. To speak of *relating*, however, is to offer another slant, by folding the critic's persona—commitments, sympathies, and identifications—into the works and frameworks of the humanities. Perhaps we can even redeem the language of the "relatable"—a word that is virtually guaranteed to trigger grimaces and pained expressions among any group of academics. To think of interpreting as relating is to foreground a thematics and poetics of attachment.

This chapter, then, turns to questions of method: *how* actor-network theory ways of thinking can be taken up in the humanities and to what end. Answering this question will require a consideration of both *scale* and *stance*. It's become evident that differing things come together to affect responses to art. But will attending to these factors draw us too far into the terrain of sociology or history? The humanities are traditionally anchored in the study of individual works: most classes, most of the time, delve deeply into a few texts or objects rather than scanning or surveying many. For many scholars of literature, for example, a critical approach does not really count unless it can deliver a new way of reading. Is interpretation an intrinsically small-scale endeavor? Can it be sized up or sized down? Does looking at the things around a work run the risk of weakening or diminishing the work? Here I describe three possible scales of ANT-ish criticism while clarifying my own preference for the midlevel perspective of the "work-net."

Does interpretation, meanwhile, imply a certain stance or posture? What kind of dispositions should scholars and teachers adopt, and what kind of entailments follow? What should we make, for example, of the recent interest in metaphors of listening? And what might it mean to interpret generously or to be more receptive?

Does a choice of stance have implications for what is known and how one comes to know it? And what does knowledge have to do with acknowledgment? Here I supplement my ANT-ish line of thinking by drawing on the insights of David Scott, Toril Moi, and others.

It's worth reiterating that ANT is not a shiny new theory that will redeem us from all the errors of the past. The approaches outlined in this chapter are not especially radical or startling. Rather, I draw out affinities with existing ways of thinking and doing in the humanities, even while proposing a reorientation at the level of language, method, and stance. The point is not to sweep away all other approaches in a war of positions but to forge stronger ties within and beyond academic networks. Such a line of thinking has consequences for teaching as well as research, resonating with the surge of interest in pedagogy. As Rachel Buurma and Laura Heffernan have shown in a series of groundbreaking essays, the history of literary studies looks very different if one focuses on how scholars teach rather than on what they write. (Even the most ardent disciple of impersonality or prophet of antihumanism may contravene their convictions when engaging in a passionate conversation with other humans.) The classroom, after all, is a place where amateur and professional attachments collide and commingle—in ways that speak directly to the concerns of *Hooked*.

Attaching to Works, Attaching to Methods

In a well-known essay, George Steiner offers a gloss on the two figures of the critic and the reader. He contrasts the judicial authority of the critic, who steps back from the text in order to scrutinize and analyze it, to the dynamic passivity of the reader, who wants to be taken over by the text and merge with it. For critics the text is an object to be appraised; for readers it is an encounter defined by closeness and vulnerability.[3] Steiner is talking about ideal types rather than real persons; how has this division between critic and reader been realized in practice? To establish English as a legitimate discipline, for example, it was crucial to distinguish between the everyday enjoyment of literature and its scholarly study—whether as philology, literary history, or close attention to complex form. Yet this institutional stress on rigor was countermanded, for much of the twentieth century, by a belief that literature mattered for society as a whole: that a broad swathe of persons could benefit from its ethical value and transformative power. The postures of what Gerald Graff calls the Scholar and the Generalist—the one committed to rigorous and solitary research, the other to a charismatic style of teaching—could coexist in a single person; René Wellek spoke of professors who "taught graduate students bibliography and sources . . . and meanwhile they read poetry to undergraduates in a trembling or unctuous voice."[4]

Joseph North's *Literary Criticism: A Concise Political History* laments the loss of this dual role: the professional scholar has triumphed over the generalist eager to inspire undergraduates or address larger publics. Over the last few decades, scholarship has become increasingly specialized, its language ever more knotty and forbidding. Publication-for-tenure is skewed toward exercises in contextual explanation that are of interest only to a small cadre of fellow specialists—very few readers, remarks North, read a novel by Virginia Woolf because they want to learn more about the cultural history of the 1920s.[5] It may also involve lengthy accounts of how a text sustains or subverts hegemonic thinking; not many readers open a book, North might have added, because they are anxious to decipher its ideological subtext. That such methods are removed from everyday response is the point—not only because they function as a form of academic credentialing but because scholars often profess their eagerness to countermand the commonsensical and alienate from the ordinary. It is a striking feature of current thought that being scholarly and being subversive are felt to go hand in hand. Such a perception, James Jiang drily remarks, "allows English academics to sleep comfortably at night, safe in the knowledge that their politics vindicates their vocation and their vocation their politics."[6]

Even those who are less sanguine about the political impact of criticism attest to the growing scission of scholarly from lay response. Such a separation seems irreversible; it is via professionalization and specialization that scholarly fields can sustain themselves as scholarly fields and stake claims to being legitimate forms of knowledge. James English puts it bluntly: achieving disciplinary status is a matter of "demonstrating a commitment to requirements, standards, examinations, and credentials."[7] Literary studies, art history, film studies, musicology: such disciplines have carved out a presence by introducing students to significant works, by elucidating the history of these works, and by transmitting advanced skills of interpretation and analysis. That students need to be *trained* to become better readers of books or viewers of paintings—becoming acculturated into new ways of thinking, forms of perception, habits of response—is uncontroversial. Studying literature or art or music is not equivalent to appreciating them; it serves different functions and purposes.

How, then, is a fondness for *Stella Dallas* or Maria Callas relevant to the classroom or the journal article? Indeed, it has often been held that attachment is an *obstacle* to interpretation—that a felt closeness to a work of art will hamper one's ability to analyze it. "Those who are discovering for the first time that poetry can cause them emotion," writes I. A. Richards, "do often, for this very reason, pay little attention to the poetry." Pursuing Richards's line of thought, John Guillory remarks that "much of what we mean now by close reading involves, as we all know, resistance to the seductions of the literary work itself, even the great work."[8] Emotion and seduction, then, as the antithesis of criticism; feeling as a precipitous derailing of thought. Another worry: doesn't the language of attachment buy into the consumerist mind-set that is now plaguing universities, thanks to the corporatization of higher education? Literary studies, especially, has often seen itself as a bulwark against the encroachments of commerce. Yet nowadays, some academics lament, students feel empowered to demand relevance and insist on relatability: enrollments in hip-hop and Harry Potter classes soar while Chaucer and Milton languish. The task of educators is surely to unsettle students—requiring them to grapple with what they find off-putting, opaque, or intractable—rather than pander to their existing likes and dislikes.

Yet attachments, I've argued, encompass far more than immediate gratifications or visceral pleasures: blending, in varying degrees, feeling and thought, the affective and the normative. As conditions of being in the world, they cannot be nailed down to a single cause or culprit, whether the self-absorption of the young or the covert manipulations of capital. As we saw in chapter 2, for example, scholars identify like mad; they are no less invested than others in the works they respond to—indeed, they are often *more* invested—even if the reasons for their investments, and the idioms in which they express them, differ. Meanwhile, Zadie Smith allowed us to see that education is not just a matter of acquiring knowledge or being schooled in critical thinking; it is also a matter of honing sensibilities and sensitivities, of becoming attuned to music or paintings or novels that once left us cold.

Any strong distinction, then, between amateur attachment and scholarly detachment does not hold up. The student who reappraises her youthful enthusiasm for *Jane Eyre* by engaging in a stringent interrogation of its racial politics has not ascended a one-way path from affective surrender to ascetic distance. Rather, she has traded certain ties for others: a newfound pleasure in advanced techniques of reading; the intellectual satisfaction of outwitting a text by reading between the lines; a felt solidarity with Edward Said or with Gayatri Spivak's "Three Women's Texts and a Critique of Imperialism." To point to these attachments is not to minimize the learning that has taken place but to grant that education is also sentimental—that is, involving the sentiments. Critique and interpretation are not opposed to attachment; they are built upon it. As Matt Hills points out, everyone is stuck on something—if not Harry Potter or Jane Austen, then the dogma of Lacanian lack or Deleuzian philosophy.[9]

Yet these are different *kinds* of attachments, someone might object; commitments to methods are intellectually or politically salient in a way that youthful enthusiasms for novels or movies are not. Perhaps—but in weighing up the merits of specific ties, we should keep in mind that there are intellectual and political alternatives to the method of "critical reading." To pin all one's hopes on the analytical payoff of exposing and unmasking is to overlook the possibility that a work of art, approached in a less wary spirit, might also serve as a source of knowledge and a means of acknowledgment. Clarifying what such an observation might entail is one of the tasks of this chapter.

Meanwhile, attachment should not be confused with rubber-stamping what students already like; rather, it faces toward the future as well as the past. Teachers can inspire students to look more closely at images they failed to notice, attune them to sounds they were once unable to hear. We cannot take attachment for granted, as if those who wander into our classrooms are already sold on Beckett or Botticelli, so that we can focus on reining in and disciplining their artless enthusiasm. Our task is not only to teach them to interpret but also—if we want to see them again in our classes—to make them care about what they interpret, to *become* affected and invested. Of course, such an impetus may come from students themselves, who sense the potential value of something they do not yet know how to value. Aspiration is often read cynically as nothing more than social climbing or a desire for economic betterment. Yet it is key to clarifying the puzzle of how we come to care for things we did not previously care for. As philosopher Agnes Callard shows in an illuminating study, it is not about getting what one wants but about learning what one wants: coming to imagine oneself as a different kind of person. And here, forces beyond our control—an inspiring teacher, a charismatic friend, a fortuitous event, getting older—play their part, but so do our own efforts. We need to work our way into having different values, learn to care about new things.[10]

Interpretation, then, cannot be hived off or segregated from the other styles of engagement we've considered. What we choose to decipher, how we decipher it, and to what end—these decisions are driven by what we feel affinity for, what resonates. Interpreting is far from being a purely cognitive exercise. Yet it is also a distinctive kind of activity, honed by long histories of engagement with sacred and secular works. And here two issues come to the fore. Interpretation—in the sense used in this chapter—is *deliberate*, a product of will and intent. Experiences of identifying or becoming attuned, as we saw, are often shaped by factors beyond one's control; they cannot be summoned into existence by sheer force of will. Yet it is possible, as any student knows, to interpret something without caring very much about it. Furthermore, interpretation is *deliberative*; it is not just a matter of assigning meaning but of weighing up the processes by which meaning is assigned. And here, our own attachments can be scrutinized, turned from motives for interpretation into objects of interpretation. This kind of second-order reflection is something that scholars in the humanities routinely engage in—and that also, of course, drives the argument of this book.

And yet being treated in this way does not cause our attachments to vanish. Reflective thought is not like acetone or nail-polish remover, an unsticking agent that miraculously dissolves all ties. Especially salient here is that such ties cut across the line between active and passive; we may feel impelled to think and write in a certain way and yet see this compulsion not as a constraint but as a necessity that we gladly embrace. External pressures on academic thought, such as institutional norms or struggles for professional status, have been amply documented, but there are also more subtle influences at work. As the philosopher Harry Frankfurt remarks, one can feel that one's caring about something—an idea, a person, a work of art—is not altogether under one's own control and yet simultaneously experience this caring, not as an external imposition or burden, but as defining, in a deep sense, who one takes oneself to be. (Luther's declaration: "Here I stand: I can do no other.") It has become what he calls a volitional necessity: something that we feel compelled by, and yet that we hold to be a strength rather than a weakness. An attachment, in short, may turn into a commitment.[11]

If our attachments affect how we interpret, can interpreting alter our attachments? More concretely: is it possible to teach students ways of analyzing texts that open up new experiences of these texts? Methods of analysis are, after all, linked to attitudes and dispositions; they are not just ways of thinking but a means of orienting. The most influential critical schools of the last half century have prized a certain ethos: knowing, vigilant, skeptical, wary. Many scholars are now calling for less guarded postures; there has been a surge of interest in the language of generosity, receptivity, hope, vulnerability. How might such calls be actualized? Even if becoming-attuned cannot be conjured up at will, for example, might certain ways of reading make it more likely? Can we encourage students to become more attached—or differently attached—to literature and art?

Here the example of critique proves instructive. That it promoted a certain ethos or attitude was not the rationale for teaching critical theory but its consequence. Let's read *Discipline and Punish* or *The Political Unconscious* in order to become more paranoid—

said no one ever. Rather, the view of critique as a uniquely rigorous form of thought helped to ensure its uptake across humanistic disciplines. Calling for more positive affects or less guarded postures will not, by itself, provide a compelling alternative unless their intellectual payoff can be clarified. Caring about works of art can prime us to approach them differently—but it is not, in itself, a *replacement* for thinking. How exactly does aesthetic experience connect up to ways of knowing? Is it feasible to interpret in a fashion that is less defensive but still reflective? And can changes in attitude involve a rethinking of method rather than a repudiation of method?

As such phrasing suggests, the focus should remain squarely on practices rather than persons. Teaching as a therapeutic exercise; education as a form of personality management—such ambitions strike me as misplaced. We should think twice—or three times— before requiring students to bare their souls in the classroom: you don't have to be a card-carrying Foucauldian to worry about yoking confessions of feeling to regimes of assessment. Stressing doing rather than being can also help guard against bouts of unearned complacency: humanists patting themselves on the back for creating empathic persons or democratically minded citizens. A tradition of critical theory is at hand to remind us that humans are often self-deluding, intractable, destructive and self-destructive, opaque to themselves and others. Yet concluding that aesthetic response is therefore nothing more than power play is not just cynical but intellectually empty, in erasing differences that matter. We should not be trying to manufacture generous persons, but we can conceivably teach more generous forms of interpretation. What approaches might best align with such an ambition? And how can the insight we've been working toward in this book—that aesthetic experiences are *forged* rather than just *felt*—afford a clearer grasp of what is at stake?

"Interpretation"—a term at the heart of the humanities—has been endlessly defined and debated. According to one line of thought, it underlies everything we might conceivably think, feel, or do. Richard Rorty insists that interpretation goes all the way down; that all awareness is a linguistic awareness; that there is no access to the world that is not filtered via words. For Charles Taylor, human beings are self-interpreting animals, enmeshed within skeins of language, for whom personhood is fundamentally a matter of narrative and self-description. This line of thinking is aptly defined by Richard Shusterman as "hermeneutic universalism": the belief that interpretation subtends and sustains the full spectrum of human experience, that it is inevitable and inescapable.[12]

For others, interpretation is just one option among others, associated with a certain stance: preening, arrogant, overreaching. Susan Sontag, assessing the ascent of Marxist and Freudian methods of reading in the 1960s, famously judged that interpretation had become "reactionary, impertinent, cowardly, stifling."[13] It is tied to a certain topology of the text; digging down below deceptive appearances; prizing core truths or stable foundations. Interpretation differs from poetics, Jonathan Culler remarks, in its pursuit of the meaning (singular) of a work.[14] Wielding their decoder rings, critics hunt down hidden truths and brush past sensuous surfaces. They are oblivious to everything that is *not* interpretation, offering pedestrian or ham-fisted accounts of the subtleties of aesthetic encounters. According to this second line of thought, interpreting is something from which we could—and probably should—desist.

Much of the confusion dissipates once we realize that people are talking about different things or, rather, differing ends of a spectrum. What we can call "strong interpretation" draws out counterintuitive meanings in the service of large-scale explanation and judgment: reading a Hollywood musical, perhaps, as an allegory of post-Fordist America. Weak interpretation, meanwhile, limits itself to less contested aspects of a text: what Sharon Marcus and Stephen Best call its surface. Ellen Rooney takes Best and Marcus to task for their intellectual naivete—for believing that "texts can reveal their own truths because texts mediate themselves."[15] And yet Best and Marcus are hardly denying the elementary hermeneutic point that any engagement with a work relies on assumptions and conventions. What they are challenging, rather, is a certain picture: that the critic's task is to brush past deceptive surfaces in order to excavate hidden truths.

My concern in this chapter is with the loose assortment of hermeneutic methods that make up the contemporary humanities. This optic is narrower than the "interpretation goes all the way down" thesis in its focus on research and teaching, yet it is broader than the equation of interpretation with a single set of metaphors, such as the presumption of depth. Literary studies, art history, film, musicology—all these fields include genres of writing that range from the micro- to the mid- to the macroscale; from fine-grained accounts of a single painting or poem to analyses of genres or artistic movements (film noir, the bildungsroman, Dada, opera), to the placing of works in historical, philosophical, or other contexts. Critics routinely engage in quite varied techniques of describing, deciphering, documenting, commenting, and contextualizing. If we think of interpretation as "treating texts as meaningful" rather than as "assigning a (single) meaning," then all these practices qualify as forms of interpretation. My focus is literary studies, where debates about method have been especially heated in recent years, but I also bring in examples from musicology and film studies that use ANT in illuminating ways.

As becomes vividly clear to anyone who glances at the history of criticism, scholars feel strongly, even passionately, about their methods. Interpretation is not just a mechanism of attachment; it is an *object* of attachment. The New Critics were deeply invested in the intellectual and ethical virtues of irony, paradox, and ambiguity, while waving away any reference to authors' intentions or how readers feel. More recently, critics have wrangled over the merits of Marx versus Foucault, feminism versus queer theory, distant versus close reading. What counts as a good interpretation? What forms of commentary are critically passé? What should we teach our students? Such questions—not just theories in the narrow sense but frameworks, approaches, methods—are of consuming concern, defining a professional persona and forming a sense of intellectual self. They are, to reprise an earlier phrase, what keep scholars up at night.

Lay audiences, meanwhile, have no reason to share such investments; what matters to them are specific books or movies or songs that entertain or educate or, very occasionally, change a life. It is not that such attachments are unmediated—as we've seen, they are forged out of many things coming together. But the effect of these mediations is to increase the allure of the object, to heighten its presence. Faced with examples of academic criticism, such audiences are likely to feel that the artwork is being overshadowed or even obliterated by the apparatus of scholarship. Why such clotted syntax and arcane vocabulary? Why the obsession with turning works of art into *problems*: paradoxical, perplexing, riven by aporias, and in need of investigation? The difference between academic and lay audiences is not one of detachment versus attachment; it is, rather, the difference between attachment to an object and attachment to a method.

Yet, the often-heard complaint that a love of literature has been replaced by "professional strategies of unsentimental analysis" misses a key point: for many scholars from the 1970s onward the turn to political and philosophical approaches was exhilarating and transformative—not the antithesis of love but another form of love. We glommed on to theory not because we were following the diktat of hiring committees but because we were profoundly energized by the questions that theory was asking. Queer theorist Didier Eribon, for example, reflects on the affective impact of Foucault's work on his own life, of the power of books that "call to us" and that "help us to overcome the effects of domination in our own selves."[16] Critical theory was an object of intense cathexis and emotional investment. Things became trickier, however, when "theory" was institutionalized as the obligatory framework for any form of engaging with literature or art. Little room was left for reckoning with the force of aesthetic experience, including its potential to remake thought as well as feeling. Not all knowledge stems from theory.[17]

Humanists, of course, also care deeply about the works they study and teach. Indeed, these attachments are often heightened by the labor of interpretation, fueled by the time and effort that goes into poring over and explicating works of art. Weeks, months, or even years are often spent in conditions of physical proximity and intensive interaction: repeated treks to an art museum to stare intently at a Dürer engraving; scribbling countless notes in the margins of a battered copy of *The Mysteries of Udolpho*; endlessly rewinding and watching the final scene from *Vertigo*. Through ongoing exposure and unflagging attention, the particles of a painting or novel or film get under the skin or seep into the bloodstream; they become an integral part of who we are.

Yet such attachments are rarely professed outright, though they can be glimpsed in the margins of criticism—evident, perhaps, in the meticulous care and detail with which a work is explicated. To pass professional muster, however, they must first be translated into the language of method. An early love of *Jane Eyre* or *Great Expectations* leads a student to graduate school and identification as a Victorianist; at which point it turns out—*mirabile dictu!*—that these same works, when read in the correct manner, will yield up the signs of dissidence or subversion that justify their study. In the contemporary humanities, evaluations of methods or frameworks outnumber—by far—attestations to the merits of individual novels or poems or paintings. Belief in the universality of aesthetic value—the intrinsic superiority of some works to others—was badly shaken up by the culture wars of past decades; there is now a much greater awareness that aesthetic judgments vary. Rather than grasping the nettle of competing values, however, critics took the easier route of a full-scale retreat from value. The question "Is it any good?" has come to sound utterly retrograde, the province of the elderly curmudgeon on the hiring committee rather than a live intellectual issue.

This avoidance of judgment is one of the most obvious differences between professional and lay audiences. Unburdened by authority and worries about being exclusionary, ordinary readers and viewers can be unstinting in their praise and eloquent about their disappointment. Of course, that academics steer clear of explicit judgment does not mean they wriggle free of questions of value. Implicit assessments about artworks (Does this work repay detailed study? Is it aesthetically interesting?) are no less prevalent than in the past. Every syllabus, in a certain sense, constitutes a judgment. Aesthetic evaluation, as Timothy Aubry points out, did not disappear from academic life; it just went underground.[18]

The current hesitation about the humanities can be reframed, in this sense, as a paralysis about how to distribute one's attachments. Is it possible to balance care for a work with care for method? Or is conflict inevitable—a result of the schism between appreciation and serious scholarship? Do current ways of writing have the effect of obscuring or overshadowing our objects rather than allowing them to shine forth? Should we be experimenting with style or voice in order to capture what we care about? Reflecting on the history of cultural studies, Ben Highmore writes that its most striking examples are notable for their vividness and accessibility: blending intellectual seriousness with lightness of presentation and mixing genres (autobiography, history, philosophy) as well as moods. "Should we shift our attention from terms like 'method' and 'theory,'" Highmore wonders, "to thinking about size, shape, angle, breadth, connection, attitude, tone?"[19] Perhaps our critical languages need to become more attuned to their objects.

Scale

Taking up Highmore's invitation, I begin by looking at scale. Humanists have often felt that to do justice to a work of art, it must occupy the fullness of one's attention. What this means, in practice, is devoting one's time and energy to the repeated reading of a handful of works: "tiny portions, meticulously chewed," as Peter Rabinowitz puts it.[20] And yet caring for something can also mean caring for what it's connected to. Generosity and receptivity can manifest themselves at different scales. One of the effects of ANT is to question the assumption that criticism must orient itself to either the very small (a discrete work) or the very large (society, global capitalism). Because associations occur at many different levels, ANT involves no orthodoxies of size, shape, or dimension. In this sense, it speaks directly to the current interest in diversifying the scales of criticism.[21]

Yet this lack of prescription does not free us from choosing but necessitates it. Let's cast our minds back to the passage from Wayne Koestenbaum quoted in chapter 1. Mulling over the puzzle of his affinity with a musical phrase from Brahms, Koestenbaum traces out a tangle of ties: the charisma of a music teacher, the force of a specific performance, memories of his childhood, psychosexual patterns of attraction, knowledge of other composers and music history. Rather than being traceable to a single cause, his attachment is woven out of multiple influences, their relative weight and impact hard to pin down. Koestenbaum's account seems preternaturally attuned to ANT's way of thinking, to what Kyle McGee describes as Latour's mantra: *everything counts.*[22]

And yet—for this very reason—it crystallizes the potential challenges of translating ANT into the protocols of the humanities. Elevated to the status of an interpretive principle and a classroom practice, such a mantra might seem to spell disaster. Squawks of protest from teachers can be anticipated: rather than looking closely at "The Metamorphosis," students would feel inspired to reflect on why Gregor reminds them of an anxious roommate or how their feelings about Kafka were shaped by study abroad in Prague. How could such issues ever be relevant? (An ANT-ish approach would ask a slightly different question: could such factors be *made* relevant?) Factoring in all the ties that shape aesthetic experience is a tall, perhaps an impossible, order, raising questions of scope and manageability.

How, then, are we to choose? One ready-to-hand solution—for literary scholars—is to restrict one's focus to the *networks within literary works*. And here they can draw inspiration from Latour's remark that literature is a vital resource for illustrating the messiness of agency. "Great novels," he writes, "disseminate the sources of actions in a way that the official philosophy available at their time is unable to follow."[23] Such novels drive home how many actors are needed to make things happen while documenting the miscalculations, gaffes, and omissions that characterize even the most successful action. Latour's go-to example is *War and Peace*. Tolstoy's portrayal of a decisive battle in the Napoleonic Wars brilliantly captures the chaos and disorder of war: how solders are unprepared, orders are misunderstood, and events fail to unfold as planned. It takes Tolstoy eight hundred pages, Latour remarks, to give back to the multitude the agency that the historians of his century placed in the hands of a few great men. Not only does Tolstoy poke holes in a hagiographic history (which reduces the battle to an encounter between Napoleon and Kutuzov), but he serves Latour as a model for rethinking how science works. Ideas do not propel themselves forward by their own power; scientists, however brilliant, are helpless if their experiments are not supported by a gaggle of allies, accomplices, and helpers; and in being mediated, their ideas are inevitably translated and transformed.

Picking up on this line of thought, Gabriel Hankins pursues what he calls a compositionist aesthetics of reading that traces out the entanglement of humans and nonhumans within the borders of literary works. How, for example, might ANT enrich our understanding of modernism? Turning to *Jacob's Room*, Hankins looks at the part played by everyday objects in Woolf's novel; although supporting actors rather than stars, they are indispensable for all kinds of action. A character writes a letter and ferrets in her bag for a stamp—nothing could be simpler than a stamp, Hankins remarks, and yet nothing is more modern or globalizing, linking her to worldwide networks. The letter cannot carry out its anticipated function without the aid of a stamp, an envelope, a writing instrument, an address; the agency of Woolf's character is displaced downward to the overlooked yet essential pen as well as upward to the institutional structures of the postal service. Awarding attention to the most commonplace of objects, novels give eloquent testimony to the force of things, weaving their characters into dense meshes of dependence on the material world.

Shifting his attention to Rilke's poem "Archaic Torso of Apollo," Hankins again traces out a constellation of human and nonhuman actors, noting a "binding together of its vividly disjunctive elements: torso, god, organ of sight; household object, genitals, fur of a wild animal; fragmented stone, exploding star; ethical injunction."[24] Here phenomena are connected not via narrative— humans and nonhumans working together to engineer chains of cause and effect—but through metaphor—the dissident yoking and splicing together of disparate worlds. The damaged statue is juxtaposed to furred pelt and astral explosion; Rilke's poem forges ties—of symbolism and sound, of assonance and rhyme—between humans, gods, animals, art, ethics. Rather than being graspable via a single framework—as a subjective expression of lyrical consciousness or a culpable evasion of economic conditions—Rilke's poem reassembles phenomena from multiple worlds. It slices across divisions of nature/culture, sacred/profane, human/animal, and thought/matter, bringing differing modes of being into intimate coexistence.

Focusing on a discrete work and looking closely at how it composes a world out of specific combinations of words—such an approach resonates with what many critics care about. Close reading remains a preferred method in literary studies, an object of intense cathexis and a defining aspect of intellectual identity and claims to expertise. "Throughout the twentieth century," remarks Barbara Herrnstein Smith, "whatever the mood, motive, or materials, if one was teaching literature or doing literary criticism in the Anglo-American literary academy, one was likely to be reading at least some individual texts closely."[25] (There are analogous formalist traditions in musicology and art history.) Yet this way of reading can take on very different colorations, depending on the second-order frameworks that sustain it. Jonathan Culler, for example, wants to underscore the opacity of literary texts: their resistance to interpretation. Reading closely—which is, for Culler, synonymous with reading deconstructively—becomes a matter of testifying, over and over, to the sheer difficulty and intractability of language.[26] A close reading beholden to a Freudian or Marxist schema, meanwhile, acknowledges a resistance only to finally overcome it, wresting counterintuitive truths from the depths of the text.

An ANT-ish close reading does not conceive of language as opposed to meaning or assume that texts are bent on deception or fraud. Rather, it asks: What is connected to what? What are the salient actors and how are they attached? And here nothing can be automatically excluded: fictional characters, figures of speech, physical objects, supernatural beings, philosophical ideas, generic conventions, physical landscapes, or patterns of metaphors. These are very different kinds of phenomena, to be sure—and their differences are to be respected—but they are connected and coexistent rather than parceled out into opposed realms. In tracing these entanglements, Hankins strives to account for what is present rather than reading against the grain. This is one form of receptivity: not interpreting a text without preconceptions—a sheer impossibility—but striving to pay attention to what Rilke and Woolf pay attention to. As a form of reading, it is close but not deep; it describes rather than explains.[27]

While ANT is passionately interested in things, lumping it under the "new materialist" banner misses the mark: hammers and tables are no more real than Harry Potter and the goddess Athena. As we've seen, ANT's flat ontology is designed to skirt dichotomies of language versus matter, subjects versus objects, fiction versus reality, or humans versus things. At one point, Hankins remarks that "a constant swirl of furniture, books, lovers, prejudices, social institutions, and landscapes" surrounds the protagonist of *Jacob's Room*. Such jumbled lists of seemingly random phenomena are a much-favored ANT technique, a way of wrenching us out of familiar ways of sorting and classifying. Like a good Latourian anthropologist, "Woolf gives us individuals, institutions, objects, and ideologies in the process of formation, in active co-articulation."[28] Networks are hybrid; they involve many kinds of actors working together.

Yet to conclude that ANT's only relevance for humanists lies in delivering new styles of close reading would be to halt the trade far too soon. Networks do not end at the borders of texts; things pass in both directions. Any perception of a single work as a self-contained unit—its walls impermeable and unscalable—clashes with ANT's emphasis on the primacy of relations. What about the ties that bind aspects of one text or work to another? Or to their creators, to audiences, to reviewers, to institutions? Close reading directs us to the words on the page; yet critics may want to raise their eyes from the page and ask how these words connect to a larger world.

To look, in other words, at *works within networks* and to ask: How do novels, paintings, films, songs, hook up to other kinds of actors? How do these ties facilitate art's uptake and its influence? Again, such questions are hardly unprecedented. ANT's interest in the empirical details of how art is made, disseminated, and received links up to existing traditions of historical and archival work in the humanities. In nineteenth-century literary studies, for example, Leah Price's *How to Do Things with Books in Victorian Britain* and Tom Mole's *What the Victorians Made of Romanticism* offer the kind of richly textured attention to material artifacts and their movements that an ANT scholar might applaud. And in the context of art history, Svetlana Alpers's *Rembrandt's Enterprise: The Studio and the Market* is lauded by Latour for its meticulous tracing of how visual culture changed over time: the simultaneous transformation of science, art, the theory of vision, and the organization of crafts and economic powers.[29]

There are parallels here to Benjamin Piekut's creation of what he calls an ANT-inspired historical ecology of music. What is required for music to exist? Piekut asks. Instruments built with care, craft, and materials; techniques of annotation, recording, and amplification that extend its reach across space and time; humans and machines that translate musical codes into sound; the training and rehearsing of performers; regimes of meaning that allow music to be interpreted; audience reactions that swirl together physical, emotional, and mental response. Fully in the spirit of ANT, he observes that music is a powerful actor—it makes a massive difference—yet it can gain this strength only through its many associations with other phenomena. The task of the critic is to trace out, with empirical precision, these "promiscuous associations that spill across conventional parsings of the world."[30]

Neither *The Magic Flute* nor "Blowin' in the Wind," then, can be viewed in isolation; coactors are needed to discern the metaphysical subtleties of Mozart or to fuel an obsession with hunting down Dylan bootlegs. Yet the salience of these coactors is specified by the music they interact with; we cannot know in advance which networks will count. ANT's tracing of relations differs from a traditional view of context, as an enframing reality that is already given, that precedes—historically and analytically—the phenomenon being analyzed, which only needs to be shoehorned into the relevant container. Things, Latour remarks, routinely escape their boxes; arrows of causality get twisted or torn; actors do not line up in orderly fashion for a group photo.[31] Rather than treating an artwork as a microcosm of the world—a faithful or deceptive reference to a prior reality—we need to trace out how it hooks up with audiences to *make* worlds.

That a musical avant-garde appeared in Europe in the late nineteenth century, for example, was a matter not just of the Hegelian bent of influential music critic Karl Franz Brendel but of its mediation via printed copies of the *Neue Zeitschrift für Musik*, which reached certain readers but not others: pulled together, perhaps, in a network that included a late-afternoon reading of the newspaper plus a *Wiener mélange* at Café Central. A young guitarist named Fred Frith stumbled across a work by John Cage in a Cambridge bookstore and incorporated its ideas into compositions for his experimental rock group Henry Cow; yet these ideas took on different shadings in hooking up with Frithian idées fixes that were entirely unknown to Cage. Things drift; they get twisted up, misconstrued, repurposed, compromised, or revised.[32] The Jazz Composers Guild in the United States—another of Piekut's examples—decided in the 1960s to remain an all-black organization. The guild acted as a collective agent, yet its agency was dispersed, both internally (individual members disagreed about the risks of interracial membership) and externally, its ideas translated via various collaborators, including a much-noted issue of the US jazz magazine *Downbeat*. Individuals, collectives, and materials come together to make things happen; agency is delegated and distributed; it unfolds fitfully in time and space.[33]

Piekut's analysis of how music comes to exist is highly illuminating, yet it's possible, I've suggested, to think along similar lines without mentioning ANT. In *The Afterlives of Walter Scott*, for example, Ann Rigney traces out the national and international networks that proliferated around Scott's work—how he became an immortal writer, and then ceased to be one. Her topics include critical commentaries, dramatizations of his plays, and oil paintings of iconic scenes from *Waverley* and *Rob Roy*, but also how his novels inspired the names of ships and streets, roses and potatoes, and were turned into movies and computer games. The name of Scott became a way of shaping space (the Scott monument in Edinburgh, his home Abbotsford as tourist destination, discourses of nation building and Scottish exceptionalism) as well as time (attitudes to modernization, cultural memory, and nostalgia). Instead of taking a discrete text as her unit of analysis, Rigney follows Scott's works as they travel across media and spin out into material culture and everyday life. Here again, entanglements are conceived of as a strength rather than a weakness; the *mobility* of Scott's work (its transportability and ability to hook new audiences) was tied to its *monumentality* (its exemplary status as a cultural reference point and source of collective values).[34]

Rigney's book and Piekut's essay embody a style of thinking that moves easily between interpretive and empirical methods. Similar ways of proceeding can be found in British cultural studies, which contests the view—an article of faith among some humanists—that a close reading of a novel, film, or painting will somehow disclose the essence of the social reality in which it is embedded. (As if the ingenious interpretation of a handful of artworks could replace all the accumulated insights of the social sciences! This is the kind of disciplinary hubris that Larry Grossberg dubs "reading the world in a grain of sand.")[35] If we are interested in how works relate to the world, cultural studies insists, the answer cannot be found by burrowing into a single work in search of hidden links between society and artistic form that will reveal themselves to the prescient critic. Rather, we need to read *across* texts, audiences, institutions—benefiting from the resources of sociology, anthropology, and history in order to trace how works link up to the world. (Cultural studies is also fond of hooks!)

Looking at things around the work, it should be stressed, need not imply any diminishing or lessening of respect for the work. Rigney's book, for example, demonstrates ample care and concern for Scott—not by a close analysis of passages from his novels but by tracing the many paths of their movement through the world. Here Joseph North's depiction of cultural history as a form of dry scholasticism aimed at tenure committees that sails over the heads of ordinary readers needs to be qualified. Everything depends on how such material is presented; think, for example, of the waves of enthusiasm for literary tourism and the avid consumption of authors' biographies. When pitched appropriately, historical materials can incite public interest in literature and art rather than dampen it—see the recent success of Devoney Looser's *The Making of Jane Austen*.

And yet, in the days when I'd proselytize for cultural studies and its tracing of the ties between works and the world, I'd get occasional pushback from my academic audience. "What you are saying is all very well and good," someone would grumble, "you may even be right—but how can I possibly *teach* this way?" Curricula in the humanities, as I've noted, are still largely organized around engagements with exemplary works. Teachers of literature, for example, may feel they have their work cut out for them in transmitting the basics of textual analysis: point of view, narrative structure, forms of irony, conventions of genre, how sound affects meaning. Literary works are complicated enough in themselves! How can students read *Beloved* with the sustained attention and effort that such a challenging work demands if much of the class time is being allotted to tracing the cultural or material networks in which *Beloved* is positioned? And how can English majors—drawn to the subject, after all, by an interest in literature—juggle analysis of a work with attention to institutions, the reactions of reviewers or disparate audiences, and the history of ideas in the space of a five- to ten-page essay?

I used to wave away such questions as tangential, but I've come to appreciate that they are fundamental. When it comes to the merits of paying close attention to novels, paintings, or films, most humanists are unlikely to budge, insisting that meaning cannot be disentangled from the precise details of form and figuration. Clarifying the mode of existence of art, I argued in chapter 1, means honoring the form of the work and the experience of the work. Yet it also involves the "ways of doing" of the relevant scholarly fields, which shape how knowledge of literature and art is conceived, established, and passed on. Institutional and disciplinary ties are no less salient than any other kind. In literary studies, for example, close reading retains a defining place, while film studies, art history, and musicology also pay meticulous attention to individual works. This orientation toward the single object is one that many humanists are attached to: that they see as fundamental to their discipline and that they will passionately defend. One might call it a felicity condition for the creation of humanistic knowledge.

Work-Nets

Can we balance concern for specific works with attention to how these works are co-made? Can we speak well of art and literature while also redescribing them in ANT-ish ways? I'm moving here, as readers will realize, toward a rationale for my own way of going about things. *Hooked* has enlisted a throng of novels, plays, films, and memoirs as sources of insight, attending to their affordances and their presence, but it has not vaulted from one extended close reading to the next. And while it occasionally gestures toward broader constellations—such as the role of *Thelma and Louise* in forming a feminist public sphere—the argument is not built around large-scale historical or sociological analysis. (My next book will come at some of these issues via an engagement with the contemporary Frankfurt School.) Rather, I've adopted a midlevel perspective that links works to the fine-grained analysis—phenomenological and sociological—of aesthetic experiences.

Looking at things closely is not guaranteed to make us more ethical, subtle, or sensitive; surveying things from afar does not automatically deliver greater insight or command of the field. The choice of optic can be made only on pragmatic grounds: what questions are being asked and why do they matter? And here, my preference for a midscale perspective in this book has been driven by two convictions. First, such a perspective gets short shrift in the recurring spats between formalists and historicists; humanities scholars are more comfortable dealing with either the very small (individual poems, paintings, films) or the very large (society, capitalism, imperialism) than with interfaces between works and persons.[36] And second, these interfaces are nonetheless key to clarifying why literature and art are worth attending to. People become attached to novels or films or songs because of how they are made to think or feel, because their sensibility is reattuned or their mental coordinates are shifted.

Rather than looking at networks within works or works within networks, *Hooked* has hovered in the space between, at the level of the *work-net*: the cluster of relations that most directly impact aesthetic experience. Latour once joked that we should talk about "worknets" rather than networks—a flip that could help defamiliarize an overused word while also highlighting the sheer amount of labor and effort needed to keep any group of actors connected. In a recent book, Anne-Marie Mai flips this coinage again to refurbish it and make it newly salient for humanists. The quasi-religious fervor with which Dylan fans talk about *Blood on the Tracks* attests to the irreplaceable role of his voice, lyrics, and guitar playing—but what, Mai wonders, of the somber tone of the album cover, the vibe in the record store where it was bought, the reactions of friends, that it was the first record bought with one's own allowance or to protest against one's parents' tastes in music? How did these various aspects come together?[37]

To speak of the work-net, then, is to emphasize those ties that form *around* works of art and that pertain most directly to their effects, to investigate the forms and textures of aesthetic experience. This means attending to the affordances of novels and paintings and paintings and films, but also to how artworks are co-made. It is to draw from the resources of aesthetics, phenomenology, and sociology without pledging one's allegiance to any one of these fields, to acknowledge the force of aesthetic immediacy while tracing mediations. Such a midlevel scale, in short, is best suited to delving into the specifics of attachment.

Let's see how this line of thinking plays out in the field of film studies. What is admirable about ANT, contends Claudia Breger, is a democratic ethos that bridges divisions between studies of film technology, production, reception, and film aesthetics. Breger is interested in what she calls cinematic world making: a process of assembling "heterogeneous but entangled elements—including affects, associations, bodies, gestures, matter, memories, perceptions, sensations, things, topoi, and tropes—via images, words, and sounds in the communicative networks of composition, production, and spectatorship."[38] All kinds of things influence what a film is and what it does: the guiding force of genre schemas; the hard work of film editors or light technicians; the buzz of anticipation that is created by agents or advertisers; whether a movie is watched at the Cineplex or on a smartphone screen.

Yet even as she gestures to the many actors that help make film's meanings and effects, Breger hews, for the most part, to a midscale focus on films and persons. And here she points to affinities between ANT and the phenomenological aesthetics of Vivian Sobchack, who connects material aspects of film, including the camera and projector, to the involvement of viewers. Both ways of thinking assume what Breger calls a "non-sovereign subject"—that is to say, persons being shaped by the very phenomena with which they interact. While ANT steers clear of a phenomenology that plumbs deep structures of consciousness, it is deeply interested in accounting for what people are attached to. "That persons are networked does not prevent us from respecting what is given in their experience"— here Breger's remark resonates with my own case for giving equal weight to forms of mediation and the sense of immediacy.

Breger applies this stance of "critical proximity" to *Western* (2017), directed by Valeska Grisebach. At the diegetic level Breger shows how ANT's tracing of networks resonates with the themes of her chosen film. No strenuous reading against the grain is needed to see *Western*'s portrayal of German workers building a hydroelectric power station in rural Bulgaria as dealing with asymmetrical relations between human and nonhuman actors and neocolonial ties between the inhabitants of Western and Eastern European states. Yet Breger also folds film analysis into a consideration of audience response, suggesting that *Western*'s narrative and expressive use of close-ups solicits a diffuse array of affective reactions that have little to do with critical distance—even as Grisebach's deployment of the conventions of the Western genre is respectful, even loving, rather than parodic. As a result, any preconceptions "about racist working-class (East) German men are broken down into ambivalent relations with the complicated protagonist and the real-life actor embodying him," inviting audience responses that may encompass interest, empathy, anger, disconcertment, and more.[39] It is only in being actualized that the film's repertoire of affective and cognitive possibilities can unfold.

Receptive/Reflective

This midlevel focus requires an explicit reckoning with stance: How does orientation shape one's relation to novels and paintings and films? What *difference* does stance make? What, for example, might it mean to be receptive to a work of art? Receptivity has often been equated with the passivity invoked by George Steiner, with the intense absorption and surrender that are hallmarks of recreational reading. It might seem, in this sense, to imply an abdication of agency and thought. But being receptive, as Jonathan Mayhew points out, is not synonymous with being appreciative; it involves a translation of experience into an intellectual register, as well as an openness to what may seem alien or off-putting—a reflective receptivity, perhaps, that takes the form of clarifying what it means to be reoriented by a work of art.[40]

Being open or receptive is a longstanding theme in the history of hermeneutics. Here, however, it is sometimes kitted out with a host of assumptions that might cause any ally of ANT to blanch. The disclosure of aesthetic truth is opposed to a soulless use of technique or method; a hermeneutic openness to the nature of being is exalted over the instrumental calculations of the sciences. Yet we can jettison any such claims to exceptionalism and their idealist baggage—what Latour calls the dichotomy of warm feeling versus frozen knowledge—while retaining certain insights from Gadamer, Ricoeur, and others. From a hermeneutic perspective, for example, the fixation on otherness and difference that characterizes much current thinking about literature and ethics—for example, in its deconstructive versions—can only seem misplaced. Critics strive to efface their own presence in order to throw the spotlight onto the form and language of a text. By stressing the alterity of literature, they strive to render it tamper-proof, to protect it from any form of appropriation, to honor its opacity as a linguistic artifact.

Here hermeneutics and ANT would gang up to insist that such an approach misses the mark. Works cannot be cordoned off from those who actualize them; they are *constituted* via the act of reception. This interaction is not just a one-sided violation; it can also be an act of exposure, as Michel Chaouli points out, where one puts oneself into a position to be affected in ways one cannot entirely predict.[41] Influence, in short, goes in both directions: in appropriating a work of art, we may also be disappropriated of parts of ourselves, altered by an encounter with unexpected possibilities. Such a change is a matter not just of the disorienting qualities of art—the shock of the unfamiliar—but also of the reorienting force of narratives, forms, ideas, values, and meanings. And for a work to (partially) remake who we are, we must also co-make it.

While Chaouli writes from a hermeneutic perspective, his argument chimes with the ANT-ish line of thinking embraced by art historian Dan Karlholm. "The default mode of artworks is *sleep mode*. Age-old or brand-new, they all await the wake-up call of actualization . . . based on the motivated interest we bestow upon them, to disrupt their inherent sleepiness and to realize their being through our encounter with them."[42] Rather than threatening or destroying works of art, our "motivated interests" allow them to come to life. To be sure, there is no guarantee of illumination through such encounters, and certainly not the slightest hope of levitating out of our condition as finite, error-prone beings. And yet such an actualization offers one possible way of learning new things about oneself and the world.

A recent book that left its mark on me—and that speaks eloquently to the question of stance—is *Stuart Hall's Voice: Intimations of an Ethics of Receptive Generosity*. Here David Scott offers a testimony to the life and work of Stuart Hall, a founding figure of British cultural studies. Their long friendship, Scott remarks, was defined by familiarity and difference: a sense of kinship in the shared condition of being Jamaican émigrés, yet a displacement that was experienced differently in terms of generation and location, as well as intellectual allegiances. "Our conceptual languages," writes Scott, "though not necessarily at odds, were never identical to each other, were never seamlessly in harmony"; "they stood somewhat at an angle to each other."[43] The book is an attempt to find a register for honoring this similarity-in-difference.

Stuart Hall's Voice is made up of six chapters written as letters—a format chosen, Scott writes, to capture the virtues and sentiments of an intellectual friendship, the ebb and flow of a decades-long conversation. These letters call up Hall's way of speaking and thinking, pose questions to him, reminisce about evenings spent around a dining table in London. And they avoid the usual format for engaging another scholar's ideas: registering points of agreement before turning to the inevitable tally of shortcomings and omissions. Scott writes: "in the following letters I will offer you a contrast between a 'critical self' who is an agent of critique, and a 'listening self' who is an agent of attunement and receptivity, and suggest that you, Stuart, were as much the latter as the former, possibly even more so the latter than the former."[44]

While Hall is often hailed as the consummate example of a politically engaged intellectual, Scott is less interested in Hall's views than in his way of having views. Not his theory of contingency but his attunement to the contingent. Irrespective of the point he was making, Scott writes, there was something distinctive about Hall's way of *taking his bearings*. For Hall, speaking was a mode of thinking on the move, not a delivery system for already formulated ideas but an ingrained responsiveness. What he embodied, above all, was a distinct manner of listening-thinking-being. The terms that Scott returns to repeatedly, that make up the scaffolding of his book, are "voice," "listening," "style," "ethos," "disposition." What he prizes in Hall is an "an ethics of receptivity and reciprocal attunement."[45]

Here we begin to see how a term we've considered in an aesthetic sense—experiences of coming to "get" Joni Mitchell or Matisse or Tarkovsky—might also bear on the textures of thought and argument. Becoming-attuned, Scott suggests, is necessary in order fully to hear what someone is saying. It is a precondition for the receptive generosity that is crystallized in Hall's example: where generosity is not about giving but receiving, about allowing oneself to be reoriented by others. A similar ethos inflects Scott's own writing: its use of the second person; its reliance on italics to simulate the strains and stresses of speech; its circling rhythms of venturing-testing-querying-describing, as he checks in with Hall to see if he has got something right. Scott models a form of thinking that is effortful and deeply engaged—and yet that declines to stand over or to see through.

A style of writing, then, that strives toward something other than critique—and yet no one would call Scott, who's written on topics ranging from Jamaican politics to tragic finitude, a naively upbeat or optimistic thinker. *Stuart Hall's Voice* cites other writers interested in listening and receptivity—Adriana Cavarero, Romani Coles, and David Levin—and these citations could easily be multiplied. Lamenting that philosophy has become a forensic process of detecting flaws in other thinkers' ideas, Michelle Boulos Walker calls for a turn to slow reading as a "wondrous appreciation rather than an authoritative account; as an attentive listening rather than a closed mind."[46] And writing to his fellow political theorists, Nikolas Kompridis objects to the assumption that receptivity is akin to passivity, that "being receptive is akin to being mindless, to being in a state of unmindedness."[47] Being receptive may require *more* thought and effort rather than less.

That philosophers, political theorists, and anthropologists (Scott's home discipline) are turning to questions of listening and receptivity is worth noting. But how, we might wonder, can such ways of thinking be translated into the study of art, literature, or music? They often stress attitude rather than method—they may even claim to be against method. And yet humanists are, after all, specialists in interpretation. We cannot simply shrug off the question of *how* to explicate works of art, even if we have qualms about applying prefabricated templates: a Marxist reading of X or a Foucauldian reading of Y. A stress on sensibility may simply be too thin for our purposes; telling students to be more generous or receptive will not, itself, get us very far. How can these ideas be translated into specific practices? How, for example, might we take Adriana Cavarero's reflections on inclination—as denoting a taste or preference and a physical posture of leaning toward—and turn them into something students can use? Rather than fragmenting subjects, Cavarero remarks, perhaps we could try bending them, explore ways of relating that do not deny affiliation and vulnerability.[48] Can such postures of caring and inclining be reconciled with an institutional boilerplate of "critical thinking" and "transferable skills"? The implications of stance for higher education and scholarly knowledge need to be thought through.

It is hard to object, for example, to Kathleen Fitzpatrick's recent rallying cry for more generosity in academia: her diagnosis of an overly competitive mind-set that rewards snark, suspicion, and styles of argument that are bent on proving everyone else wrong.[49] And yet demanding that students perform generous readings seems oddly counterproductive: how generous can such readings be when they are carried out at the teacher's behest or to safeguard one's GPA? Indeed, what could it even mean to assess an essay for its generosity? Here the gap between ethical and bureaucratic-administrative spheres is at its widest; they stare at each other in incomprehension across an abyss. Heather Love writes: "literary scholars have been in the business of asking people to care more, and care better. This is the kind of thing that is easy to claim but hard to test, prove, or teach. We might focus instead on teaching people the arts of noticing, or concrete techniques for how to pay attention to texts and the world."[50] (Fitzpatrick goes in a related direction when she focuses on practices rather than persons.) For similar reasons I prefer the language of orientation to that of ethically inflected emotion; while "receptivity" involves attention and a willingness to reassess one's beliefs, it does not further stipulate the content of response.

An example may prove clarifying. In a recent seminar I assigned Eva Hoffman's memoir *Lost in Translation* alongside classic essays of transnational and postcolonial theory by Kwame Anthony Appiah, Linda Hutcheon, and Arjun Appadurai that I've often taught before. The cumulative effect of these essays is to implant a sharpening skepticism about ideas of nation, race, and ethnicity—now relegated to cultural constructs in need of sustained interrogation. Class discussion soon turns into a relentless questioning of the desire to belong, exposing the Romantic-regressive underpinnings of the desire for home. We find ourselves sliding toward a language of hybridity over identity, of transnational flows over rooted selves.

Adding *Lost in Translation* to the syllabus altered, and enriched, the tenor of our discussion. Hoffman's account of a young Polish-Jewish woman who moves to Canada and later to the United States is certainly concerned with conflicting allegiances, yet it also captures the anguish of dislocation and the losses of migration in ways that the theoretical essays do not begin to acknowledge. Describing her departure from Poland at the age of fifteen, Hoffman writes: "I am suffering my first severe attack of nostalgia, or *tesknota*, a word that adds to nostalgia the tonalities of sadness and longing. . . . [I]t comes upon me like a visitation from a whole new geography of emotions, an annunciation of how much an absence can hurt."[51] The phrase "geography of emotions" is telling; Hoffman's attachment to the country of her birth is not just mental but affective and visceral: not in the sense of unmediated but in being emotionally compelling and impossible to brush off. While nostalgia often gets a bad press in the humanities, *Lost in Translation* purposefully dwells on the affective force of what it means to be tied to a country and a language. Hoffman remarks that for her, as a Jewish person, Polish patriotism is not an option, and yet "the country of my childhood lives within me with a primacy that is a form of love."[52]

Hoffman's memoir has been taken to task for its shortcomings, such as its failure to thoroughly engage the history of Polish anti-Semitism. Her "passionate attachment to her idealized image of Cracow, her loyalty to Polish culture," laments Madeline Levine, "seem part and parcel of this avoidance."[53] Marianne Hirsch writes of being moved by Hoffman's memoir—experiencing a tearful moment of recognition—only to ultimately resist any identification, coming to see Hoffman's nostalgia for Poland as a form of denial. "Thinking about my own experience, I want her to see that in Poland, as a child, she was already divided, already, in some ways, not uniquely, not fully herself."[54] Hoffman's memoir, she suggests, is based on misperceptions that need correction. But another possibility offers itself: that one might *come* to identify with Hoffman's perspective or find oneself reattuned by the sensuous gravity and clarity of her style. In doing so, one might discern not an avoidance of truth but another form of truth. What would it mean, in Scott's terms, to *listen* to *Lost in Translation*?

Hoffman comments on the glibness with which ideas of difference are sometimes invoked in literary theory. Otherness is easily entertained as an intellectual proposition, she remarks, while turning out to be far more painful in practice: when one is engaging with another human being who is clamoring to be understood. And how much more so when one is a stranger in a new country, thrown into a world governed by unfathomable rules and opaque conventions! "For all our sophisticated deftness at cross-cultural encounters," she writes, "fundamental difference, when it is staring at you across the table from within the close-up face of a fellow human being, always contains an element of violation."[55] Speaking back to a critical discourse that idealizes disruption and disorientation, Hoffman suggests that such terms have a limited purchase as touchstones for living a life. Nostalgia is not an intellectual mistake but an emotional reality that *Lost in Translation* conveys in all its affective complexity and poetic intensity, its loving exaggerations and its melancholic attachments. Not only does Hoffman care about Poland, but—to reprise an earlier motif—she cares that she cares about Poland.

And if a reader is drawn to Hoffman's work, these attachments may impinge upon her and perhaps reorient her. It is here that we begin to see how receptivity can have consequences for thought. If a work exists only as an object to be deciphered, its impact will be attenuated; as Ricoeur writes in a harsh but vivid metaphor, it is treated as a "cadaver handed over for autopsy."[56] Any knowledge is circumscribed by parameters that are already given. And yet a work of art has the potential to alter what we know and how we know it. There is not just a disorientation but a reorientation, a shifting of affective, perceptual, or mental coordinates. Such a shift cannot occur if interpreting is nothing more than decoding, but neither is it a matter of allowing oneself to be carried away by one's feelings. (This is another way of not listening.) Tobias Skiveren notes that what touches or moves us is not simply pre-given; we can learn to be affected by literature if we engage with it in certain ways.[57] To "learn to be affected" is something other than critical knowingness or mindless absorption.

Lost in Translation, for example, reoriented my perspective, schooling me in a different sensibility. As someone with two passports, a green card, and no strong affiliation to a country (I left England in my early twenties without regret or even reflection), I came to Hoffman's memoir as a stranger. Her intense attachment to the home of her childhood is affectively foreign to me. But *Lost in Translation* allowed me to grasp more fully—in the sense of inhabiting from within, knowing *how* something is rather than *that* something is—what it means to have ties to a home, a language, a country. Such a reattunement does not occur automatically—as we've seen, many factors shape whether we get or fail to get a work of art. But if it happens, it has implications for what we know and how we know it. And as philosopher Jenefer Robinson points out, readers' attitudes can be changed not only by adopting new beliefs but also by "unexpected physiological responses, non-cognitive affective appraisals, shifts in focus of attention, the perception of new aspects of situations, and the revelation of previously hidden wants and interests."[58] We do not need to reach for grandiose claims about literature and art making us more ethical or fully human—but we *can* argue that they offer ways of knowing that are harder to access by other means.

In *Uses of Literature* I tackled the question of what it is that literature allows us to know. Among its many affordances are a tracing of the unspoken or subterranean nuances of human interaction; a capacity to ventriloquize many different languages, idioms, and styles of expression; and techniques of description that allow ordinary objects to shimmer in a transformed light.[59] Yet the possibility of gaining any kind of knowledge through literature requires a prior acknowledging, a willingness to be receptive. Rather than asking, "What does this work fail to see?" one can ask, "What is this work forcing me to notice?" Rather than deploying political or philosophical perspectives to interpret a work, one considers how it might alter or reframe those perspectives.

Reading as a practice of acknowledgment is discussed by Toril

Moi; it is a way of freeing our minds, she writes, from the belief that the critic's task is to impose theories or frameworks on literature. (The same argument can easily be extended to art and music.) The distinction between knowledge and acknowledgment is central to Stanley Cavell's work; the skeptic, who is fixated on the problem of knowledge (how can anything ever be known?), is oblivious to the question of acknowledgment: the relations and obligations in which he or she is entangled. As Moi points out, acknowledgment is not an operation performed by a subject on an object; nor is it driven by a desire for certainty (even the certainty that there is no certainty). "If reading is a practice of acknowledgment, then reading requires us to discover our own position in relation to the work."[60] Here the question of stance is unavoidable rather than optional or peripheral.

Acknowledgment is not a replacement for, or supplement to, knowledge; rather, as Moi points out, it *"changes the dimension in which we assess our understanding of others"*—including those "others" that are novels or films or pieces of music.[61] In acknowledging the claims of *Lost in Translation* I find myself reattuned—acquiring a deeper understanding of a desire for home that has implications, both existential and political, extending well beyond Hoffman's work. I am rather more favorably inclined than Moi appears to be to the language of method; skills of humanistic analysis—attending to composition or narrative style or mise-en-scène or point of view—can be formalized and taught and they help make acknowledgment possible. They are, however, repurposed to different ends—not to decipher an object but to make sense of a relation. For example, Michaela Bronstein remarks, style is no longer viewed as "a static object of analysis, but as . . . managing and controlling a reader's experiences and mental processes. Style is . . . the underlying cause of readerly symptoms and sympathies."[62] We are impelled to ask what the affordances of art *do* (a question built into the idea of affordances, as distinct from the language of form). And this "doing" cannot be explained via a giant's leap from a single work to a social structure; it must account for the audiences—those unavoidable intermediaries!—through which a novel or a film or a painting must pass. How does a text solicit certain forms of identifications? Or stimulate new sensations, perception, and thought?

And we can begin to see how differing forms of attachment are intertwined. That critics are drawn to decipher certain works depends on what takes hold. How does a work hook up with the inclinations or affinities of those who engage with it? Reckoning with such successful or failed connections can give us a more comprehensive picture of how interpretation happens. And yet education—not only of students but of those who teach them—can also mean coming to appreciate what one was previously indifferent to. The student who arrives in graduate school as a modernist is converted, after a memorable Chaucer class, into a passionate medievalist; the professor drafted into teaching an introduction to film studies becomes, to her own surprise, a devotee of *Imitation of Life* or *Mildred Pierce*. Such reorientations are less a matter of making things happen than of letting things happen: a letting-happen that, as Nikolas Kompridis remarks, is not a denial of agency but another form of agency. Receptivity is a thought-filled rather than thoughtless engagement.[63] Being exposed to unfamiliar works or being exposed differently to familiar ones; learning new languages of analysis and habits of attention; becoming attuned to the formal composition and intricate subtleties of a previously unnoted poem or painting—such practices of engagement and interpretation can alter the vectors of our attachments.

To the Classroom

We are seeing a surge of interest in the practice of teaching; once seen as unglamorous and intellectually unsexy, it is now hailed as a key to clarifying the aims and methods of humanistic study. The classroom, after all, is a space where the humanities are always already public. Rachel Buurma and Laura Heffernan trawl through the syllabi, course descriptions, scribbled reminders, and lecture notes of well-known literary scholars to show that their interactions with students were a messier and richer affair than their critical manifestos might lead us to think. For example, T. S. Eliot—a byword for modernist impersonality and austere formalism—was deeply engaged with his working-class students at the University of London extension school. He revised assignments to speak to their interests, drew on anecdotes to render literature more accessible, and made connections between the labor of writing and his students' working lives. Buurma and Heffernan remark that here, as elsewhere, "students and teachers have come together to study literature in ways that violate both the implicit and explicit tenets of most of the official and informal stories about the discipline."[64] And Joseph North looks to the pedagogy of I. A. Richards as a model for a rebooted literary studies that would center on aesthetic education rather than the transmission of historical knowledge— though he never clarifies how cultivating sensibility in the classroom will result in the Marxist politics he wishes for.

What might an ANT-ish approach add to this conversation? I've proposed that it can be carried out at a variety of scales. A critic invested in close reading might inspire her students to trace out the entanglements of human and nonhuman actors as they are disclosed in a single work, reflecting on how they shed light on the complexities of agency. Meanwhile, ANT also has affinities to large-scale approaches ranging from the digital humanities to the tracing of transnational linkages. We might consider, for example, Jacob Edmond's experiments in introducing his students to unconventional objects of literary study, such as the seven-thousand-volume research library of a well-known New Zealand writer. Perhaps we should be less quick to assume, writes Edmond, that some things are too big to teach. Here I'm inclined to agree with Ted Underwood's remark that variations of scale should not be treated as mutually exclusive options to be pitted against each other in an increasingly tired debate about close versus distant reading.[65]

Yet I also remain—unsurprisingly—an advocate of a midlevel focus on attachment, especially in the classroom. A seminar, after all, is the quintessential example of a work-net. *People are bound together by a work*; it is the rationale for students and teacher coming together and the conduit through which their words are channeled. Creating a fragile collective with its own habits, quirks, and rhythms that will dissolve at semester's end, they address each other via a poem, a painting, or a film, which mediates their interaction. As Yves Citton remarks, a form of ventriloquism takes place; many kinds of opinion can be hazarded in the classroom, but they must be routed via the text, which is shown to contain them or at least relate to them. Rather than speaking directly of the world, participants engage with the work as it relates to that world.[66] They reflect on individual responses while also fashioning collective ones—shaped by the teacher's guidance, to be sure, but also by the relay of affinities and antipathies, sparks and synergies, among the students themselves.

A defining aspect of this work-net, I would argue, is its impurity. Students who have previously read novels or watched films or listened to music in certain ways are now expected to do so differently: to attend to things they did not previously notice, to learn unfamiliar terms and struggle with new techniques. Both defenders and critics often portray this training as a unidirectional shift: from enthusiasm or distaste to dispassionate appraisal. Janice Radway, for example, reflects on the shame she experienced as a graduate student—not just about the middlebrow novels she had previously loved but about the enthusiasm and absorption with which she had read them.[67] While I'd hardly deny that professional reading can shore up antiemotionalism and snobbery, it also overlaps at certain points, I've suggested, with lay response. The classroom is a heterogeneous and messy space: a contact zone where differing languages, attitudes, and dispositions coexist and sometimes collide

How might a midlevel approach be suited to capturing this messiness? Evidently, it is no longer possible to insist on looking only at the words on the page or letting the work speak for itself. But we also decline to teach the-work-as-product-of-a-context—a body stretched out on an operating table on which we exercise our diagnostic skills. Instead, we center attention on the ties most salient to the classroom: those shaping interactions between works and students. Here we come closer to grasping the force of Ricoeur's idea of "standing in front of a text." The meaning of a work is not *behind* it; it does not precede it temporally or spatially, as the expression of an individual or the masked voice of a conglomerate author (a social structure or system). Rather, any meaning can be activated only by its audiences—though, as we've seen, not under conditions entirely of their own making. The picture of a work as a container for hidden meanings no longer holds us captive; yet a view of works of art as actors in the world is reaffirmed. Johan Fornäs writes: "It is finally in front of the text that its users imagine its meanings and use them in interactive and interpretative practices to construct identities and social worlds."[68] As this phrasing suggests, such practices can hook readers (or viewers or listeners) up to larger concerns, yet any ties must be *traced* rather than simply assumed.

What about the worry that—without the sturdy guardrail of critical theory—students will fall back into aimless chitchat or banal confession, an unreflective outpouring of opinions: "I love this book" or "I hate this character"?[69] Having taught in this way for several years, I've found that students are more than able to rise to the challenge if provided with relevant models. Triangulating between analysis of a work, reflections on the making of their response, and engagement with relevant debates—on the complexities of recognition, say, or the value and limits of empathy—they write insightful and sometimes revelatory essays.

At Virginia I teach upper-level theory courses, where students experiment with such approaches after having cut their teeth on Freud and Foucault, Adorno and Butler. However, PhD student Jessica Swoboda has had success introducing similar forms of analysis to first-years. A composition class devoted to the theme of music, for example, delved into the puzzle of attunement, using Zadie Smith's essay and Carl Wilson's book on musical taste as reference points. Reflecting on her relation to "Take Me Home, Country Roads," one student—Olivia Goodrich—grapples with the disjuncture between her friends' delight in belting out the John Denver song and her own visceral distaste; reflects on how her own preferences were shaped by having classical musicians as parents; considers her failure to get the song—even after repeated efforts—as being linked to hierarchies of taste. And yet she clicks, surprisingly, with "Rocky Mountain High"—another Denver hit—when it appears on autoplay while she's studying in the library:

> This one was telling a story, and the guitar did this back-and-forth thing, and my thinking brain was finally occupied with something technical to follow, just long enough for the very soul of the music to sneak in and hit me like a gut punch. I started hearing it the way I hear Velvet Underground, or a really good rendition of unaccompanied Bach, or Joni Mitchell, where at every moment of the music I am fully absorbed and cannot think behind or beyond. This kind of instantaneous transcendence reminded me of Zadie Smith's experi-

ence with Mitchell. For both of us, the experience happened under conditions of exhaustion or distraction, when our "critical mind[s] lay undefended" (Smith). However, unlike Smith, I knew exactly what I had found in that one song that made it suddenly so profound to me. It was skill and complexity, the weaving sound of the instrumentation, which made all the difference between the unpalatable feelings-fest of "Country Roads" and this other song by the same singer-songwriter with many of the same themes.[70]

Far from mindless emoting, Goodrich delivers a beautifully handled reflection on aesthetic attachments and how they are formed in predictable and less predictable ways, without ever losing sight of the music she is discussing.

And here, any lingering accusations of "naive humanism" can easily be deflected. In the way of thinking I've outlined, actors and networks are reversible terms: not labels for different entities but a result of shifting one's vantage point. Any actor, if one zooms in close enough, becomes a network: what look like stable units turn out to be fragile composites made up of many parts. The point holds for persons as well as institutions; internally differentiated as well as externally connected, human beings are unstable compounds with permeable borders. Here ANT would concur with Ricoeur's assertion that to "say self is to say not-I"—but also with his insistence that this self is not just a textual effect or a political symptom. We are given a means of understanding how readers or viewers or listeners are "constructed"—yet without the heavy-handed determinism that often accompanies use of this term.

The advantage of an ANT-ish approach, then, lies in its openness to the different ties that shape aesthetic experiences—its refusal to presort them into those that count and those that can be summarily discounted. Identifications around gender, race, or sexuality, for example, can possess significant force, shaping responses to works of art as well as to the world. Rather than either affirming or deconstructing identity, an ANT-ish line of inquiry would ask: What do such identifications do? What gets connected to what? How might a student's affinity with an Asian American author, for example, be shaped by shared experiences, techniques of literary solicitation, forms of marketing and promotion, or academic or institutional framing? The purpose of such questions is not to dismiss or downgrade specific ties but to more fully understand them by attending to the details of how they are made. Yet other affinities may prove to be equally salient: perhaps to a style, a mood, a tone, a texture, a rhythm, an atmosphere. Aesthetic responses, as we've seen, can be hard to predict: whether someone will get a painting or a piece of music, whether they find themselves identifying with a character, and on what grounds. Differing affinities—aesthetic, political, intellectual, ethical—do not line up next to each other in orderly fashion. As Hennion remarks, this is one area where scholarship lags behind common sense; we all know the sense of surprise when an artwork does not provide the payoff we were hoping for. We do not *relate* to it as we had expected.

In a recent essay, Brian Glavey reflects on what it means for art to be relatable. Could there be a word more likely to dissolve intellectual inquiry into a soupy haze of sentiment and feel-good generalities? One of his students chances on a poem by Frank O'Hara ("Having a Coke with You") that's not listed on the syllabus of his queer poetics class and writes about it on the course blog—and most of the other students end up following her lead. "The consensus reverberating through all their posts was resounding," Glavey writes; "the Coke poem's celebration of infatuation and fun was irrepressibly *relatable*."[71] This enthusiasm, he ruefully notes, was accompanied by a certain lack of attention to its poetic qualities. He quotes Rebecca Mead's complaint that the language of relatability has the effect of turning an artwork into a selfie, the act of reading into an exercise in narcissism.

And yet, rather than engaging in scholarly finger-wagging—a response even more predictable than what it's reacting to—Glavey gives his argument another twist. Being relatable, he points out, has a double referent: it denotes not only what a reader can connect with but also what can be communicated—that is to say, told or related—to others. And here it speaks to the question of whether aesthetic experiences are transitive or intransitive, a relation to others or to the self. His students, Glavey realizes, are onto something, given O'Hara's intense interest, in his poetry and criticism, with the sociability of art. The essay pursues this theme of relatability both in O'Hara's work and in its reception, including its uptake in social media and in the second series of *Mad Men*. Aesthetic relations do not exist outside commodification—the O'Hara poem is featured on the Coca-Cola website—but many other ties are also at play, including forms of queer sociability and affective attachment that connect persons to artworks via lovers and friends.

Glavey's essay ends with these words:

> My student, who found herself "incessantly talking" about the poem all afternoon, was on the right track, amplifying the poem's own voluble enthusiasm. . . . For O'Hara, the value of the art object is constituted by the social relationships that go into its creation and sustain its reception, and the best way to attest to that value is to talk, to write, to compose a poem or post a video, which is, after all, why I am telling you about it.[72]

Like any form of criticism, Glavey's essay links to a network, adding a new strand to the weave of ties that have formed around O'Hara's work. To write about poetry is to prolong its existence by connecting actors to each other. And receptivity can be extended to students or lay readers as well as to texts; respecting the distinctiveness of literature does not have to mean arching an eyebrow at the naive responses of neophytes. Glavey deftly clarifies how his students' concerns are picked up and refracted in "Having a Coke with You." Rather than squelching their attachments, he reorients, redescribes, and extends them.

While the relations between academic and lay response have long interested me, they've only recently begun to attract serious attention in the mainstream of scholarly thought. Why now? Proximate causes include the increasingly beleaguered condition of the humanities; the defunding of public universities and drastic drop in tenure-track positions; a rising class of para-academics who can sustain their intellectual passions only by writing in online venues such as *LARB*, *Public Books*, or *The Point*; and, in some cases, an eagerness to break free of scholarly straitjackets in order to experiment with voice, form, and genre. While interrelated, these factors are very different in kind; the economic, political, and institutional attacks on the humanities cannot be resolved—it should not be necessary to point out—by rethinking method or by writing in different ways. And yet, even as they mourn or rage against the loss of academic careers, some younger scholars welcome the growing interest in reaching wider publics. Ragini Srinivasan, for example, reflects on his own self-identification as a writer as well as a scholar, his difficulties in graduate school and beyond in fitting into disciplinary boxes, and his interest in what he calls "semi public writing" that "pursues moments of recognition, values readerly pleasures, catalyzes moments of understanding," and "opens something up for and in its readers."[73]

Srinivasan's essay is published in a new collection of essays called *The Critic as Amateur*. I can't help feeling a twinge of unease at the appeal to amateurism: for those of us who grew up in England at a certain time, the word has hard-to-eradicate connotations of social class, conveying a sense of aristocratic hauteur toward all those engaged in the grubby business of earning a living. Looking back on his student days, for example, Terry Eagleton remarks that writing books was felt to be a vulgar, publicity-seeking affair by Cambridge dons who saw their life's work as chairing the college wine committee.[74] Meanwhile, at a time when the legitimacy of humanistic knowledge is being assailed, embracing the language of amateurism may not be the savviest or most strategic response. We need to defend intellectual authority rather than downplay it.

Yet *The Critic as Amateur* is a stimulating collection that points its finger at a crucial issue: the missed connections between humanities scholarship and lay audiences. Can such connections be strengthened? Is it feasible to engage the features of everyday response more fully, yet without denying the hard-earned expertise of art historians, literary critics, film scholars, or musicologists? Could such engagement help provide stronger public rationales for why the humanities matter? And what about the messy mixtures that characterize our own lives? Academics, after all, are not always "on" professionally—reading a novel to relax, we may respond quite differently than we do in the classroom. Can we forge a better balance between attention to objects and attention to methods? Finally, can we do better justice to the varieties of aesthetic experience—their forms, their feel, their textures—yet without scanting the actors and factors that make such experience possible? Can some of the divisions between the affective and the reflective, the phenomenological and the sociological, be broken down? And can the resulting insights deliver more compelling accounts of why literature and art matter that hook up to the concerns of both academics and lay audiences? The idea of attachment, I've suggested, offers one possible avenue for tackling these questions.

Acknowledgments

Let me first express my deep gratitude to the Danish National Research Foundation for awarding me a Niels Bohr Professorship that gave me the freedom to spend five years at the University of Southern Denmark on a half-time basis, leading a collective research project, "Uses of Literature: The Social Dimensions of Literature." I thank Liselotte Højgaard, Søren-Peter Olesen, and Jens K. Nørskov at the Danish National Research Foundation for their trust in me and their consistent encouragement. Thanks also to Vice-Chancellor Henrik Dam, Dean Simon Møberg Torp, and department chairs Anne Jensen and Per Krogh Hansen for their kind support. How is it, I wonder, that a US-based scholar can be so generously supported by Danish largesse while humanities researchers back home scrabble for a few pitiful crumbs of funding?

My time at Odense would not have been possible without the initiative and enthusiasm of friends and colleagues at the University of Southern Denmark. I owe a special debt to Anne-Marie Mai for her extraordinary energy, acumen, and generosity of spirit as well as to good friends and fellow organizers Peter Simonsen and Klaus Petersen. The experience of working as part of a large research group has been eye-opening and life-transforming: conversations unfolding over time, moments of laughter and sometimes passionate debate, a sense of collective commitment and being part of something larger than oneself. *Hooked* bears the imprint of this history. I am especially grateful to Patrick Fessenbecker and John Helt Haarder for their detailed comments on specific chapters. I also received a great deal of helpful feedback from other members of the group: Mathies Græsborg Aarhus, Anne-Marie Søndergaard Christensen, Lars Handesten, Emily Hogg, Marie-Elisabeth Holm, Sophy Kohler, Alastair Morrison, Anders Juhl Langscheidel Rasmussen, Johanne Gormsen Schmidt, Moritz Schramm, Camilla Schwartz, Anita Wohlmann, and Bryan Yazell. Pernille Hasselsteen deserves an award for her superhuman efficiency, her extraordinary problem-solving skills, and her kindness and thoughtfulness. Marianne Lysholt was a great help to me in my first year. I am deeply grateful to Luna Kyung Keller Larsen for helping me to surmount what seemed like a never-ending series of bureaucratic hurdles.

It was a great pleasure to collaborate with Toril Moi and Amanda Anderson over several months while writing this book: I learned much from their example and treasure their friendship. I also give warm thanks to Elizabeth Anker, Jonathan Flatley, Jon Najarian, and Ika Willis, who offered very detailed and helpful feedback on specific chapters and helped make my arguments stronger. Meanwhile, valuable suggestions and encouragement came from many other interlocutors: Elaine Auyoung, Michaela Bronstein, Rita Charon, Elizabeth Fowler, Brian Glavey, Ben Highmore, Günter Leypoldt, Benjamin Piekut, Carl Plantinga, Rosa Maria Rodriguez Porto, Ralph Rodriguez, Shaun Ross, Simon Stern, Jeff Wallace, and Ross Wilson. I talked through the ideas of *Hooked* while giving many lectures at colleges and universities and want to thank my audiences for their interest. It has been a revelation to see how much intellectual energy and enthusiasm the topic of attachment can inspire, among junior as well as senior researchers. For similar reasons this book draws on the ideas of current and former students—undergraduates, graduate students, and those who are now established scholars—to a far greater extent than any previous book I've written.

I am eternally grateful to Antoine Hennion, who responded to my various questions with good humor and expansive replies. And I received useful leads, references, and examples from a great many individuals, including Matthew Affron, Gregory Chase, Francesca Coppa, Nicholas Dames, John Kulka, Riin Magnus, Mathew Ratcliffe, Namwali Serpell, Richard Shusterman, Caitlin Smith, Victor Szabo, and Keith Vincent. As I was starting on this book, I benefited from the research assistance of Samantha Wallace; Jessica Swoboda has been a valued interlocutor as I complete it.

My thinking and my life have also been enriched by conversations with David Alworth, Ben Bateman, Laura Bieger, Winfried Fluck, Susan Fraiman, Susan Stanford Friedman, Julika Griem, Aaron Hanlon, Krishan Kumar, Michael Levenson, Heather Love, Kate Makarova, Rei Magosaki, Stephen Muecke, John Portmann, Sophie Rosenfeld, and Mollie Washburne. I want to thank Alan Thomas and Randolph Petilos, at the University of Chicago Press, for their consistent support and encouragement, the reviewers of the manuscript for their helpful suggestions, Pamela J. Bruton for her excellent copyediting, and Derek Gottlieb for the index. Allan Megill and Maria Felski lived with this book as it came to fruition; my greatest debts are to them.

✻ ✻ ✻

Most of chapter 3 first appeared in *Character: Three Inquiries in Literary Studies*, by Amanda Anderson, Rita Felski, and Toril Moi (Chicago: University of Chicago Press, 2019). Some of the arguments of *Hooked* are briefly summarized in my "Postcritical Reading," in *Further Reading*, ed. Matthew Rubery and Leah Price (Oxford: Oxford University Press, 2020).

This book was written with financial support from the Danish National Research Foundation (grant no. DNRF 127).

Notes

Preface

1. Rita Felski, *The Limits of Critique* (Chicago: University of Chicago Press, 2015).

Chapter 1

1. Annemarie Mol, "Actor-Network Theory: Sensitive Terms and Enduring Tensions," *Kölner Zeitschrift für Soziologie und Sozialpsychologie*, Sonderheft, 50, no. 1 (2010): 261.

2. Luc Boltanski and Eve Chiapello, *The New Spirit of Capitalism* (London: Verso, 2005), 38.

3. Lauren Berlant, *Cruel Optimism* (Durham, NC: Duke University Press, 2011); Sara Ahmed, *The Cultural Politics of Emotion* (New York: Routledge, 2004).

4. Joli Jensen, "Fandom as Pathology: The Consequences of Characteriza-

tion," in *The Adoring Audience: Fan Culture and Popular Media*, ed. Lisa A. Lewis (London: Routledge, 1992), 26.

5. Deidre Lynch, *Loving Literature* (Chicago: University of Chicago Press, 2015).

6. Carl Wilson, *Let's Talk about Love: Why Other People Have Such Bad Taste* (London: Bloomsbury, 2007), 157.

7. Antoine Hennion, "From ANT to Pragmatism: A Journey with Bruno Latour at the CSI," *New Literary History* 47, nos. 2–3 (2016): 297.

8. Bruno Latour, *An Inquiry into Modes of Existence: An Anthropology of the Moderns*, trans. Catherine Porter (Cambridge, MA: Harvard University Press, 2013), 241.

9. Latour, *Inquiry*, 248.

10. Rebecca Solnit, *The Faraway Nearby* (New York: Penguin, 2013), 63.

11. Antoine Hennion, "Pragmatics of Taste," in *The Blackwell Companion to the Sociology of Culture*, ed. Mark D. Jacobs and Nancy Weiss Hanrahan (Oxford: Blackwell's, 2005), 137.

12. Wayne Koestenbaum, "Affinity," in *My 1980s and Other Essays* (New York: Farrar, Straus and Giroux, 2013), 279.

13. Koestenbaum, "Affinity," 279.

14. Eva Illouz, *Why Love Hurts: A Sociological Explanation* (Cambridge: Polity, 2012).

15. Hiro Saito, "An Actor-Network-Theory of Cosmopolitanism," *Sociological Theory* 29, no. 2 (2011): 124–49.

16. I felt absurdly pleased at having coined (I thought) the idea of semidetachment, only to see it appear, six months later, in the title of John Plotz's new book. Plotz deploys it to talk about aesthetic experience as a partial absorption in a fictional world. See his *Semi-detached: The Aesthetics of Virtual Experience since Dickens* (Princeton, NJ: Princeton University Press, 2018).

17. Michael Polanyi, *The Tacit Dimension* (Chicago: University of Chicago Press, 2009), 18.

18. Clive Bell, "Art," in *Aesthetics: Classic Readings from the Western Tradition*, ed. Dabney Townsend (Boston: Jones and Bartlett, 1996), 332–33.

19. For a helpful overview of these debates, see Sam Rose, "The Fear of Aesthetics in Art and Literary Theory," *New Literary History* 48, no. 2 (2017): 223–44.

20. Paul C. Taylor, *Black Is Beautiful: A Philosophy of Black Aesthetics* (Oxford: Wiley Blackwell, 2016), 2.

21. Richard Shusterman, "The End of Aesthetic Experience," *Journal of Aesthetics and Art Criticism* 55, no. 1 (1997): 30.

22. Noel Carroll, "Four Concepts of Aesthetic Experience," in *Beyond Aesthet-*

ics: *Philosophical Essays* (Cambridge: Cambridge University Press, 2001); Derek Attridge, *The Work of Literature* (Oxford: Oxford University Press, 2015), 1; Derek Attridge, *The Singularity of Literature* (London: Routledge, 2004), 167.

23. Winfried Fluck, "Aesthetics and Cultural Studies," in *Aesthetics in a Multicultural Age*, ed. Emory Elliott, Louis Freitas Caton, and Jeffrey Rhyne (Oxford: Oxford University Press, 2002), 87. See also Heinz Ickstadt, "Toward a Pluralist Aesthetic," 263–77, in the same volume; and, from a more analytical perspective, see Alan H. Goldman, "The Broad View of Aesthetic Experience," *Journal of Aesthetics and Art Criticism* 71, no. 4 (2013): 323–33.

24. Jean-Marie Schaeffer, *Art of the Modern Age*, trans. Steven Rendall (Princeton, NJ: Princeton University Press, 2000), 301. See also Norman Kreitman, "The Varieties of Aesthetic Disinterestedness," *Contemporary Aesthetics* 4 (2006), https://www.contempaesthetics.org/newvolume/pages/article.php?articleID=390. Bence Nanay makes a case for replacing the idea of "disinterested attention" with "distributed attention"—yet aesthetic attention is surely often highly focused rather than evenly distributed. See his *Aesthetics as a Philosophy of Perception* (Oxford: Oxford University Press, 2016).

25. James Wood, *The Nearest Thing to Life* (Boston: Brandeis University Press, 2015), 75.

26. The point is not entirely new—Dewey spoke of "mediated immediacy"—but it has yet to be fully assimilated and taken on board.

27. Bruno Latour, *Reassembling the Social: An Introduction to Actor-Network-Theory* (Oxford: Oxford University Press, 2005), 237.

28. Noel Carroll, "Friendship and Yasmina Reza's 'Art,'" *Philosophy and Literature* 26, no. 1 (2002): 202–3. There is a great deal of research on book clubs and on fans, but not much else. See, however, Alexander Nehamas, *On Friendship* (New York: Basic Books, 2016).

29. James Elkins, *Pictures and Tears* (New York: Routledge, 2004); Michael White, *Travels in Vermeer: A Memoir* (New York: Persea, 2015); Dario Gamboni, *The Destruction of Art: Iconoclasm and Vandalism since the French Revolution* (London: Reaktion Books, 2007).

30. Yasmina Reza, *"Art": A Play* (New York: Farrar, Straus and Giroux, 1997), 63.

31. Quoted in Amanda Gigeure, *The Plays of Yasmina Reza on the English and American Stage* (Jefferson, NC: McFarland, 2010), 47. For a brief but insightful reading of the play, see the afterword to Hannah Freed-Thall, *Spoiled Distinctions: Aesthetics and the Ordinary in French Modernism* (Oxford: Oxford University Press, 2015), 143–48.

32. Tim Parks, *The Novel: A Survival Skill* (Oxford: Oxford University Press, 2015).

33. Bruno Latour, "On Actor-Network Theory: A Few Clarifications," *Soziale Welt* 47, no. 4 (1996): 371.

34. Bruno Latour, "Why Has Critique Run Out of Steam? From Matters of Fact to Matters of Concern," *Critical Inquiry* 30 (2004): 227.

35. For the phone booth example and other helpful clarifications, see Latour, "On Actor-Network Theory."

36. Latour, *Reassembling the Social*, 142.

37. Bruno Latour, "On Recalling ANT," in *Actor Network Theory and After*, ed. John Law and John Hassard (Oxford: Wiley-Blackwell, 1999), 24.

38. Caroline Levine, *Forms: Whole, Rhythm, Hierarchy, Network* (Oxford: Oxford University Press, 2015), 18.

39. Levine, *Forms*, 13.

40. Latour, *Inquiry*, 35.

41. Kimberly Chabot Davis, *Postmodern Texts and Emotional Audiences* (West Lafayette, IN: Purdue University Press, 2007).

42. Leah Price, *How to Do Things with Books in Victorian Britain* (Princeton, NJ: Princeton University Press, 2013).

43. Orhan Pamuk, *The New Life* (New York: Vintage, 1998), 3–4.

44. Pamuk, *New Life*, 7.

45. Susan Fraiman, *Extreme Domesticity: A View from the Margins* (New York: Columbia University Press, 2017).

46. Peter Conrad, "*Late Turner: Painting Set Free* Review—Prepare to Be Dazzled," *Guardian*, September 13, 2014, https://www.theguardian.com /artanddesign/2014/sep/14/late-turner-painting-set-free-tate-britain -review-prepare-to-be-dazzled.

47. Wai Chee Dimock, "Literature for the Planet," *PMLA* 116, no. 1 (2001): 175.

48. Ross Posnock, review of *The Limits of Critique*, by Rita Felski, *American Literary History*, online review, series 6 (2016), https://academic.oup .com/DocumentLibrary/ALH/Online%20Review%20Series%206/Ross %20Posnock%20Online%20Review%20VI.PDF.

49. Lawrence Grossberg, "Is There a Fan in the House? The Affective Sensibility of Fandom," in Lewis, *Adoring Audience*, 50.

50. Carl Plantinga, *Moving Viewers: American Film and the Spectator Experience* (Berkeley: University of California Press, 2009), 3.

51. Robyn Warhol, *Having a Good Cry: Effeminate Feelings and Pop-Culture Forms* (Columbus: Ohio State University Press, 2003), 67; Lynne Pearce, *Feminism and the Politics of Reading* (London: Arnold, 1997), 106.

52. Alexander Nehamas, *Only a Promise of Happiness: The Place of Beauty in a World of Art* (Princeton, NJ: Princeton University Press, 2010), 74.

53. Susan Sontag, "The Decay of Cinema," *New York Times*, February 25, 1996. See also Christian Keathley, *Cinephilia and History, or The Wind in the Trees* (Bloomington: Indiana University Press, 2006).

54. Jerrold Levinson, "Falling in Love with a Book," in *Aesthetic Pursuits: Essays in Philosophy of Art* (Oxford: Oxford University Press, 2016), 79. See, however, the interesting discussion by David Aldridge in "Education's Love Triangle," *Journal of Philosophy of Education* 53, no. 3 (2019): 531–46.

55. Ronald de Sousa, *Love: A Very Short Introduction* (Oxford: Oxford University Press, 2015), 3.

56. Pearce, *Feminism and the Politics of Reading*.

57. Ben Anderson, *Encountering Affect: Capacities, Apparatuses, Conditions* (London: Routledge, 2016), 19, 165. For another good account of affect as "heuristically *distinguished* but not sharply *separated* from emotion," see "Introduction: Affect in Relation," in *Affect in Relation—Families, Places, Technologies: Essays on Affectivity and Subject Formation in the 21st Century*, ed. B. Röttger-Rössler and J. Slaby (New York: Routledge, 2018), 1–28.

58. Charles Taylor, "What Is Human Agency?," in *Human Agency and Language: Philosophical Papers 1* (Cambridge: Cambridge University Press, 1985).

59. Günter Leypoldt, "Social Dimensions of the Turn to Genre: Junot Díaz's *Oscar Wao* and Kazuo Ishiguro's *The Buried Giant*," *Post45*, March 31, 2018, http://post45.research.yale.edu/2018/03/social-dimensions-of-the -turn-to-genre-junot-diazs-oscar-wao-and-kazuo-ishiguros-the-buried -giant/. For more on the relevance of "strong values" to literary reception, see his "Degrees of Public Relevance: Walter Scott and Toni Morrison," *Modern Language Quarterly* 77, no. 3 (2016): 369–89.

60. Leypoldt, "Social Dimensions of the Turn to Genre."

61. bell hooks, "An Aesthetics of Blackness: Strange and Oppositional," in *Yearning: Race, Gender, and Cultural Politics* (Boston: Southend Press, 1990).

62. See Rita Felski, "The Role of Aesthetics in Cultural Studies," in *Aesthetics and Cultural Studies*, ed. Michael Berubé (Oxford: Blackwell, 2004); Rita Felski, "Modernist Studies and Cultural Studies: Reflections on Method," *Modernism/Modernity* 10, no. 3 (2003): 501–17.

63. Günter Leypoldt, "Knausgaard in America: Literary Prestige and Charismatic Trust," *Critical Quarterly* 59, no. 3 (2017): 58.

64. Jeffrey T. Nealon, *I'm Not like Everyone Else: Biopolitics, Neoliberalism, and American Popular Music* (Lincoln: University of Nebraska Press, 2018), 110.

65. Anna Poletti et al., "The Affects of Not Reading: Hating Characters, Being

Bored, Feeling Stupid," *Arts and Humanities in Higher Education* 15, no. 2 (2016): 10.

66. Amit Chaudhuri, *The Origins of Dislike* (Oxford: Oxford University Press, 2018), 14–15.

67. Deborah Root, *Cannibal Culture: Art, Appropriation, and the Commodification of Difference* (New York: Routledge, 1996), 136.

68. There is already some writing along these general lines. See, e.g., Geoff Dyer, *Out of Sheer Rage: Wrestling with D. H. Lawrence* (London: Picador, 2009); or Jonathan Gray on anti-fans: "New Audiences, New Textualities: Anti-fans and Non-fans," *International Journal of Cultural Studies* 6, no. 1 (2003): 64–81.

69. Or more precisely, little *academic* attention has been paid to the personal reactions solicited by "high" art. A flood of books with titles like *My Life in Middlemarch* or *How Proust Changed My Life* or *My Life in Vermeer* points to a strong public interest in autobiographical accounts of attachments to artworks. That these books are rarely referenced in scholarly articles seems related to two factors: their encroachment onto academic terrain, combined with styles of thought that are often dismissed as middlebrow or belletristic.

70. Jackie Stacey, *Stargazing: Hollywood Cinema and Female Spectatorship* (London: Routledge, 1994); David S. Miall, *Literary Reading: Empirical and Theoretical Studies* (New York: Peter Lang, 2006); Daniel Cavicchi, *Tramps like Us: Music and Meaning among Springsteen Fans* (Oxford: Oxford University Press, 1998).

71. The phrase "hesitancies and inarticulacies" is drawn from Matt Hills's impressively argued *Fan Cultures* (London: Routledge 2002), 7. Some ethnographers, such as Kimberly Chabot Davis, include much longer passages of audience commentary.

72. This point is developed in more detail in Rita Felski, "Everyday Aesthetics," *minnesota review* 71–72 (2009): 171–79.

Chapter 2

1. David Freedberg, *The Power of Images: Studies in the History and Theory of Response* (Chicago: University of Chicago Press, 1989), 440.

2. Erik Wallrup, *Being Musically Attuned: The Act of Listening to Music* (London: Ashgate, 2015), 6.

3. James English, "Prestige, Pleasure, and the Data of Cultural Preference: 'Quality Signals' in an Age of Superabundance," *Western Humanities Review* 70, no. 3 (2016), http://www.westernhumanitiesreview.com /fall-2016-70-3/prestige-pleasure-and-the-data-of-cultural-preference -quality-signals-in-the-age-of-superabundance/.

4. Michael Gallope, *Deep Refrains: Music, Philosophy, and the Ineffable* (Chicago: University of Chicago Press, 2017), 16.

5. W. J. T. Mitchell, *What Do Pictures Want? The Lives and Loves of Images* (Chicago: University of Chicago Press, 2005), 8.

6. Nicholas Cooke, *Analysing Musical Multi-media* (Oxford: Oxford University Press, 1998).

7. See Sara Ahmed, *Queer Phenomenology* (Durham, NC: Duke University Press, 2006); Steven Connor, "CP; or, A Few Don'ts by a Cultural Phenomenologist," *Parallax* 5, no. 2 (1999): 17–31; Don Ihde, *Postphenomenology and Technoscience* (Albany: State University of New York Press, 2009); and my references to neophenomenology in *Uses of Literature* (Oxford: Blackwell, 2008). There is also Thomas Rickert, *Ambient Rhetoric: The Attunements of Rhetorical Being* (Pittsburgh, PA: University of Pittsburgh Press, 2013); and Lisbeth Lipari, *Listening, Thinking, Being: Toward an Ethics of Attunement* (University Park: Pennsylvania State University Press, 2014).

8. Michiko Kakutani, "From Kazuo Ishiguro, a New Annoying Hero," *New York Times*, October 17, 1995. For an overview of negative responses, some no longer available online, see Suzie Mackenzie, "Between Two Worlds," *Guardian*, March 25, 2000.

9. Connor, "CP," 26.

10. Antoine Hennion, "Pragmatics of Taste," in *The Blackwell Companion to the Sociology of Culture*, ed. Mark D. Jacobs and Nancy Weiss Hanrahan (Oxford: Blackwell's, 2005), 133.

11. Antoine Hennion and Line Grenier, "Sociology of Art: New Stakes in a Post-critical Time," in *The International Handbook of Sociology*, ed. Stella Quah and Arnaud Sales (London: Sage, 2000), 344.

12. Claudio E. Benzecry, *The Opera Fan: Ethnography of an Obsession* (Chicago: University of Chicago Press, 2011); Tia DeNora, *Music in Everyday Life* (Cambridge: Cambridge University Press, 2000); Howard S. Becker, *Art Worlds*, rev. ed. (Berkeley: University of California Press, 2008); Maria Angelica Thumale Olave, "Reading Matters: Towards a Cultural Sociology of Reading," *American Journal of Cultural Sociology* 6, no. 3 (2018): 417–54. See also Rita Felski, "My Sociology Envy," *Theory, Culture, and Society*, July 25, 2019, https://www.theoryculturesociety.org/rita-felski-my-sociology-envy/.

13. Tony Bennett, "*Habitus Clivé*: Aesthetics and Politics in the Work of Pierre Bourdieu," *New Literary History* 38, no. 1 (2007): 206. Here Bennett is giving an overview of an argument by one of the most important critics of Bourdieu, Bernard Lahire, as articulated in Lahire's *La culture des individus: Dissonances culturelles et distinctions de soi* (Paris: Editions la

Découverte, 2004). And see also Jeffrey C. Alexander, "The Reality of Reduction: The Failed Synthesis of Pierre Bourdieu," in *Fin-de-Siècle Social Theory: Relativism, Reduction, and the Problem of Reason* (London: Verso, 1995), 128–217.

14. Janice Radway, "What's the Matter with Reception Studies?," in *New Directions in American Reception Studies*, ed. Philip Goldstein and James L. Machor (Oxford: Oxford University Press, 2008), 339.

15. Zadie Smith, "Some Notes on Attunement," in *Feel Free* (New York: Penguin, 2018), 100. Further citations appear in parentheses in the text.

16. Hennion, "Pragmatics of Taste," 136.

17. Matthew Ratcliffe, "Heidegger's Attunement and the Neuropsychology of Emotion," *Phenomenology and the Cognitive Sciences* 1 (2002): 289.

18. Stanley Cavell, "Aesthetic Problems of Modern Philosophy," in *Must We Mean What We Say? A Book of Essays* (Cambridge: Cambridge University Press, 2002), 93.

19. Robert Escarpit, *Sociology of Literature*, trans. Ernest Pick (London: Frank Cass, 1971), 87.

20. Morris Beja, *Epiphany in the Modern Novel* (Seattle: University of Washington Press, 1971), 25.

21. Ben Green, "Peak Music Experiences: A New Perspective on Popular Music, Identity, and Scenes" (PhD diss., Griffith University, 2017), 106. Similar descriptions of conversion to Springsteen can be found in Daniel Cavicchi, *Tramps like Us: Music and Meaning among Springsteen Fans* (Oxford: Oxford University Press, 1998). For an earlier, and still important, critique of high versus popular culture oppositions, see Simon Frith, *Performing Rites: Evaluating Popular Music* (Oxford: Oxford University Press, 1996). Frith writes: "I would argue, at least as a starting premise, that in responding to high and low art forms, in assessing them, finding them beautiful or moving or repulsive, people are employing the same evaluating principles. The differences lie in the objects at issue (what is culturally interesting to us is socially structured), in the discourses in which judgements are cast, and in the circumstances in which they are made" (19).

22. Stanley Cavell, *Must We Mean What We Say?* (New York: Scribner, 1969), 52; Daniel N. Stern, *The Interpersonal World of the Infant* (New York: Basic Books, 1985).

23. Zadie Smith, *NW* (London: Penguin, 2013), 36.

24. Patrica Hampl, *Blue Arabesque: A Search for the Sublime* (New York: Mariner, 2007), 2–5.

25. Peter de Bolla, *Art Matters* (Cambridge, MA: Harvard University Press, 2003), 57.

26. Geoff Dyer, *Zona: A Book about a Film about a Journey to a Room* (London:

Vintage, 2012), 142–43. I am grateful to Namwali Serpell for bringing this book to my attention.

27. Dyer, *Zona*, 10.

28. Virginia Woolf, "How Should One Read a Book?," in *The Second Common Reader* (London: Harvest, 2003), 266.

29. Karl Heinz Bohrer, *Suddenness: On the Moment of Aesthetic Appearance* (New York: Columbia University Press, 1994).

30. Jean-François Lyotard, "The Sublime and the Avant-Garde," in *The Inhuman: Reflections on Time* (Stanford, CA: Stanford University Press, 1992).

31. T. J. Clark, *The Sight of Death: An Experiment in Art Writing* (New Haven, CT: Yale University Press, 2006), 5.

32. Clark, *Sight of Death*, 12.

33. Jean-Marie Schaeffer, *L'experience aesthetique* (Paris: Gallimard, 2015).

34. Bence Nanay, *Aesthetics as Philosophy of Perception* (Oxford: Oxford University Press, 2016), 16.

35. Mark Doty, *Still Life with Oysters and Lemon: On Objects and Intimacy* (New York: Beacon, 2002), 4.

36. Rebecca Mead, *My Life in Middlemarch* (New York: Broadway, 2015), 16.

37. Vladimir Jankélévitch, *Music and the Ineffable*, trans. Carolyn Abbaté (Princeton, NJ: Princeton University Press, 2003), 102.

38. Carolyn Abbaté, "Music—Drastic or Gnostic?," *Critical Inquiry* 30 (Spring 2004): 505–6.

39. Freedberg, *Power of Images*, 1.

40. Alfred Gell, *Art and Agency: An Anthropological Theory* (Oxford: Oxford University Press, 1998), 6.

41. Caroline Van Eck, "Living Statues: Alfred Gell's *Art and Agency*, Living Presence Response, and the Sublime," *Art History* 33, no. 4 (2010): 646. On Gell's confusion of the agency of art with poisoned arrows and land mines, see Richard Layton, "*Art and Agency:* A Reassessment," *Journal of the Royal Anthropological Institute* 9, no. 3 (2003): 447–64.

42. James Elkins, *Pictures and Tears: A History of People Who Have Cried in Front of Paintings* (New York: Routledge, 2004), 248.

43. Antoine Hennion, "Objects, Belief, and the Sociologist: The Sociology of Art as a Work-to-Be-Done," in *Roads to Music Sociology*, ed. Alfred Smudits (Wiesbaden: Springer, 2018), 50.

44. Emilie Gomart and Antoine Hennion, "A Sociology of Attachment: Music Amateurs, Drug Users," in *Actor Network Theory and After*, ed. John Law and John Hassard (Oxford: Wiley-Blackwell, 1999), 220–47.

45. Hennion, "Pragmatics of Taste," 135.

46. George Steiner, *Real Presences* (Chicago: University of Chicago Press, 1989), 183.

47. Steiner, *Real Presences*, 186.

48. Steiner, *Real Presences*, 183.

49. Hans Ulrich Gumbrecht, *Production of Presence: What Meaning Cannot Convey* (Stanford, CA: Stanford University Press, 2004), 117.

50. Janet Wolff, "After Cultural Theory: The Power of Images, the Lure of Immediacy," *Journal of Visual Culture* 11, no. 1 (2012): 3–19. Where Wolff goes badly wrong is citing ANT as an example of an approach that ignores mediation. In reality, ANT is *premised* on mediation.

51. De Bolla, *Art Matters*, 3.

52. Annemarie Mol, "Actor-Network Theory: Sensitive Terms and Enduring Tensions," *Kölner Zeitschrift für Soziologie und Sozialpsychologie*, Sonderheft, 50, no. 1 (2010): 3.

53. Alva Noë, *Varieties of Presence* (Cambridge, MA: Harvard University Press, 2012), 115.

54. Nadine Hubbs, *Rednecks, Queers, and Country Music* (Berkeley: University of California Press, 2014), 97.

55. Toril Moi, *Revolution of the Ordinary: Literary Studies after Wittgenstein, Austin, and Cavell* (Chicago: University of Chicago Press, 2017).

56. Clark, *Sight of Death*, 184.

57. Vivian Sobchack, *Carnal Thoughts: Embodiment and Moving Image Culture* (Berkeley: University of California Press, 2004), 65.

58. Gilbert Ryle, "Knowing How and Knowing That," *Proceedings of the Aristotelian Society* 46 (1945–46): 1–16.

59. Elkins, *Pictures and Tears*, 87.

60. Elkins, *Pictures and Tears*, 88.

61. Hennion, "Pragmatics of Taste," 140.

62. See Isabelle Stengers, "Affinity," in *The Encyclopedia of the Enlightenment*, ed. Michel Delon (New York: Routledge, 2003); Nathalie Sarraute, *Tropisms*, trans. John Calder (New York: New Directions, 2015).

63. Gernot Böhme, "Atmosphere as the Fundamental Concept of a New Aesthetics," *Thesis Eleven* 36 (1993): 113–26; Dora Zhang, "Notes on Atmosphere," *Qui Parle* 27, no. 1 (2018): 122–23.

64. David Wellbery, "Stimmung," trans. Rebecca Pohl, *new formations* 93 (2017): 6–45.

65. For a thorough discussion of *Stimmung*'s meanings in German Romanticism and its later excoriation, see Wallrup, *Being Musically Attuned*.

66. Jonathan Flatley, *Affective Mapping: Melancholia and the Politics of Modernism* (Cambridge, MA: Harvard University Press, 2008), 19. For other helpful accounts of mood, see, e.g., Lauren Freeman, "Toward a Phenomenology of Mood," *Southern Journal of Philosophy* 52, no. 4 (2014): 445–76;

Ratcliffe, "Heidegger's Attunement"; and Rita Felski and Susan Fraiman, eds., "In the Mood," special issue, *New Literary History* 43, no. 3 (2012).

67. Kathleen Stewart, "Atmospheric Attunements," *Rubric* 1 (2010): 5.

68. David James, "Critical Solace," *New Literary History* 47, no. 4 (2016): 481–504.

69. Anna Jones Abramson, "Joseph Conrad's Atmospheric Modernism: Enveloping Fog, Narrative Frames, and Affective Attunement," *Studies in the Novel* 50, no. 3 (2018): 350. I thank Jessica Swoboda for bringing this essay to my attention. And see also Ben Anderson, "Affective Atmospheres," *Emotion, Space, and Society* 2 (2009): 77–81.

70. Robert Sinnerbrink, "*Stimmung*: Exploring the Aesthetics of Mood," *Screen* 53, no. 2 (2012): 148–63.

71. See Paul Roquet, *Ambient Media: Japanese Atmospheres of Self* (Minneapolis: University of Minnesota Press, 2016); Anderson, "Affective Atmospheres."

72. Antoine Hennion, "From ANT to Pragmatism: A Journey with Bruno Latour at the CSI," *New Literary History* 47, nos. 2–3 (2016): 296.

Chapter 3

1. Faye Halpern, "In Defense of Reading Badly: The Politics of Identification in *Benito Cereno, Uncle Tom's Cabin,* and Our Classrooms," *College English* 70, no. 6 (2008): 56.

2. For activation and motivation as defining features of character, see the introduction to *Characters in Fictional Worlds*, ed. Jens Eder, Fotis Annidis, and Ralf Schneider (Berlin: De Gruyter, 2010), 10.

3. Susan Sontag, "Notes on 'Camp,'" in *Against Interpretation and Other Essays* (New York: Picador, 2001), 286.

4. A generalization, admittedly, though not an inaccurate one. I should emphasize, however, that I have found the ideas of some film scholars working under the general rubric of cognitive psychology very helpful, especially the work of Murray Smith and Carl Plantinga.

5. Jackie Stacey, *Stargazing: Hollywood Cinema and Female Spectatorship* (London: Routledge, 1994), 126.

6. Berys Gaut, "Emotion and Identification," in *A Philosophy of Cinematic Art* (Cambridge: Cambridge University Press, 2010), 258. The phrase "Vulcan mindmeld"—often cited in accounts of identification by analytical philosophers—comes from Noel Carroll, *The Philosophy of Horror; or, Paradoxes of the Heart* (New York: Routledge, 1990), 89.

7. Douglas Crimp, "Right on Girlfriend!," in *Fear of a Queer Planet: Queer Politics and Social Theory* (Minneapolis: University of Minnesota Press,

1993), 316; Diana Fuss, *Identification Papers: Readings on Psychoanalysis, Sexuality, and Culture* (New York: Routledge, 1995), 8.

8. All quotations are from Michael Montlack, ed., *My Diva: 65 Gay Men on the Women Who Inspire Them* (Madison, WI: Terrace Books, 2009). See, respectively, 140, 24, 46, 23.

9. Timothy Aubry, "Afghanistan Meets the *Amazon*: Reading *The Kite Runner* in America," *PMLA* 124, no. 1 (2009): 30.

10. For a good discussion of this issue, see Marco Carraciolo, *Strange Narrators in Contemporary Fiction: Explorations in Readers' Engagements with Character* (Lincoln: University of Nebraska Press, 2016).

11. Jeanette Winterson, *Why Be Happy When You Could Be Normal?* (London: Grove Press, 2013), 117.

12. Winterson, *Why Be Happy?*, 61.

13. Winterson, *Why Be Happy?*, 220.

14. Blakey Vermeule, *Why Do We Care about Literary Characters?* (Baltimore: Johns Hopkins University Press, 2011).

15. Or perhaps I am speaking only of myself here.

16. Mario Vargas Llosa, *The Perpetual Orgy: Flaubert and Madame Bovary* (New York: Farrar, Straus and Giroux, 1987), 7. For an account of reader fascination with immoral or unpleasant characters, see Katherine Tullmann, "Sympathy and Fascination," *British Journal of Aesthetics* 56, no. 2 (2016): 115–29.

17. Vargas Llosa, *Perpetual Orgy*, 13.

18. Bruno Latour, *An Inquiry into Modes of Existence* (Cambridge, MA: Harvard University Press, 2014), 240.

19. Jeremy Rosen, *Minor Characters Have Their Day: Genre and the Contemporary Literary Marketplace* (New York: Columbia University Press, 2016).

20. Francesca Coppa, *The Fanfiction Reader: Folk Tales for the Digital Age* (Ann Arbor: University of Michigan Press, 2017), 13.

21. [Daniel] Mallory Ortberg, *Texts from Jane Eyre and Other Conversations with Your Favorite Literary Characters* (New York: Henry Holt, 2004).

22. For a helpful discussion of *Umwelt*, see Riin Magnus and Kalevi Kull, "Roots of Culture in the Umwelt," in *The Oxford Handbook of Culture and Psychology,* ed. Jaan Valsiner (Oxford: Oxford University Press, 2012), 649–66.

23. See Jon Helt Haärder, "Knausenstein's Monster Portraits of the Author in a Post-anthropocentric Mirror," *Textual Practice*, 2019, https://doi.org/10.1080/0950236X.2019.1655472; and also Toril Moi, "Describing *My Struggle*," *The Point, December 27, 2017,* https://thepointmag.com/2017/criticism/describing-my-struggle-knausgaard.

24. Stacey, *Stargazing*, 146.

25. Erwin Panofsky, "Style and Medium in the Motion Pictures," in *Film: An Anthology,* ed. Daniel Talbot (1959; Berkeley: University of California Press, 1970), 29.

26. Richard Dyer, *Stars* (London: British Film Institute, 1979), 178.

27. Hélène Mialet, *Hawking Incorporated: Stephen Hawking and the Anthropology of the Knowing Subject* (Chicago: University of Chicago Press, 2012).

28. Jon Najarian, "Response to Rita Felski, 'Identifying with Characters,'" paper presented at PALS workshop, Duke University, March 2018.

29. Richard Lea, "Fictional Characters Make 'Experiential Crossings' into Real Life, Study Finds," *Guardian*, February 14, 2017, https://www.theguardian .com/books/2017/feb/14/fictional-characters-make-existential-crossings -into-real-life-study-finds.

30. Latour, *Inquiry*, 242.

31. T. W. Adorno, "The Position of the Narrator in the Contemporary Novel," in *Notes to Literature,* vol. 1, trans. Shierry Weber Nicholsen (New York: Columbia University Press, 1991), 30–36.

32. Julian Murphet, "The Mole and the Multiple: A Chiasmus of Character," *New Literary History* 42, no. 2 (2011): 255–76.

33. Hans-Robert Jauss, *Aesthetic Experience and Literary Hermeneutics,* trans. Michael Shaw (Minneapolis: University of Minnesota Press, 1982), xxix.

34. See Murray Smith, "On the Twofoldedness of Character," *New Literary History* 42, no. 2 (2011): 277–94.

35. Rebecca Solnit, "Men Explain *Lolita* to Me," *Literary Hub*, December 17, 2015, https://lithub.com/men-explain-lolita-to-me/.

36. Murray Smith, *Engaging Characters: Fiction, Emotion, and the Cinema* (Oxford: Clarendon Press, 1995). My differences from Smith can be summarized as follows: I retain the term "identification," which he rejects in favor of a (in my view, overly broad) notion of engagement; he devotes a chapter to recognition as a perceptual matter but does not address its phenomenological or sociological aspects; he draws a strong distinction between empathy and sympathy, whereas I see the differences between these two terms as much less significant. Nonetheless, I have found Smith's overall approach very helpful.

37. Emily Nussbaum, "The Great Divide: Norman Lear, Archie Bunker, and the Rise of the Bad Fan," *New Yorker*, April 7, 2014, 64–68. For an account of a reader identifying with Casaubon, see Suzanne Keen, *Empathy and the Novel* (Oxford: Oxford University Press, 2007), 75. Scholars in cultural studies have written at great length about audiences reading against the

grain of conservative texts, but little attention has been paid to the opposite scenario: conservative readings of progressive works.

38. Steven Connor, *Theory and Cultural Value* (Oxford: Blackwell, 1992).

39. Carl Plantinga, *Screen Stories: Emotion and the Ethics of Engagement* (Oxford: Oxford University Press, 2018).

40. On the links between aesthetic and political representation as they play out in the field of literary studies, see John Guillory, *Cultural Capital: The Problem of Literary Canon Formation* (Chicago: University of Chicago Press, 1993).

41. See Rita Felski, *Beyond Feminist Aesthetics: Feminist Literature and Social Change* (Cambridge, MA: Harvard University Press, 1989).

42. Sheila Benson, "Thelma & Louise Just Good Ol' Boys?," *Los Angeles Times,* May 31, 1991; Margaret Carlson, "Is This What Feminism Is All About?," *Time*, June 24, 1991.

43. Bernie Cook, ed., *Thelma and Louise Live! The Cultural Afterlife of an American Film* (Austin: University of Texas Press, 2007), 34.

44. Kim Chabot Davis, *Postmodern Texts and Emotional Audiences* (West Lafayette, IN: Purdue University Press, 2007), 65.

45. For an account of the many obstacles that had to be overcome before the film could be made, see Becky Aikman, *Off the Cliff: How the Making of Thelma and Louise Drove Hollywood to the Edge* (New York: Penguin, 2017).

46. Interview with Callie Khouri, in Cook, *Thelma and Louise Live!*, 184. On limited views of identification in debates about the film, see Sharon Willis, "Hardware and Hardbodies, What Do Women Want? A Reading of *Thelma and Louise*," in *Film Theory Goes to the Movies: Cultural Analysis of Contemporary Films,* ed. Jim Collins et al. (New York: Routledge, 2012), 120–28.

47. Paul Ricoeur, *Time and Narrative,* vol. 1, trans. Kathleen McLaughlin and David Pellauer (Chicago: University of Chicago Press, 1984), 59. Dorothy J. Hale argues that poststructuralist critics who profess their distrust of ethical norms are nonetheless attributing an ethical content to radical otherness. Dorothy J. Hale, "Fiction as Restriction: Self-Binding in New Ethical Theories of the Novel," *Narrative* 15, no. 2 (2007): 187–206; Dorothy J. Hale, "Aesthetics and the New Ethics: Theorizing the Novel in the Twenty-First Century," *PMLA 124, no. 3* (2009): 896–905.

48. Rita Felski, *Uses of Literature* (Oxford: Blackwell, 2008), 25.

49. Robert Cohen, "'The Piano Has Been Drinking': The Art of the Rant," *Georgia Review* 59, no. 2 (2005): 234.

50. Thomas Bernhard, *The Loser*, trans. Jack Dawson (New York: Vintage, 1991), 38.

51. Gary Indiana, "Saint Bernhard: Preface to a Multi-volume Suicide Note," *Village Voice Literary Supplement,* March 5, 1996.

52. Ethan Reed, "Forms of Frustration: Unrest and Unfulfillment in American Literature after 1934" (PhD diss., University of Virginia, 2019).

53. For a helpful overview of the relevant debates, see the introduction to *Empathy: Philosophical and Psychological Perspectives*, ed. Amy Coplan and Peter Goldie (Oxford: Oxford University Press, 2017).

54. Ann Jurecic, "Empathy and the Critic," *College English* 74, no. 1 (2011): 10.

55. Jurecic, "Empathy and the Critic," 27. For a recent critique of empathy, see Namwali Serpell, "The Banality of Empathy," https://www.nybooks.com /daily/2019/03/02/the-banality-of-empathy/.

56. Kiley Garrett was an undergraduate student in my Theories of Reading class at the University of Virginia in the spring of 2017. This sentence is drawn from her essay on empathy.

57. Mohsin Hamid, *Exit West: A Novel* (New York: Riverhead Books, 2017), 4.

58. Hamid, *Exit West*, 167.

59. Viet Thanh Nguyen, "A Refugee Crisis in a World of Open Doors," *New York Times,* March 10, 2017.

60. Kate Vane, amazon.com, March 2, 2017.

61. Nguyen, "Refugee Crisis."

62. Kim Chabot Davis, *Beyond the White Negro: Empathy and Anti-racist Reading* (Urbana: University of Illinois Press, 2014), 12.

63. Davis, *Beyond the White Negro*, 13.

64. Michelle Cliff, *No Telephone to Heaven* (New York: Plume, 1996), 116.

65. Keen, *Empathy and the Novel*.

66. Alice Kaplan, *Looking for "The Stranger": Albert Camus and the Life of a Literary Classic* (Chicago: University of Chicago Press, 2016), 2.

67. Jauss, *Aesthetic Experience and Literary Hermeneutics*, 181–88.

68. Joanna Gavins, *Reading the Absurd* (Edinburgh: Edinburgh University Press, 2013), 28.

69. R. M. Hare, "Nothing Matters," in *Applications of Moral Philosophy* (London: Macmillan, 1972), 105. I am grateful to John Kulka for pointing me to this example.

70. Aaron Gwyn, "Albert Camus' Poker-Faced 'Stranger' Became a Much Needed Friend," *PG-13: Risky Reads*, August 10, 2014, http://www.npr.org /2014/08/10/336823512/albert-camus-poker-faced-stranger-became-a -much-needed-friend.

71. Neal Oxenhandler, *Looking for Heroes in Postwar France: Albert Camus, Max Jacob, Simone Weil* (Hanover, NH: University Press of New England, 1996), 20.

72. English Showalter Jr., *"The Stranger": Humanity and the Absurd* (Boston: Twayne, 1989), 17.

73. Deborah Nelson, *Tough Enough: Arbus, Arendt, Didion, McCarthy, Sontag, Weil* (Chicago: University of Chicago Press, 2017).

74. For a detailed analysis of this dynamic, see James Phelan, "Estranging Unreliability, Bonding Unreliability, and the Ethics of *Lolita*," *Narrative* 15, no. 2 (2007): 222–38.

75. Kamel Daoud, *The Meursault Investigation* (New York: Other Press, 2015), 131.

76. Lee Konstantinou, *Cool Characters: Irony and American Fiction* (Cambridge, MA: Harvard University Press, 2016), 31.

77. Halpern, "In Defense of Reading Badly."

78. Ludwik Fleck, *Genesis and Development of a Scientific Fact* (Chicago: University of Chicago Press, 1981), 42.

79. Amber Jamilla Musser, "BDSM and the Boundaries of Criticism: Feminism and Neoliberalism in *Fifty Shades of Grey* and *The Story of O*," *Feminist Theory* 16, no. 2 (2015): 126.

80. Mikaella Clements, "Moby-Dick and Me: A Teenaged Love Story," *The Toast*, November 12, 2015.

81. David Shumway, "Disciplinary Identities," in *Affiliations: Identity in Academic Culture*, ed. Jeffrey di Leo (Lincoln: University of Nebraska Press, 2003), 93. On the relations between irony, character, and the ethos of criticism, see Amanda Anderson, *The Way We Argue Now: A Study in the Cultures of Theory* (Princeton, NJ: Princeton University Press, 2006).

82. José Esteban Muñoz, *Disidentification: Queers of Color and the Performance of Politics* (Durham, NC: Duke University Press, 1999), 18.

83. Miriam Hansen, "Pleasure, Ambivalence, Identification: Valentino and Female Spectatorship," *Cinema Journal* 25, no. 4 (1986): 6–32. Muñoz's model of disidentification is also very close to the idea of articulation, originally developed by Laclau and Mouffe, that became a founding category of cultural studies. See Jennifer Daryl Slack, "The Theory and Method of Articulation in Cultural Studies," in *Stuart Hall: Critical Dialogues in Cultural Studies*, ed. David Morley and Kuan-Hsing Chen (London: Routledge, 1996), 112–27.

84. Summer Kim Lee, "Too Close, Too Compromised: Killing Eve and the Promise of Sandra Oh," *Los Angeles Review of Books*, December 2018.

85. Kingsley Amis, *The James Bond Dossier* (London: Jonathan Cape, 1965), 43.

86. For recent, if rather different, defenses of flat characters, see James Wood, *How Fiction Works* (New York: Farrar, Straus and Giroux, 2008); Marta Figlerowicz, *Flat Protagonists: A Theory of Novel Character* (Oxford: Oxford University Press, 2016).

Chapter 4

1. James M. Jasper, *The Emotions of Protest* (Chicago: University of Chicago Press, 2018).

2. See Rita Felski, *The Limits of Critique* (Chicago: University of Chicago Press, 2015), 34, 174.

3. George Steiner, "'Critic'/'Reader,'" *New Literary History* 10, no. 3 (1979): 423–52.

4. René Wellek, "American Literary Scholarship," in *Concepts of Criticism* (New Haven, CT: Yale University Press, 1963), 304; Gerald Graff, *Professing Literature: An Institutional History* (Chicago: University of Chicago Press, 1987).

5. Joseph North, *Literary Criticism: A Concise Political History* (Cambridge, MA: Harvard University Press, 2017).

6. James Jiang, "So Far So Left?," *Sydney Review of Books*, March 6, 2018.

7. James English, "Literary Studies," in *The Sage Handbook of Cultural Analysis*, ed. Tony Bennett and John Frow (London: Sage, 2008), 127.

8. John Guillory, "Close Reading: Prologue and Epilogue," *ADE Bulletin* 142 (2010): 14.

9. Matt Hills, *Fan Cultures* (London: Routledge, 2002), 112.

10. Agnes Callard, *Aspiration: The Agency of Becoming* (Oxford: Oxford University Press, 2018).

11. Harry G. Frankfurt, "The Importance of What We Care About," in *The Importance of What We Care About: Philosophical Essays* (Cambridge: Cambridge University Press, 1988), 80–94.

12. Richard Shusterman, "Beneath Interpretation," in *The Interpretative Turn: Philosophy, Science, Culture*, ed. David R. Hiley, James F. Bohman, and Richard Shusterman (Ithaca, NY: Cornell University Press, 1992).

13. Susan Sontag, "Against Interpretation," in *Against Interpretation and Other Essays* (New York: Octagon, 1978), 7.

14. Jonathan Culler, *Theory of the Lyric* (Cambridge, MA: Harvard University Press, 2015), 5.

15. Ellen Rooney, "Live Free or Describe: The Reading Effect and the Persistence of Form," *differences* 21, no. 3 (2010): 123.

16. Didier Eribon, *Returning to Reims* (London: Allen Lane, 2018), 214.

17. Both of these positions are articulated in Paul Jay, *The Humanities Crisis and the Future of Literary Studies* (New York: Palgrave, 2014), 120, 4.

18. Timothy Aubry, *Guilty Aesthetic Pleasures* (Cambridge, MA: Harvard University Press, 2018).

19. Ben Highmore, "Aesthetic Matters: Writing and Cultural Studies," *Cultural Studies* 32, no. 2 (2018): 244.

20. Peter Rabinowitz, "Against Close Reading," in *Pedagogy Is Politics: Lit-*

erary Theory and Critical Teaching, ed. Maria-Regina Knecht (Urbana: University of Illinois Press, 1992), 2.

21. James F. English and Ted Underwood, "Shifting Scales: Between Literature and Social Science," *Modern Language Quarterly* 77, no. 3 (2016): 277–95; Rebecca L. Walkowitz, ed., "What Is the Scale of the Literary Object?" *Modernism/Modernity* 3, cycle 4 (February 1, 2019), https://modernism modernity.org/forums/what-scale-literary-object.

22. Kyle McGee, *Bruno Latour: The Normativity of Networks* (London: Routledge, 2014), 26.

23. Bruno Latour, "Agency at the Time of the Anthropocene," *New Literary History* 45, no. 1 (2014): 8.

24. Gabriel Hankins, "The Objects of Ethics: Rilke and Woolf with Latour," *Twentieth-Century Literature* 61, no. 3 (2015): 339.

25. Barbara Herrnstein Smith, "What Was 'Close Reading'? A Century of Method in Literary Studies," *minnesota review* 87 (2016): 58.

26. Jonathan Culler, "The Closeness of Close Reading," *ADE Bulletin* 41, no. 3 (2011): 8–13.

27. Heather Love, "Close but Not Deep: Literary Ethics and the Descriptive Turn," *New Literary History* 41, no. 2 (2010): 371–92; Sharon Marcus, Heather Love, and Stephen Best, "Building a Better Description," *Representations* 135 (Summer 2016): 1–21.

28. Hankins, "Objects of Ethics," 344.

29. Bruno Latour, "Visualization and Cognition: Thinking with Eyes and Hands," *Knowledge and Society* 6 (1986): 9.

30. Benjamin Piekut, "Actor-Networks in Music History: Clarifications and Critiques," *Twentieth-Century Music* 11, no. 2 (2014): 1–2.

31. Quoted in Piekut, "Actor-Networks in Music History," 15. See also Rita Felski, "Context Stinks!," *New Literary History* 42 (2011): 573–91.

32. Piekut, "Actor-Networks in Music History," 9.

33. Piekut, "Actor-Networks in Music History," 8.

34. Ann Rigney, *The Afterlives of Walter Scott: Memory on the Move* (Oxford: Oxford University Press, 2012).

35. See Rita Felski, "Modernist Studies and Cultural Studies: Reflections on Method," *Modernism/Modernity* 10, no. 3 (2003): 501–17.

36. Such midscale approaches appear sporadically—reader-response theory, for example—but none have managed to gain long-term traction.

37. Anne-Marie Mai, *Bob Dylan the Poet* (Odense: University of Southern Denmark, 2018), 119–23.

38. Claudia Breger, "Cinematic Assemblies: Latour and Film Studies," in *Latour and the Humanities*, ed. Rita Felski and Stephen Muecke (Baltimore: Johns Hopkins University Press, forthcoming).

39. Breger, "Cinematic Assemblies."

40. Jonathan Mayhew, "What Lorca Knew: Teaching Receptivity," *Hispanic Issues On Line* 8 (Fall 2011): 161, 163. On "reflective receptivity," see also Nikolas Kompridis, "Receptivity, Possibility, and Democratic Politics," *Ethics and Global Politics* 4, no. 2 (2011): 255–72.

41. Michel Chaouli, "Criticism and Style," *New Literary History* 44, no. 3 (2013): 323–44.

42. Dan Karlholm, "Is History to Be Closed, Saved, or Restarted?," in *Time in the History of Art: Temporality, Chronology, and Anachrony*, ed. Dan Karholm and Keith Moxey (New York: Routledge, 2018), 21.

43. David Scott, *Stuart Hall's Voice: Intimations of an Ethics of Receptive Generosity* (Durham, NC: Duke University Press, 2017), 11.

44. Scott, *Stuart Hall's Voice*, 5.

45. Scott, *Stuart Hall's Voice*, 17.

46. Michelle Boulos Walker, *Slow Philosophy: Reading against the Institution* (London: Bloomsbury, 2016), 33.

47. Nikolas Kompridis, *Critique and Disclosure: Critical Theory between Past and Future* (Cambridge, MA: MIT Press, 2006), 203.

48. Adriana Cavarero, *Inclinations: A Critique of Rectitude* (Palo Alto, CA: Stanford University Press, 2016).

49. Kathleen Fitzpatrick, *Generous Thinking: A Radical Approach to Saving the University* (Baltimore: Johns Hopkins University Press, 2019).

50. Heather Love, "Care, Concern, and the Ethics of Description," in Felski and Muecke, *Latour and the Humanities.*

51. Eva Hoffman, *Lost in Translation: A Life in a New Language* (New York: Penguin, 1989), 4.

52. Hoffman, *Lost in Translation*, 74.

53. Madeline Levine, "Eva Hoffman: Forging a Postmodern Identity," in *Living in Translation: Polish Writers in America*, ed. Stephan Halina (Amsterdam: Rodopi, 2003), 227.

54. Marianne Hirsch, *Family Frames: Photography, Narrative, and Postmemory* (Cambridge, MA: Harvard University Press, 1997), 224.

55. Hoffman, *Lost in Translation*, 209–10.

56. André LaCoque and Paul Ricoeur, preface to *Thinking Biblically: Exegetical and Hermeneutical Studies* (Chicago: University of Chicago Press, 1998), xii.

57. Tobias Skiveren, "On Good Listening, Postcritique, and Ta-Nehisi Coates' Affective Testimony," in *Affect Theory and Literary Critical Practice: A Feel for the Text*, ed. Stephen Ahern (London: Palgrave, 2019), 217–33.

58. Jenefer Robinson, *Emotion and Its Role in Literature, Music, and Art* (Oxford: Oxford University Press, 2005), 157.

59. Rita Felski, *Uses of Literature* (Oxford: Blackwell, 2008).

60. Toril Moi, *Revolution of the Ordinary: Literary Studies after Wittgenstein, Austin, and Cavell* (Chicago: University of Chicago Press, 2017), 209.

61. Moi, *Revolution of the Ordinary*, 208.

62. Michaela Bronstein, "How Not to Re-read Novels: The Critical Value of First Reading," *Journal of Modern Literature* 39, no. 3 (2016): 79.

63. Kompridis, *Critique and Disclosure*, 207–8.

64. Laura Heffernan and Rachel Sagner Buurma, "The Classroom in the Canon: T. S. Eliot's Modern English Literature Extension Course for Working People and *The Sacred Wood*," *PMLA* 133, no. 2 (2018): 265. See also their essay "The Common Reader and the Archival Classroom: Disciplinary History for the Twenty-First Century," *New Literary History* 43, no. 1 (2012): 113–35.

65. Jacob Edmond, "Too Big to Teach? Sizing Up Global Modernism," *Modernism/Modernity* 3, cycle 4 (February 1, 2019), https://modernismmodernity .org/forums/posts/too-big-teach-sizing-global-modernism; Ted Underwood, *Distant Horizons: Digital Evidence and Literary Change* (Chicago: University of Chicago Press, 2019).

66. Yves Citton, *L'avenir des humanities: Economie de la connaissance ou cultures de l'interprétation?* (Paris: La Découverte, 2010), 85–87.

67. Janice Radway, *A Feeling for Books: The Book-of-the-Month Club, Literary Taste, and Middle-Class Desire* (Chapel Hill: University of North Carolina Press, 1999).

68. Johan Fornäs, *Defending Culture: Conceptual Foundations and Contemporary Debates* (London: Palgrave, 2017), 214.

69. See Juliane Romhil, "'How Does This Book Relate to Me?' Personal Engagement and Critical Enquiry in the Literary Studies Classroom," *Higher Education Research and Development* 38, no. 1 (2018): 51–62.

70. Olivia Goodrich, "Country Roads, Take Me to Attunement," essay, 2018.

71. Brian Glavey, "Having a Coke with You Is Even More Fun Than Ideology Critique," *PMLA* 134, no. 5 (2019): 996.

72. Glavey, "Having a Coke with You," 1009.

73. Ragini Tharoor Srinivasan, "It's All Very Suggestive, but It Isn't Scholarship," in *The Critic as Amateur*, ed. Saikat Majumdar and Aarthi Vadde (London: Bloomsbury, 2019), 69.

74. Terry Eagleton, *The Gate Keeper: A Memoir* (London: St. Martin's, 2003), 131–32.

Index

Afterlives of Walter Scott, The (Rigney), 141–42

agency, viii, 61–67, 136–37, 139–41; of artworks, xiii. *See also* distributed agency

Ahmed, Sara, 3, 44

alignment, xiii, 94–95, 109–11. *See also* identification

allegiance, xiii, 84, 94, 96, 98–101, 109–11, 115–16. *See also* identification

Alpers, Svetlana, 139

amateurism, 162–63

American Psycho (Ellis), 110

American studies, 114–16

Amis, Kingsley, 119

Anderson, Ben, 32

Andrews, Julie, 91

Ang, Ien, 82

Animal Farm (Orwell), 105

ANT (actor-network theory), 21, 38; audiences and, 147–48; close reading and, 138–39; descriptions of, x–xiii, 6–9, 21–24; education and, 156–63; flat ontology of, 10, 21–22, 27, 31–32, 138; methodological attachments and, 123–24, 135–37, 154; musicology and, 139–40; scale and, 135–37, 139–45, 156; work-net concept and, 143–46, 156–57. *See also* Latour, Bruno

anthropology, 142

Appadurai, Arjun, 150–51

Appiah, Kwame Anthony, 150

"Archaic Torso of Apollo" (Rilke), 137

Arendt, Hannah, 113

"Art" (Reza), xii, 2, 16–19

Art and Agency (Gell), 63

articulation, 139, 184n83

Art Institute of Chicago, 56–57

Art Matters (de Bolla), 68

aspiration, 127–28

atmosphere, 43, 71–77, 105, 159–60

attachment: aesthetics and, viii–xi, xiv, 6–7, 15–16; affect and, 28–32, 161–63; amateur-professional dichotomies in, 124–25, 132–33, 162–63; audiences and, 4, 7–8, 38–39; definitions of, ix, 1–9; devices of, 19–28; education and, 16–17, 127–28, 153–63; institutions' role in, 33–34; judgment and, ix, xi, 3–4; methodologies and, 124–35, 142–43, 154; political motivation and, 2, 9–10, 29–30; reflectiveness and, 128–29, 146–55, 162–63; scholarly resistance to, viii, x, xiii, 2–5, 9–19, 28–29, 35–37, 62, 72, 81, 85–86, 97, 114–17, 121–23, 126–27, 133–34; value and, 28–29, 32–37. *See also* ANT (actor-network theory); audiences; detachment; methods and methodologies; modernity; psychology; sentiments

attachment theory, 19

attending, xii, 44–46, 122, 135, 142–44, 153–54

Attridge, Derek, 13

attunement, 122, 148; definitions of, xii, 41–50, 74–78; education and, 127–28, 153–63; methods and, 122; receptivity and, 148–50; temporality of, 54–61

Aubry, Timothy, 83, 134

audiences, 47, 106–8, 147, 157; aesthetic activation and, 7; characters and, 75–77, 79–94; fandom and, viii, 4, 10, 25, 38–39, 54, 66, 69, 91, 95–97, 118, 144; lay, 132–33; research on, 4–5. *See also* attachment; empathy; sentiments

counter-public spheres, 98
"Country Roads" (Denver), 158–59
Crime and Punishment (Dostoyevsky), 48
Crimp, Douglas, 82
critical proximity, 145–46
critical theory, 59, 81, 129–33
Critic as Amateur, The (Srinivasan), 162–63
critique, 10–11, 17–23, 32–33, 40, 61–63, 81, 97, 101–6, 125–33, 149, 158. *See also* ideology; political motivation; *and specific theorists*
Critique of Judgment (Kant), 11
Cruise, Tom, viii
Cujo (King), 6
Culler, Jonathan, 131, 138
cultural politics, 97
cultural studies, 37–38, 82, 141–42, 181n37, 184n83

Danto, Arthur, 12
Daoud, Kamel, 113–14
Davis, Geena, 98
Davis, Kim Chabot, 25, 82, 98, 108
death of the author, 90
de Bolla, Peter, 68
deconstruction, 116, 122, 138, 147, 182n47
de Heem, Jan Davidsz, 61
delayed categorization, 60
Deleuze, Gilles, 32
deliberativeness, 128
DeNora, Tia, 47
Denver, John, 158–59
de Sousa, Ronald, 31
detachment, xii, xiii, 9–19. *See also* attachment; methods and methodologies; modernity
Dewey, John, 15, 171n26
difference, 147, 182n47

Dimock, Wai Chee, 27
Dion, Celine, 17
disassociation, xiii, 2, 111–14
Discipline and Punish (Foucault), 129–30
disciplines (scholarly), 124–35. *See also* humanities; psychology; sociology
disenchantment, viii, 9–19, 30; ironic identification and, xiii
disidentification, 117–18, 184n83
dispositions, 17, 49, 104, 114, 122, 148
distancing (from aesthetic objects). *See* detachment
distant reading, 132, 156
distributed agency, 9, 64, 140–41
doing justice, xii, xiv, 6, 12, 41, 77, 135, 162–63
domesticity, 26–27
Dostoyevsky, Fyodor, 48
Doty, Mark, 61
Duchamp, Marcel, vii
Dumont, Margaret, 83
dwelling, 10–11
Dyer, Geoff, 2, 57–58, 103
Dyer, Richard, 91
Dylan, Bob, 144

Eagleton, Terry, 162
Eastwood, Clint, 98
Eco, Umberto, 110
Ecstasy of St. Francis, The (Bellini), 73
Edmond, Jacob, 156
education, 56, 119–20, 124, 126–30, 142–43, 153–63
Elective Affinities (Goethe), 74
Eliot, T. S., 155
Elkins, James, 18, 64, 73
Elledge, Jim, 82

Root, Deborah, 37
Rorty, Richard, 105, 130–31
Rushdie, Salman, 13
Ruskin, John, 73
Ryle, Gilbert, 72

Said, Edward, 127
Saito, Hiro, 10
Sarandon, Susan, 97–98
Sarraute, Nathalie, 74
scale, xiii, 123, 135–46, 156
Schaeffer, Jean-Marie, 14, 60–61
science studies, xi, 136. *See also* ANT
    (actor-network theory); Latour,
    Bruno
Scott, David, xiii, 2, 124, 148–49,
    152
Scott, Ridley, 97, 100
Sebald, W. G., 76, 102
Sedgwick, Eve, 118
Semi-detached (Plotz), 170n16
semidetachment, 10–19, 170n16
sensibilities, 28, 49, 54, 114, 122, 144,
    150–53
sentiments: affect and, 28–29; em-
    pathy and, xiii, 2, 79–80, 94, 101,
    105–11, 114–15; feminism and, 29–
    30; gendering of, 105–6; judgment
    and, ix; mistrust of, viii, 66–67.
    See also attachment; attunement;
    identification
Serpell, Namwali, 176n26
Sherlock (series), 88
Shumway, David, 117
Shusterman, Richard, 12, 131
Sight of Death, The (Clark), 59–60
Sinnerbrink, Robert, 77
skepticism, 40, 70–71, 153–54
Skiveren, Tobias, 152–53
slow reading, 149

Smith, Barbara Herrnstein, 138
Smith, Murray, 81, 100–101, 179n4,
    181n36
Smith, Zadie, xii–xiii, 2, 39, 42, 48–
    61, 78, 127, 158–59
Sobchack, Vivian, 71–72, 145
sociology, 16–19, 38, 46–47, 123, 142,
    163
solicitations, 29
solidarity, 14, 84, 100, 105–6, 127
Solnit, Rebecca, 7, 94
Sontag, Susan, 12, 30, 80, 113, 131
Sound of Music, The (film), 90–91
Souriau, Etienne, 65
Spinoza, Baruch, 32
Spivak, Gayatri, 127
Srinivasan, Ragini, 162–63
Stacey, Jackie, 81–82, 90
Stalker (Tarkovsky), 2, 37, 57–58
stance, 122–25, 146, 153–55
status distinctions, xii
Steiner, George, 66–67, 124, 146
Stengers, Isabelle, 74
Stern, David, 55
Stewart, Kathleen, 76
Still Life with Oysters and Lemon
    (Doty), 61
Stimmung, 43, 49–50, 74–75
Stone Butch Blues (Feinberg), 26–27
Story of O, The (Desclos), 115
Stranger, The (Camus), 2, 110–13
strong evaluation, 33–34
strong interpretation, 131–32
Stuart Hall's Voice (Scott), 148–49
style, 76, 154–55
stylization, 80
surface reading, viii, 131
Swift, Taylor, ix
Swoboda, Jessica, 158, 179n69
symbolic violence, 17–18